# Spiritual Being & Becoming

# Spiritual Being & Becoming

*Western Christian and Modern Scientific Views of Human Nature for Spiritual Formation*

ERIC J. KYLE

PICKWICK *Publications* · Eugene, Oregon

SPIRITUAL BEING & BECOMING
Western Christian and Modern Scientific Views of Human Nature for Spiritual
Formation

Pickwick Publications
An Imprint of Wipf and Stock Publishers
199 W. 8th Ave., Suite 3
Eugene, OR 97401

www.wipfandstock.com

ISBN 13: 978-1-4982-0168-1

*Cataloguing-in-Publication Data*

Kyle, Eric J.

Spiritual being & becoming: Western Christian and modern science views of human nature spiritual formation / Eric J. Kyle

xviii + 290 pp. ; 23 cm. Includes bibliographical references and index.

ISBN 13: 978-1-4982-0168-1

1. Spiritual Life—Christianity. 2. Theological anthropology—Christianity. 3.
Philosophical anthropology—History. 4. Religion and science. I. Title

BV4490 K94 2014

Manufactured in the U.S.A.                                      03/06/2015

To Parents, Teachers, and Mentors

# Contents

# Figures

# Acknowledgments

I WOULD LIKE TO thank Frank Rogers Jr., Andrew Dreitcer, Phillip Dreyer, and Philip Clayton for their discerning support and guidance in formulating and reviewing various parts of this project. I would also like to thank Lindsey Sikes whose editorial work was a tremendous blessing to this project. In addition, I would like to give thanks to my patron saint and inspiration for this work, Thomas Aquinas, who sought to integrate the historical and contemporary intellectual movements of his own era just as I have sought to in these pages. AMDG, "For the greater glory of God."

# Introduction

IT IS REPORTED THAT there are as many as 100 billion neurons that make up the human nervous system.[1] It has also been noted of the brain's operation that the "number [of possible states of activation] is thought to be larger than the number of atoms in the known universe."[2] It is therefore an understatement to say that this biological organ is quite complex. And, yet, it is a fundamental part of what makes us who we are as human beings.

There is more to human nature than our biological functioning as well. The field of psychology, as we shall see, contains a number of schools of thought that study the human psyche from different perspectives. From psychodynamic theorists, to social-cognitive researchers, to transpersonal explorers, psychology in and of itself is quite complex.

However, we must also know that the study and exploration of human nature did not begin in contemporary times. History, particularly western Christian history, is full of texts that offer detailed explorations of the human condition from both internal reflections and external observations. The *Conferences* of John Cassian, for instance, contain intrapersonal insights and reflections reported by monks living in the deserts of North Africa of early Christian history.[3] Thinkers such as Augustine of Hippo, Maximus the Confessor, Martin Luther, and Immanuel Kant all offer discussions on the nature and essence of the human condition as we shall see in this book.

Yet, given this voluminous body of knowledge, there doesn't yet seem to be a consensus that has emerged either in relation to the basic components that appear to be more commonly experienced and

1. Bear, Connors, and Paradiso, *Neuroscience*, 24.

2. Siegel, *Mindsight*, 38.

3. Cassian, *John Cassian: The Conferences*.

enduring elements of human nature or in relation to the terminology that is used in referring to these components and their interrelationships. While there are common models that are used in today's religious and spiritual circles, such as "body-mind-spirit,"[4] many of these still leave questions relating to what these terms mean and how these components are related to one another. There is, therefore, still work to be done to parse out what the basic elements of human nature might be and to address their interrelationships.

Nevertheless, those working religious education and spiritual formation positions are tasked with working for the spiritual upliftment of the individuals and communities that they are called to work with. On the surface, it might initially seem to be a relatively simple vocation: journey with people towards the greater fulfillment of their lives with God. However, as one begins to work closely with individuals, one can begin to realize just how complex humans are. In other words, we can begin to see how the insights of the historical and contemporary thinkers and theorists mentioned above might help to shed insight into our work.

Consider for a moment that your car has broken down and that you have no prior knowledge of how vehicles work and that you cannot afford to pay someone else to fix it. In this situation, you could pop the hood and begin trying to figure out what all of the different components are and how they work all on your own. Or, you can seek the help of others who are more knowledgeable in this area who can help you to learn at least enough about your car to get it running again. Clearly, the second option is the more preferable one.

Apply this now to our work as religious educators and spiritual formators. In order to help others (as well as ourselves) to grow in their lives with God, it will be very helpful to have some foundational background in relation to human nature. As we have already seen, and will see in much more detail below, human beings are infinitely complex (literally, given our inherent connections to our Infinite Creator); far more than the vehicles that carry us around on a regular basis. If we would benefit from the insights and support of others in better understanding our cars, how much more might we benefit from an education on human nature in our formation work with others?

However, as asserted above, there does not yet seem to be consensus in relation to the basic elements of human nature and their

---

4. For examples of this, see such works as Hauser, *Moving in the Spirit*; Van Kaam, *Fundamental Formation*; Wilber, *Integral Spirituality*.

inter-relationships. In light of this, we might wonder at what can be done. First, we can simply choose one of the theories of human nature from our own communities or from others and use it as is in our ministries. Or, we can attempt to create our own based mostly on our own personal experiences and background. Finally, we can seek to synthesize a more unified theory from among two or more other models. Anyone of these methods would provide us with a model that could then be used to help guide our formative work. But which of these methods should we use? How will we know that the theory we are using is really helpful for our specific programs and communities? When we do choose or synthesize one, how might we go about applying it to our specific formation programs?

This book is an attempt to help answer these questions and to provide some of the background and education to support this ministerial work. The following are the primary goals of this text: 1) To provide an exploration of the diverse views of human nature as they are found in both western Christianity and modern science; 2) To see how we might begin to construct our own generalized theological anthropology in lights of these views; and 3) To see how we might apply these synthesized models of human nature to our own specific spiritual formation and religious education programs. In addition, this book will construct and offer a generalized theory that may be used more broadly beyond the human person.

In order to pursue these ends, we must first understand that there are multiple levels at which most congregational, non-profit, and educational ministries operate: individual, relational, and communal.[5] We can work with individuals to help them with their own personal spiritual lives, lives that filled with compassion, self-worth, connection, service, joy, et cetera. Secondly, we need to work with the relationships that are formed and are forming in our communities. From close intimate ones, to cliques and small groups, these relationships should embody and manifest God's intimacy, forgiveness, healing, support, self-differentiation, et cetera. Finally, we can work with communities and organizations as a whole. This entails working with the social, political, and economic aspects so that they are more fully in-line with God's Life of justice, stewardship, et cetera. Each of these comprises the work of those in ministry and each level must be attended to with the same intentionality and discernment as any of the others.

5. For further discussions of these levels, see the introductory chapters of Kyle, *Living Spiritual Praxis*; Kyle, *Sacred Systems*.

Within this scheme, this work is located primarily at the individual level. It is an effort to help us to better understand some of the rich array of dynamics and movements that comprise our spiritual being and becoming as humans. Towards these ends, this book will unfold along the following lines. In the first chapter, we will explore a series of theological anthropologies that have been a part of western Christian history. Our goal here is not an in-depth study of each of these various thinkers, but rather an attempt to identify what some of the common elements of human nature that have been identified across this history. Immediately following these explorations, we will identify what some of these common elements are as well as the theories of change and theologies latent within and among them, both of which are central for the work of spiritual formation.

In the second chapter, we will then turn our attention to some of the modern science schools of thought that have and continue to offer insights into the human condition. Again, we are not seeking an extensive education in each of these fields, but rather a brief introduction to some of the main aspects of human nature that have been identified. As with the first chapter, we will then identify the common elements that the various schools have studied. We will also reflect on the nature of change found among them and compare some of the common elements with those found in our western Christian thinkers.

With this historical and contemporary background in place, we will then walk through a process to create a more unified and synthesized theological anthropology. As we shall see, what is most important here is not so much the model of human nature that is presented but rather the processes that were engaged to synthesize such a model. Readers are not expected to accept this theory as *the* unified model that still seems to be missing in relation to human nature as discussed above. Instead, you are encouraged to follow along and create your own model, one that is more appropriate to your own locale and all that God is doing therein.

The fourth chapter then takes us on more of an abstracted side-step wherein I take the unified model from the previous chapter and inductively generate a more universal model for formation work. With what could be categorized as a "universal theory of organism," this model is intended to help derive and articulate more generalized principles and guidelines for our ministries. The primary goal of this abstracted chapter is really to help us to better understand the nature and essence of spiritual formation and religious education.

The final chapter then brings us back to the ground where we will be learning how to use the unified model from the third chapter, as well as the principles and guidelines from the fourth, to guide our program development. Here a detailed case example will be presented in which a spirituality and peacebuilding program is designed following what may be a called "theory-based" program development method. Again, the goal here is not the specificities of the case example itself, but rather the processes that are engaged which can help to guide the creation of our own formation programs.

Overall, the work of religious education and spiritual formation is a complex endeavor. As we shall see, just focusing on a single individual and their own growth is an infinitely interconnected and complicated kind of work. If we are to do this work effectively, we must do so in well-informed ways just as we should when attempting to fix our own cars. It is therefore hoped that this book will not only provide us with a fuller understanding of some of the views of human nature that are available, but also to provide some level of guidance in how we might begin to utilize and apply this background knowledge to the ministries to which God has called us to. At their heart, these are ministries that strive towards the spiritual being and becoming of our world.

CHAPTER 1

# Western Christian Theological Anthropologies

WE BEGIN OUR MASSIVE synthesizing effort with western Christian thinkers. In particular, we will be briefly exploring the theological anthropologies of the following nine sources: the Bible (according to one author); Augustine of Hippo; Maximus the Confessor; Thomas Aquinas; Martin Luther; Immanuel Kant; Karl Barth; Karl Rahner; and contemporary anthropologies in light of modern Western science. In order to help us to better understand how their views of human nature might be relevant for spiritual formation, we will review the following three major areas: 1) their general views of human nature, including any components they identify and how they account for goodness and evil; 2) their views of the Divine in relation to humanity; and 3) their assertions related to the nature of change for humans, and God's relationship to such transformation. The first two topics address the basic elements of their theological anthropologies while the third one is of a more specific interest to the field of theistic spiritual formation. Collectively, these thinkers provide insights into some of the diverse views that may be found in this religious tradition and they conceive of how human transformation might transpire.

## BIBLICAL VIEWS (BCE—SECOND CENTURY CE)

We begin these historical explorations with where Christianity often does: the Bible. Rather than turning directly to the Bible and attempting my own summary of the theological anthropologies found therein, I instead chose to look to one resource that appeared to have already accomplished this: Joel Green's (Professor of New Testament Interpretation at Fuller Theological Seminary) book, *Body, Soul, and Human Life*.[1] Green is primarily concerned "with how the Bible portrays the human person, the basis and telos of human life, what it means for humanity, in the words of Irenaeus, to be "fully alive.""[2] Given this focus, Green claims that he is additionally interested in how such views inform our contemporary understandings of such topics as "freedom, salvation, Christian formation, and the character of the church and its mission" in light of modern scientific claims.[3] In addition to these, as we shall see, Green is additionally interested in the topic of life-after-death and what, if anything, survives.

Regarding the nature of human beings, Green highlights a number of important points that uniquely characterize us. He asserts the fundamental unity of the human person as found in both the Hebrew and Christian Testaments.[4] Turning to scriptural concepts such as "nephes," "gewiyya," and others, he claims that these concepts emphasize the wholeness of the individual.[5] Throughout these explorations, Green finds that "segregating the human person into discrete, constitutive 'parts,'" is not emphasized, but rather are persons considered in their completeness.[6]

Given this wholeness, Green further finds that the embodiedness of humanity is also stressed.[7] Jewish perspectives emphasize a "psychosomatic unity," while Christian texts, such as Luke and Peter, highlight the bodilyness of Jesus and humans in general[8]. Based upon these insights, Green asserts his own similar views when he writes, "What I want especially to underscore here, though, is that who we are, our personhood, is inextricably bound up in our physicality."[9] Humans are therefore seen to be in continuity with other animals, we share our embodiedness with the

---

1. Green, *Body, Soul, and Human Life*.

2. Ibid., 3.

3. Ibid., 15–16.

4. Ibid., 8, 69.

5. Ibid., 55, 57.

6. Ibid., 49, 69.

7. Ibid., 14, 144.

8. Ibid., 59, 151, 167–68.

9. Ibid., 179.

earth.[10] Based on the Bible, Green claims, "humanity is formed from the stuff of the earth."[11]

Equally emphasized with our physicality, is relationality; our relatedness to others, God, and creation at large. Central to human nature, following from the Genesis creation story, is our "capacity to relate to Yahweh as covenant partner,"[12] and Jesus' own life and resurrection may only be understood "with reference to relationality and mission."[13] Our personal identities, claims Green, are therefore intricately bound up with the Divine, but also the human relationships that we have.[14] So important are these relationships, that we cannot be "genuinely human and alive" without them.[15]

With these two central aspects of human nature, our embodiedness and our relationality, Green goes on to point out two potential consequences. The first is that the "soul" must not be conceived of as a separate and distinct "thing" that survives death, as it is found in Greek thought, but rather does it comprise the whole person, embodied and relational; i.e., all that constitutes who we are.[16] Secondly, deriving directly from the first, is that our understandings of resurrection, following from the Bible, therefore needs to change. His basic thesis is that "life-after-death is narratively and relationally shaped and embodied, the capacity for life-after-death is not intrinsic to humanity but is a divine gift, and resurrection signifies not rescue from the cosmos but transformation with it," rather than the liberation of a separate immortal soul.[17] These claims both further emphasize the relational and embodied nature of human existence.

Despite our deep connections to creation, Green still notes the emphasis given by the scriptures to humans as "made in the image of God."[18] "Humanity," writes Green, "thus stands in an ambivalent position—living in solidarity with the rest of the created order and yet distinct from it on

---

10. Ibid., 61.

11. Ibid.

12. Ibid., 64.

13. Ibid., 168–70.

14. Ibid., 50, 144, 169.

15. Ibid., 147.

16. Ibid., 54–55, 64, 70, 154.

17. Ibid., 144, 151, 168, 168–70, 172.

18. Ibid., 62.

account of humankind's unique role as the bearer of the divine image."[19] Being in a unique position, sin still enters into the discussion and is understood as being the denial of our own humanity, the vocation to which God continually calls us.[20] Set off by a chain of events with Adam, sin continues in the world by our on-going participation and relationship with it.[21] Nevertheless, humanity still holds the divine image as yet another core aspect of its nature.

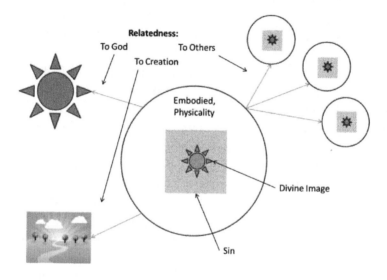

Figure 1. Green's Theological Anthropology.

Though Green's review of human nature is detailed, his explicitly theological assertions appear to be rather sketchy. While he does briefly mention the role of Wisdom in the Hebrew scriptures, "a pure emanation of the glory of the Almighty . . . a reflection of eternal light, a spotless mirror of the working of God, and an image of his goodness,"[22] most of his brief theological discussions center on the person of Jesus. As already noted above, the embodiedness and relationality of Jesus is emphasized.[23] In essence, Jesus is presented as a model for us, the image of God, and an

---

19. Ibid.

20. Ibid., 69, 89, 92.

21. Ibid., 95, 98, 100.

22. Ibid., 68.

23. Ibid., 169.

image into which we are to be molded.[24] Highlighting Peter's views specifically, Green writes, "The analogy between Christ and his followers is not
exact, since Christ's behavior provides not only the blueprint for his followers but also its basis."[25] God, in the form of Christ, is therefore highlighted
as being both a guide and a transforming foundation for human existence.

Finally, Green does spend some time, throughout his text, discussing
the nature of human transformation and God's relation to it. Given our
unique position between the "stuff of the earth," and the sinfulness that
has been perpetuated since the fall, and the "image of God," humanity is
therefore in need of transformation.[26] Directly stemming from the views
of human nature discussed above, change must involve the whole person
and not mere parts.[27] Such a transformation involves a complete turning
around and alteration of every aspect of our being, such as our imaginative frameworks and conceptual schemes.[28] It therefore includes a complete
withdrawal from sin and "a deep-seated conversion in one's conception of
God and, thus, in one's commitments, attitudes, and everyday practices."[29]

As a part of such changes, since it is also an intricate aspect of our nature, is transformation in the context of our relationships.[30] Such change
must come to include the larger communities of which we are a part.[31] It
may also require us to nest ourselves "within a new web of relationships,
a transfer of allegiances."[32] Such shifts may therefore entail "adopting the
rituals and behaviors peculiar to or definitive of that new community."[33]
In order to facilitate human change, Green therefore notes, our relationships must come to change as well.

The journey of human change is just that: a journey. Green notes
some of the metaphors for change contained within the Bible such as the
potter's wheel.[34] All of our efforts internally and relationally are "aimed
at a transformation of day-to-day patterns of thinking, feeling, believing,

24. Ibid., 59, 69.

25. Ibid., 90.

26. Ibid., 68.

27. Ibid., 69.

28. Ibid., 128, 137.

29. Ibid., 90, 102–3.

30. Ibid., 69.

31. Ibid., 70.

32. Ibid., 128–29, 133.

33. Ibid., 130.

34. Ibid., 94.

and behaving."[35] This conversion, Green notes, is not a one-time event but rather is depicted in the Bible as an on-going task to which we are invited.[36] Green also highlights the "organic" nature of change that is presented, noting how changes in one area can feed and fuel others.[37] Change in the Bible is therefore depicted by Green as one of a continuous and organic journey.

Finally, such transformations are not solely the work of humans, but stand upon the foundation of the work of God. As noted above, Christ is not just a model for change, but also an active element within it.[38] Referring to the views of Peter, Green writes, God gives "the medicine of liberation . . . through Christ's defeat of the powers arrayed against God, through his sacrificial death by which the stain of sin was cleansed, through the power of the Spirit in new birth and sanctification."[39] God's transforming life is therefore depicted, particularly in the Christian testament, as being poured out upon creation who brings an inner "transformation of human nature by means of divine wisdom."[40] In short, human change cannot transpire without the Divine work in our lives, relationships, and world.

These, then, comprise the views of human nature as described by Green in his book. Human nature is seen as a unified whole whose embodiedness and relationality are central. These views, for Green, have direct implications for our conceptions of the soul and resurrection. Also a part of our nature is the notion of our being made in the image of God. Sin derives from our unwillingness to be the life to which God is calling us, a sort of turning way from being fully human. But with Jesus as our model, and with the presence of God at work within creation, transformation is possible. Such transformations, of course, involve the whole of our being, particularly in our internal and external relationships, and we can expect such changes to transpire as an organic, on-going journey into God.

35. Ibid., 123.
36. Ibid., 126.
37. Ibid., 132.
38. Ibid., 70.
39. Ibid., 92.
40. Ibid., 98, 137.

## AUGUSTINE OF HIPPO (354–430)

From the Bible, we now move into the early institutional church, turning to Augustine's views as they are depicted in his theological treatise, *The Trinity*.[41] In this book, which took some fifteen to twenty years for him to complete,[42] Augustine presents a sort of history of his quest for the Trinity.[43] Divided into two parts, with the first focusing on the mystery of God itself and the second on the image of God in humanity, the book sets out to examine this doctrine in an intimate and extensive way.[44] While holding a more explicit theologically oriented focus, this text still provides us with insights into Augustine's views of human nature.

With an active mind like Augustine had, we can expect his anthropology to be quite detailed and complicated; and that it is. True to his Greco-Romans roots, he does conceive of humanity as having a body and a soul: with the body being conceived of in terms of unspiritual "living tissue" and having various senses through which our experiences of the world are somehow internally imprinted, and the soul is discussed in terms of wholly governing and spiritualizing the body, being rational, and having the potential for immortality.[45] These two are related in a hierarchical fashion, with the soul governing the body and with rational souls governing irrational ones, though unity can be sought through the use of the will.[46]

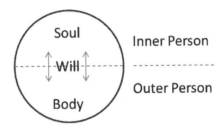

Figure 2. Augustine's Body-Soul Distinction.

41. Augustine, *The Trinity*.

42. Ibid., 17, 20, 63.

43. Ibid., 18, 20–21.

44. Ibid., 21.

45. Ibid., 131, 155, 210–11, 276, 280, 311, 374.

46. Ibid., 131–32, 311, 361.

In addition to this scheme, however, Augustine also discusses various "trinities" that are found within us that are mutually interdependent in the same way as the divine Trinity. An example of this is the trinity of mind, knowledge, and love in which the mind can focus its attention leading to knowledge, which then leads to love.[47] Knowing one's self is also asserted to lead one to a love of God.[48] Augustine further understands mind to be contained in the higher parts of the soul, uniting our "understanding and activity," and is therefore not shared with other beasts.[49] Another trinity includes memory, understanding, and will, emphasizing the will's ability to focus one's energies and unite inner fragments.[50] For both of these, he stresses their trinitarian-like unity.[51]

As if this were not complicated enough, Augustine is also found to discuss differences between the "inner and outer man," asserting that "the inner man is endowed with understanding, [and] the outer man with sensation."[52] He seems to make this distinction in order to stress the hierarchical difference between our lower "outer man" senses, which we share with animals, and our higher "inner man" abilities of reason, wisdom, and uniting our knowledge with love that can lead to deeper places of inner, and sometimes, wordless knowing.[53] Such concepts seem to be relevant for his views of sin and salvation, for things of the lower body are asserted to distort the things of truth.[54] Such distortions, Augustine asserts, are partly the result of the activities of a self-serving mind and soul, for which death is the punishment.[55] In addition to this, he also points to the power and workings of the devil, which Christ came to defeat and pay our debt to.[56] Taken collectively, these many and diverse views of human nature are quite complicated.

Turning briefly now to Augustine's theological assertions, his main hopes are to stress the inseparability of the different persons of the

47. Ibid., 273, 280, 286, 288–89, 398.

48. Ibid., 384.

49. Ibid., 323.

50. Ibid., 298, 309, 315, 376, 398.

51. Ibid., 298.

52. Ibid., 303, 322.

53. Ibid., 322–23, 329, 365, 395, 405, 413, 415, 429.

54. Ibid., 242–43.

55. Ibid., 164, 292, 330.

56. Ibid., 156, 165, 355, 357, 359.

Trinity, emphasizing that "there are not three gods but one God."[57] This united Trinity, this one God, is conceived as being totally eternal, omnipresent, unchangeable, and is of an uncreated "more excellent," invisible, and spiritual (meaning God "senses with mind not body") nature that creates all that is.[58] In this scheme, Christ and the Holy Spirit are begotten by the Father and sent on mission to serve the Creator.[59] Jesus is further asserted to be both a model to our "outer man" and a saving sacrament to our "inner man" "in order to refashion us to the image of God," standing as a mediator between us and God.[60]

Within this framework, God relates to humans through wisdom, angels, Christ, each other, and "from the inmost invisible and intelligible court of the supreme emperor, according to his unfathomable justice of rewards and punishments."[61] God is therefore asserted to be in control of all that transpires giving "power as he judges best in his sublime, spiritual, and immutable wisdom."[62] Also, even though he stresses the transcendence of God, Augustine also asserts the possibility of union with God as well, writing, "seeing that human nature could so be joined to God that one person would be made out of two substances. That in fact means one person now out of three elements, God, soul, and flesh."[63] Augustine's theological views might therefore be paradoxically characterized as simultaneously utterly transcendent and supremely immanent.

Finally, as it relates to the nature of human change, he stresses the necessity of redemption and salvation for the soul.[64] This redemption comes as a result of our being "weighed down by the accumulated dirt of our sins, which we had collected by our love of temporal things."[65] Despite this weight, the rational soul has the opportunity to be purified and therefore rises to the things of the spirit, by faith and by "cleaving" itself to the Spirit of God to see the "unchangeable illuminating light."[66]

---

57. Ibid., 69, 100, 172, 175, 195, 209, 218, 241, 426 (book 1, chaps. 3–4).

58. Ibid., 108, 153, 154, 200, 363, 383, 400, 429.

59. Ibid., 74, 82, 98, 100, 104, 174, 404 (book 2, chap. 2).

60. Ibid., 156, 158, 161, 223, 411.

61. Ibid., 132, 363–64, 399 (book 3, chap. 4).

62. Ibid., 134.

63. Ibid., 361.

64. Ibid., 155, 169, 361.

65. Ibid., 169, 311.

66. Ibid., 77, 118, 155, 170, 208, 230, 245, 280, 325, 391.

Such transformations are also aided by daily practicing the virtues and contemplation, by a "deliberate choice in order to acquire excellence," by the use of reason and self-knowing, and by embracing the love which is God.[67] This journey is therefore conceived of by Augustine as a gradual ascent from earth to heaven, from the "outer man" to the inner one.[68]

Throughout it all, God is asserted as being the source, sustainer, and culminator of this journey. Augustine asserts that our "arousing" happens by a work of the Holy Spirit and by our needing to first be shown by God how much we are loved.[69] Once aroused, we can become more a part of the climb as discussed above, but we are not able to do so without the sanctifying work of God.[70] Our salvation, ultimately, is only made possible by the redeeming and debt-paying work of Christ.[71] In the end, the summit of our journey, Augustine holds, is a state of bliss and union that will continue without end.[72]

In closing, Augustine's views of human nature are quite detailed and complex. Nevertheless, Augustine's anthropology includes such components as: body and soul; mind, knowledge, and love; memory, understanding, and will; and the inner and outer person. While there are hierarchical dichotomies among these, Augustine was also found to assert trinitarian-like unities among some of them as well. The dichotomies seemed to form part of the basis for his views of sin and salvation, with the spiritual journey being characterized as a pilgrimage from lower to higher natures and from irrational to rational abilities. Such a journey is made possible by one's focused use of their faculties as well as by the necessary and direct interventions of the Divine. In this somewhat dualistic scheme, the Sacred was found to likewise be characterized in seemingly paradoxical images of transcendence and immanence. Overall, Augustine's framework seems to depict human nature and the spiritual journey as having the potential of being one that ultimately moves in the direction of an ever increasing trinitarian unity both internally as well as externally.

67. Ibid., 155, 244, 253, 325, 334, 343, 365, 379, 383, 385, 434.

68. Ibid., 329, 434.

69. Ibid., 152–53.

70. Ibid., 167, 189, 350, 434.

71. Ibid., 156, 329.

72. Ibid., 430.

## MAXIMUS THE CONFESSOR (580–662)

With Augustine having a tremendous influence in the Western church, we now briefly turn to one influential figure in the Eastern Orthodox traditions, Maximus the Confessor, as his anthropological thoughts are depicted in the contemporary text by Lars Thunberg entitled, *Microcosm and Mediator*.[73] Born to a noble family and provided with a good education, Maximus was a secretary to Emperor Heraclius early on in his life.[74] However, he later chose to leave this lifestyle behind to live a devoted and ascetical vocation eventually ending up in Africa in 626 C.E.[75] Maximus was present at the Lateran Council in 649, but was later exiled for a theological controversy.[76] Despite this rejection during his lifetime, Maximus' influence continues to leave a lasting legacy today.

As it relates to human nature, Maximus emphasizes the unity of our whole being with our end being God; though we also clearly have various and distinct parts. For him, it is the wholeness of the individual that is stressed.[77] The goal of one's life is therefore to find our end and fulfillment in God.[78] The mind, or "nous," has the function of unifying our various parts so that the whole of our being can be deified in God, acting as sort of a microcosmic mediator of part of creation.[79] Humans as a mediator, a middle position between matter and God, is therefore central to Maximus' theological anthropology according to Thunberg.[80]

As it relates to the parts of this unified microcosm, Maximus presents at least two central "trichotomies" of which humans are comprised, though we also have other important components as well. The first is a trichotomy of mind, body, and soul.[81] He stresses the necessary interdependence of soul and body, arguing that while they are independent, one cannot exist without the other thereby reflecting the hypostatic union of Christ's nature.[82] Mind, on the other hand, "which is contemplative,

73. Thunberg, *Microcosm and Mediator*.

74. Ibid., 1–2.

75. Ibid., 2–4.

76. Ibid., 6–7.

77. Ibid., 111–12.

78. Ibid., 113, 174.

79. Ibid., 112, 170–71, 176, 331, 430.

80. Ibid., 138–39, 142, 167.

81. Ibid., 106–7.

82. Ibid., 97–98, 100, 101, 104–6.

is also the primary instrument of [a person's] relationship to God" and therefore has the task of integrating and turning one's life wholly towards the Divine.[83]

While Maximus views the soul as standing in a middle position between sensible and incorporeal aspects of creation,[84] he further envisions a trichotomy of the soul: the concupiscible, irascible, and rational parts. Thunberg summarizes Maximus' views of this trichotomy when he writes, "the concupiscible element represents man's relationship to the lower world and thus is called to express his basic direction of being, attachment to a higher cause; the irascible element represent primarily the inter-human relationship; and the rational element the relationship to God as Intellect and Spirit."[85] The concupiscible element is "mainly responsible for the fall of man" and the rational and irascible parts can be freely directed for good or evil.[86] In Maximus' scheme, these are presented in a neutral sense for they are all to be united in the journey towards God.[87]

Maximus therefore also talks about the role of the passions and the will in human nature, as well as their relationship to the origins and presence of evil in the world. The passions were introduced through the fall and the will, which is closely related to rationality and mind, is central for the directions one's life takes.[88] In fact, Maximus associates one's rational nature with the image of God in humanity, which was given to us in the beginning, while the passions make us more like irrational animals, though they are not evil in themselves.[89] The fall was therefore the result both of human's own choices and the Devil's seduction and brought pain and death; it was basically a misuse of the faculties of humanity.[90] While evil is not considered to be a substantive reality, it does derive from three sources—"ignorance, self-love, and tyranny"—and all other vices, particularly the eight vices (gluttony, fornication, avarice, grief, wrath, listlessness, vainglory, pride), result from these and cause disintegration and

83. Ibid., 109, 111, 205, 207.
84. Ibid., 171, 176.
85. Ibid., 196.
86. Ibid., 199, 201, 203.
87. Ibid., 198.
88. Ibid., 152, 209–12.
89. Ibid., 117–18, 126, 152.
90. Ibid., 155, 159, 171, 226, 227, 244.

fragmentation.[91] In all of these, evil is essentially humanity choosing to find its pleasure in sources other than God and thereby choosing to distort the natural faculties one has and destroying the unity that one can potentially have.[92]

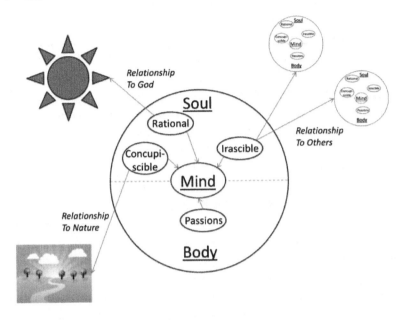

Figure 3. Maximus' View of Human Nature.

Maximus' theology, as presented in this text, primarily focuses on Christology, though the utter transcendence and source of existence is also discussed.[93] Christology, particularly the hypostatic doctrine of the union of Christ's two natures, was central for Maximus because it served as a model for deification in humans; human and divine natures becoming one.[94] In this way, Christ is depicted as unifying extremes bringing them into oneness and wholeness, something humans have failed to do.[95] Such unity is also, for Maximus, possible for creation, and Christ therefore serves as both a model and facilitator for such unity.[96] As Thunberg

91. Ibid., 155, 161, 232–33, 248, 267–79, 283.

92. Ibid., 176, 263, 278, 279, 281, 284.

93. Ibid., 81.

94. Ibid., chap. 1, specifically p. 27; see also p. 433.

95. Ibid., 91, 140.

96. Ibid., 49, 54, 391–92, 399.

writes, "man becomes god, while God becomes man; man's deification is from another point of view God's continuing incarnation."[97] Maximus' hypostatic Christology is therefore central to his theological anthropology according to Thunberg.

Finally, Thunberg talks in detail about the nature of spiritual change and the formative journeys that humanity is to embark upon. Depicted as a microcosm of the world, humans are mediating subjects through whom the Divine likeness is brought to bear in creation.[98] Such a mediation is asserted to happen in five primary arenas: "between man and woman, Paradise and the inhabited work, heaven and earth, intelligible and sensible things and finally between created and uncreated nature."[99] These mediations, which are primarily viewed as reconciling the consequences of the fall and facilitating our unification,[100] are surmounted in successive phases thereby coinciding with the three stages of the spiritual life that he holds: vita practica, vita contemplativa, and vita mystica.[101] Vita practica is primarily concerned with the "conquest of the passions" and acquisition of the virtues; vita contemplativa aims at a knowledge of the true nature of things that then leads one towards God; and vita mystica involves a "super-knowledge," which is "a supreme ignorance through which God the Unknowable is made known"; a prayer that is "formed by God alone."[102] These mediations and stages of the journey are therefore central to Maximus' views of the human spiritual transformation.

In order to make this journey and these transformations, Maximus asserts a number of necessary elements including the central role that Christ plays. All of the faculties are to be turned towards God and used in the spiritual quest.[103] Being that the mind is a mediator between diverse parts, one's free choice is therefore crucial for change and Maximus outlines seven stages of volition.[104] Also of importance are detachment, humility, self-mastery, practice of the virtues, charity, love of God and neighbor, and contemplation.[105] Of these, a great emphasis is placed on

97. Ibid., 59.

98. Ibid., 126, 138–40.

99. Ibid., 331–32, 373–427.

100. Ibid., 373, 380, 382–83, 391–92, 400, 406.

101. Ibid., 332.

102. Ibid., 338, 350–51, 358, 364.

103. Ibid., 197.

104. Ibid., 119, 138–39, 218–26, 229.

105. Ibid., 126, 231, 295, 296, 298, 306, 312–14, 323–25, 332.

the virtues, for it is through the intentional practice of these that Christ is made tangibly and deifically present in one's life and in our world; it is therefore an integral part of the deifying process.[106] As Thunberg notes of Maximus' views, "The keeping of the commandments itself makes Christ to dwell in Christians."[107] All-in-all, reintegration therefore occurs primarily by one choosing to live the ascetical life, as Christ becomes more fully manifested through these freely chosen actions, being ultimately effected by the Divine Logos.[108]

Thunberg therefore depicts Maximus' anthropology as one that is both a microcosm and a mediator, for this is what Christ Himself was and continues to be in creation. With sin primarily being a result of poorly chosen and used faculties, which eventually leads to disintegration, the way to deification and unification comes via the ascetical life. Overall, the goal of all human being and becoming is hypostatic union; humans becoming god as God becomes in humanity, and as creation is reconciled into God's very own self.

## THOMAS AQUINAS (1225–1274)

Shifting back to the West, and moving into the medieval scholastic period, we come now to one of the most influential theological thinkers, Thomas Aquinas. In particular, we will be exploring his thought as it is found in both part of Aquinas' own *Summa Theologica*[109] as well as in Jean-Pierre Torrell's *Saint Thomas Aquinas: Volume 2, Spiritual Master.*[110] With Aquinas's *Summa* being generated throughout the course of his life, Torrell emphasizes the relationship between his theology and the concept of faith.[111] "Faith," for Aquinas, Torrell tells us, "is the spiritual space where human ignorance is fashioned into divine science," or "the living attachment of the whole person to the divine Reality to which the person is united through faith by means of the formulas that convey that Reality

---

106. Ibid., 323, 325–26, 328–29.

107. Ibid., 327.

108. Ibid., 171, 231, 330, 430.

109. More specifically, I will be focusing on part I, questions 75–89.

110. Aquinas, *Summa Theologica*; Torrell, *Saint Thomas Aquinas*. Aquinas' work will be parenthetically referenced according to where it is in the *Summa*. For example, "*Summa*, Ia, q. 75, a. 3, reply 1," references the *Summa*, part Ia, question 75, article #3, reply #1. Torrell's work will more simply refer to the page number.

111. Torrell, *Saint Thomas Aquinas*, 5.

to us."[112] Aquinas' theology, and therefore his theological anthropology, is a quest to articulate how we experience and come to attach ourselves ever more fully to God.

Thomas' views of human nature are generally positive, with the Divine considered to be the central aim of one's life. In contrast to other views of human nature, as we found with Augustine, Aquinas views the person as fundamentally and inherently "good," rather than as "brutish or savage," thereby having the ability to "acquire universal and perfect goodness."[113] With each species having its own end in God, the one primary aim and desire of the human species is to attain God, to become like God, and thereby complete a sort of "circular movement of creatures who have come forth from him and are led back toward their origin."[114] Being moved by the Holy Spirit in this journey, humans are also conceived of, similar to Maximus, as a microcosm of the macrocosm.[115]

With these general views of human nature in place, Thomas further distinguishes among its various components. In Thomistic thought, the body and the soul, and their mutual interrelationship are given a central place. Torrell asserts that Aquinas emphasizes that "without the body, there is no longer man" and that the person is essentially considered to be a continuity between matter and spirit rather than being a duality (as it is in Platonic thought) with the body being the form of the soul, and the soul taking the form of the body.[116] In Thomas' own words, the soul has "an aptitude and a natural inclination to be united to the body" and it therefore needs the body; it is their composite that comprises the essence of the soul.[117]

Nevertheless, the soul is able to exist without the body, and it is conceived of as having various powers and abilities. Aquinas asserts not only the benefits of the soul's relation to the body, but also its distinction, stating that it can survive the body's destruction and possesses other ways

---

112. Ibid., 4, 8; see also 13.

113. Ibid.

114. Aquinas, *Summa Theologica*, Ia, q. 75, a. 73, reply 71; Torrell, *Saint Thomas Aquinas*, 51, 55–56, 82, 84, 86, 180, 284, 311–12, 346.

115. Torrell, *Saint Thomas Aquinas*, 200, 205.

116. Aquinas, *Summa Theologica*, Ia, q. 75, a. 77, reply 73; Ia, q. 76, a. 71, answer; Ia, q. 76, a. 78, answer; Torrell, *Saint Thomas Aquinas*, 253, 255–56, 257–59.

117. Aquinas, *Summa Theologica*, Ia, q. 76, a. 71, reply 76; Ia, q. 76, a. 75, answer; Ia, q. 79, 80; Torrell, *Saint Thomas Aquinas*, 257.

of knowing beyond the senses.[118] The soul is conceived of as incorporeal, incorruptible, and "the more noble part," in Torrell's words, for it is created by God, giving life and action to the body, and it is through the soul that the spiritual life is possible.[119] The soul is also conceived of as having multiple powers, such as "vegetative, sensible, and intellectual," and humans are said to have at least two appetites, "the irascible and the concupiscible," yet these are unified in the one soul and one person.[120] Of these various powers and parts, the "intellectual principle" in humans is emphasized, from which memory, reason, and understanding come and is considered to be "nobler than the will"; though "the will moves the intellect."[121] As we can see, Thomas' views of the soul are quite detailed and complex.

In addition to the body and the soul, Aquinas' anthropology also gives some place to free-will, community, and conscience. Addressing the contemporary debates of his time, Thomas affirms the presence of free-will in humans and can therefore acquire mastery over his acts, though these powers are limited.[122] Such freedom therefore endows humanity with the ability to choose between good or evil, and sin is conceived of as choosing counter to the God-given nature of things.[123] In all these choices, conscience, which "does not order us to do this or avoid that except because it believes that something does or does not correspond to the law of God," holds a central place for consultation and guidance of our actions.[124] In addition to these, Torrell also stresses the centrality of community for each human life, for, quoting Thomas,

118. Aquinas, *Summa Theologica*, Ia, q. 77, a. 78, answer; Ia, q. 89, a. 71, answer. (*Summa*, Ia, q. 77, a. 8, answer; q. 89, a. 1, answer)

119. Ibid., Ia, q. 75, a. 71, answer; Ia, q. 75, a. 72, answer; Ia, q. 75, a. 73, answer; Ia, q. 75, a. 75, answer; Ia, q. 75, a. 76, answer; Ia, q. 75, a. 76, reply 71; Torrell, *Saint Thomas Aquinas*, 256, 338.

120. Aquinas, *Summa Theologica*, Ia, q. 76, a. 73, answer; Ia, q. 77, a. 75, answer; Ia, q. 77, a. 78, answer; Ia, q. 78, a. 71, answer; Ia, q. 80, a. 72, answer; Ia, q. 81, a. 72, answer; Torrell, *Saint Thomas Aquinas*, 259–260.

121. Aquinas, *Summa Theologica*, Ia, q. 76, a. 75, answer; Ia, q. 79, a. 71, answer; Ia, q. 79, a. 76; Ia, q. 79, a. 78; Ia, q. 82, a. 73, answer; Ia, q. 82, a. 74, contrary; Torrell, *Saint Thomas Aquinas*, 310.

122. Aquinas, *Summa Theologica*, Ia, q. 81, a. 83, answer; Ia, q. 82, a. 84, answer; Ia, q. 83, a. 81, answer; Torrell, *Saint Thomas Aquinas*, 61, 238.

123. Torrell, *Saint Thomas Aquinas*, 244, 246, 285.

124. Ibid., 317, 321.

"friendship is what is most necessary to live."[125] Human nature is therefore a complex unified entity of body, soul, intellect, free-will, conscience, and community in Thomistic thought.

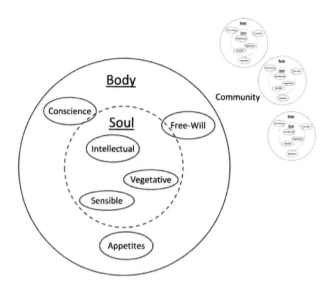

**Figure 4. Aquinas' Anthropological Elements.**

As Aquinas' theology is quite extensive, to say the least, I will only briefly summarize those aspects of it that are relevant for his theological anthropology as it has been presented in Torrell's book. Ultimately, God is conceived of as being unknowable and fully transcendent.[126] Quoting from one of Thomas' own sermons, "We know that God is perfectly known when we become aware that he is still beyond everything that we can think about him."[127] Yet God is still, asymmetrically speaking, the Creator and Redeemer of creation; an artist "who imprints upon his work a trace of his beauty" and ever seeks "the communicating of his own goodness" through the actions and given nature of creation.[128] God is therefore fully present in every part of creation as God continually works towards these ends as "God's love makes being arise from nothingness—at every

---

125. Ibid., 276–77, 281, 306.

126. Ibid., 27, 42, 46, 52, 231.

127. Ibid., 38.

128. Ibid., 57, 62–63, 67, 77, 99, 241, 250.

instant."[129] Such beauty and perfection is seen most fully in Christ, who is both the model and the mode, the very source of grace, for each of us in achieving our Divine aims.[130] In fact, Torrell asserts, "the whole *Summa* moves toward Christ" as Jesus is presented as a "friend" to humanity, "so that knowing God under a visible form, we might be enraptured by him into love of the invisible"; for we are the mystical body of Christ.[131] In this scheme, the Holy Spirit is similarly conceived of as an aid and source of life and grace in creation, as the Trinity is considered to be fully one.[132] These theological conceptions therefore capture something of God's utter transcendence and all-pervasive immanence within, through, and beyond our lives and communities.

Finally, with these views of human nature and some essential elements of Thomas' theology, we turn to his views of human transformation. Summarizing Aquinas' views of human change, Torrell writes, "[A person] is fully [her or himself] only when [she or he] is under cultivation; similarly, the image of God in [her or him] will be fully itself only in the perfected stage of its spiritual activity."[133] The basic idea is that human formation transpires by a two-fold movement wherein an individual becomes ever more like the Divine image, as seen in Christ, and God thereby comes to dwell ever more fully in the individual; i.e., the whole of our lives and communities are to be "Christianized."[134] Viewed in the "circular movement" discussed above, the spiritual journey progresses according to three stages: "First, in that [a person] has a natural aptitude to know and love God . . . Second, in that [a person] knows and loves God actually or habitually . . . Third, in that [a person] knows and loves God actually and perfectly."[135]

In order for this journey to progress, Aquinas asserts a number of necessary elements. Highlighting the need for the proper use of one's free-will, Aquinas is asserted to stress the practices of contemplation, rationality, following one's conscience, and the virtues.[136] It is particu-

129. Ibid., 68, 75.

130. Ibid., 59, 69, 101, 103–4, 116, 139, 145.

131. Ibid., 102, 109, 147.

132. Ibid., 131–32, 155, 157–61, 163, 168, 189–90, 202.

133. Ibid., 86; see also 343.

134. Ibid., 98, 101, 112, 116, 127–28, 144, 164–65, 262, 309, 331, 367, 371.

135. Ibid., 88; see also 341.

136. Ibid., 170, 182, 283, 317, 325, 343–44.

larly through the practice of the virtues—such as fortitude, temperance, prudence, justice, faith, hope, and especially charity or love—that one comes to be a "virtuous being," imitating Christ, and thereby possessing the gifts of God and raising us to our highest ends.[137] In addition to these, Thomas also emphasizes the role and rational mediation of the passions and desire, which must come to be oriented towards their final ends: God.[138] All-in-all, the very essence and nature of the spiritual journey is the complete spiritualizing, harmonizing, and re-orienting of the whole of one's life towards the Divine.[139] Of course, none of this can completely happen by one's own powers, but only through supportive community and ultimately from God, who alone gives us the potential, the path, and the ability to achieve such perfecting Divine ends.[140]

The theological anthropology of Thomas Aquinas is therefore one that depicts human nature as inherently good, comprised of various parts, but ultimately unified. It is one that sets each person on a path leading from where we currently are towards the integrating and perfecting ends towards which we are ever being invited. Whilst God is conceived as being completely transcendent to creation, God is also intimately immanent and active as well. Our spiritual journeys, in Thomistic thought, particularly because of the free-will with which we have been endowed, requires our tangible participation in this Divine life as we are drawn ever more fully into intimate union with the Sacred.

## MARTIN LUTHER (1483–1546)

From classical Catholic to rebelling Protestant, we now move into the Reformation Era with the anthropological views of Martin Luther as they are depicted in his own work, *The Freedom of a Christian*, as well as in Tuomo Mannermaa's book, *Christ Present In Faith: Luther's View Of Justification*.[141] Mannermaa's book explores questions such as: "What precisely did Luther mean by justification? How does it take place? And how are humans, who remain sinners, affected, and their salvation

137. Ibid., 91–92, 212, 268–69, 273–74, 323, 356, 368.

138. Ibid., 261–63, 265, 351, 359.

139. Ibid., 263, 312.

140. Ibid., 93–94, 104, 125–26, 141, 168, 173, 178, 192, 205, 222, 228, 270, 278, 282, 306–7, 347.

141. Luther, "The Freedom of a Christian"; Mannermaa, *Christ Present in Faith*.

effected, by justification?" In pursuit of these, Mannermaa draws on Luther's commentary on Paul's Epistle to the Galatians while also arguing for a doctrine of "theosis" and "deification" in Luther's thought.[142] Luther's text, on the other hand, was written in 1520 for the Pope against some of the Roman Curia's views at that time and, according to Luther, "contains the whole of Christian life in a brief form."[143] From these two texts, we gain a brief insight into some of Luther's views of human nature, God, and transformation.

Similar to Augustine, Luther's view of human nature is one that is dualistic and couched in conflict. "Man has a twofold nature," writes Luther, "a spiritual and a bodily one. According to the spiritual nature, which men refer to as the soul, he is called a spiritual, inner, or new man. According to the bodily nature, which men refer to as flesh, he is called a carnal, outward, or old man."[144] In this scheme, flesh is viewed as full of sin, pitted against the Spirit, and in need of redemption.[145] The inner person, on the other hand, which also seems to be conceived of as what it means to be a Christian, is secure, subject to both none and all, is created in the image of God, is totally righteous, and ultimately replaces the old self or outer person.[146] Between these two, an on-going battle wages as the Spirit of Christ fights for us against the flesh; a battle that can be lost at any time, even after years of struggle.[147] In this battle, Luther asserts, "It is evident that no external thing has any influence in producing Christian righteousness or freedom"; there is nothing a person can do of themselves to win.[148] Human nature for Luther is therefore characterized by our being caught between these two extremes, with nothing that we can do for our own redemption and liberation.

---

142. Mannermaa, *Christ Present in Faith*, vii, xii, 87.

143. Luther, "The Freedom of a Christian," 263–64, 266–67.

144. Ibid., 278.

145. Ibid., 278, 281, 286, 294; Mannermaa, *Christ Present in Faith*, 55, 58–59, 65.

146. Luther, "The Freedom of a Christian," 277, 289, 294; Mannermaa, *Christ Present in Faith*, 39, 44, 58.

147. Luther, "The Freedom of a Christian," 290–91; Mannermaa, *Christ Present in Faith*, 63, 65, 70.

148. Luther, "The Freedom of a Christian," 278, 283; Mannermaa, *Christ Present in Faith*, 26, 79.

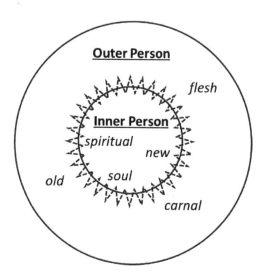

**Figure 5. Luther's Conflicted Person.**

Theologically, a primary emphasis is placed on the role and centrality of Christ.[149] Christ is viewed as bearing all our sins, winning the battle for the inner person, uniting us and all creation in substance with God.[150] He is both God's favor and God's gift, coming as God's Word; He is grace itself.[151] Christ is also viewed by Luther as, Mannermaa asserts, "a kind of "collective person," or, as the Reformer formulates it himself, the "greatest person" (maxima persona), in whom the persons of all human beings are really united," for wherever "the confidence of the heart is present, therefore, there Christ is present, in that very cloud and faith."[152] Luther, Mannermaa asserts, even conceives of the Holy Spirit as the Spirit of Christ.[153] Luther therefore seems to have a very high Christology in which Jesus holds a very central theological position.

Given these two foundations, Luther's views of human change appear to be based directly on them. The entire aim and goal of the Christian spiritual life is for each person to put off the "old self" and become

149. Mannermaa, *Christ Present in Faith*, 5.

150. Luther, "The Freedom of a Christian," 303, 305, 309; Mannermaa, *Christ Present in Faith*, 8, 13, 15–16, 40.

151. Luther, "The Freedom of a Christian," 280; Mannermaa, *Christ Present in Faith*, 19, 25, 27.

152. Mannermaa, *Christ Present in Faith*, 15, 57.

153. Ibid., 73.

one in Christ thereby allowing the new person to emerge in our lives; though it will never fully happen in this life.[154] Progressing differently for different believers, this journey proceeds by faith in Christ alone and each person must come to realize their own inability to progress unaided; faith is therefore absolutely central for Luther.[155] "Faith," writes Manner-maa, "communicates the divine attributes to the human being, because Christ himself, who is a divine person, is present in faith."[156] Faith, then, is the primary means by which Christ comes to actually live in a believer and sanctify their lives, ultimately becoming one with them.[157]

However, Luther also highlights the role of other means of grace. While he utterly denies the ability of works to justify or sanctify,[158] he does support their use in the saving journey.[159] Specifically, when they are coupled with faith, they can teach us to do good things (such as serve our neighbors), reveal our sins to us, help us to resist the desires of the flesh and thereby discipline the body, and direct us solely towards the things of God.[160] Of all the works that can be performed, Luther places a great emphasis on the hearing and the sharing of the Word of God, particularly the Gospel of Christ for He is present in us through the Word.[161] In addition to this, the interactions of a community are also important to the spiritual journey.[162] "It is the church," Mannermaa claims, "that brings Christians to "perfection," to the likeness of the form of Christ, until they come of age."[163]

Of course, none of these efforts, nor faith itself, is possible without Divine intervention; without Christ Himself.[164] In this scheme, Christ

154. Ibid., 39, 67, 86.

155. Luther, "The Freedom of a Christian," 281–83, 291, 295, 299, 311; Mannermaa, *Christ Present in Faith*, 18, 65–66.

156. Mannermaa, *Christ Present in Faith*, 22.

157. Ibid., 5, 16, 26, 29, 42–43, 45.

158. Luther, "The Freedom of a Christian," 288, 296; Mannermaa, *Christ Present in Faith*, 31–32, 36.

159. Luther, "The Freedom of a Christian," 300.

160. Ibid., 282, 294, 296, 302, 305, 308; Mannermaa, *Christ Present in Faith*, 35, 69, 86.

161. Luther, "The Freedom of a Christian," 279–80, 292–93; Mannermaa, *Christ Present in Faith*, 79, 84.

162. Luther, "The Freedom of a Christian," 314; Mannermaa, *Christ Present in Faith*, 82–83.

163. Mannermaa, *Christ Present in Faith*, 80.

164. Ibid., 16.

takes on all of the sin of our lives and transforms it along with us in the process.[165] It is, ever and always, God's life that makes us loving, righteous, and perfect.[166] And it is only through our faith that the Christian "possesses [Christ] by faith."[167] Christ is therefore seen, as He was in some of the other anthropologies we have looked at, as the author and finisher of our faith.

Luther's theological anthropology therefore depicts humanity as being trapped between flesh and Spirit. Having no means in ourselves to affect our own liberation, we must turn ourselves in faith to Christ, our sole Redeemer. While works, Word, and community can all aid us in this journey, it is faith alone that ultimately liberates and saves us according to Luther. It does so by allowing the very Person of Christ to win the battle and move us ever more fully towards union with His very own Personhood, taking on His qualities and righteousness as we do. Luther's theological anthropology is therefore found to be highly Christological and dualistic as we are called to leave the old self behind and find our new, inner, and spiritual selves in the person of Jesus.

## IMMANUEL KANT (1724–1804)

Again changing gears, like moving from night to day, we next turn to Immanuel Kant's rational-based religion with his own work, *Religion within the Limits of Reason Alone.*[168] This piece was written when he was seventy years old and was his last major work.[169] Being raised as the son of Pietist parents, the authors of the introduction assert, "while [Kant] moved from height to height in his strictly philosophical inquiries, his whole conception of Christian theology remained almost unchanged from youth to old age . . . It is invariably the pietist version of Christianity that he seems to have in view in his later writings."[170] This is therefore an

---

165. Luther, "The Freedom of a Christian," 283–284; Mannermaa, *Christ Present in Faith*, 17, 69.

166. Luther, "The Freedom of a Christian," 286; Mannermaa, *Christ Present in Faith*, 21, 49, 54, 73, 79.

167. Luther, "The Freedom of a Christian," 286; Mannermaa, *Christ Present in Faith*, 51.

168. Kant, *Religion within the Limits.*

169. Ibid., xxii, xxx.

170. Ibid., xxx.

expression, according to these authors, of his Pietist upbringing as well as his philosophical profession.

For Kant, human nature is generally conceived of in a positive light. Though we have "fallen into evil only through seduction," we, and the inclinations that we have, are still intrinsically good.[171] Kant also asserts the presence of some "mystery, i.e., something holy which may indeed be known by each single individual but cannot be made known publicly, that is, shared universally."[172] We are therefore called, in Kant's theological anthropology, to struggle against our falleness and become free according to the means by which the goodness of God makes available to us.[173]

Central to our nature, then, are two components that Kant emphasizes: our will and our predispositions. Our will is unique because of our freedom to choose which way to go in life.[174] This will, however, can only act to the extent as "far as the individual has incorporated it into his maxim (has made it the general rule in accordance with which he will conduct himself)."[175] Predispositions, on the other hand, are inclinations that are already present and active within our lives; such as: self-love, propagation of the species, making social comparisons, and the "capacity for respect for the moral law."[176] Taken together, these two concepts form a part of Kant's views of human nature.

In this scheme, goodness and evil find a rational place, as both can result from either predispositions or from the use of one's free-will, and often times both.[177] "To have a good or an evil disposition as an inborn natural constitution," Kant writes, "[means] that it has not been acquired in time (that he has always been good, or evil, from his youth up) . . . Yet this disposition itself must have been adopted by free choice, for otherwise it could not be imputed."[178] He then identifies three different degrees of the capacity for evil, all of which find their roots in free-choice, one's natural predispositions, or both.[179] Kant also highlights the significant impact that we can have on one another as it relates to the predispositions

171. Ibid., 39, 51.
172. Ibid., 129.
173. Ibid., 85, 88, 134.
174. Ibid., 19, 36.
175. Ibid., 19.
176. Ibid., 22–23.
177. Ibid., 17, 30.
178. Ibid., 20.
179. Ibid., 24.

and maxims we adopt; community is therefore a significant part of our personhood according to him.[180] All in all, however, Kant points to the centrality and role of one's free-will in evil actions; it is our choice to actively adopt evil into our own "maxims" or not, into the principles by which we live.[181] Finally, Kant asserts a view of an original "state of innocence" from which we have fallen and towards which we must strive.[182] His theological anthropology is therefore one that asserts the inherent goodness of humanity, the roles of free-will and predispositions, and importance of community for our lives.

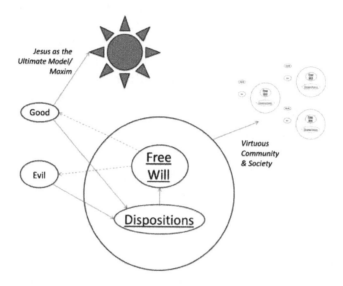

Figure 6. Kant's "Reasonable" Theological Anthropology.

As it relates to God, Kant has a Christology similar to what we have encountered previously. For him, Jesus is viewed as an example and model, "through his teachings, his conduct, and his sufferings"; He is an "archetype" for us.[183] Christ is the archetype to which we are expected to conform and He "opens the portals of freedom to all who, like him, choose to become dead to everything that holds them fettered to life on

---

180. Ibid., 88.

181. Ibid., 26, 27, 31, 50.

182. Ibid., 36, 39, 85.

183. Ibid., 54, 57, 60, 77, 119–20, 150.

earth to the detriment of morality."[184] In a sense, then, Christ is the ultimate maxim towards which we ought to strive.

More generally, Kant also speaks of God in universal terms. On this, he writes, "Now the universal true religious belief conformable to this requirement of practical reason is belief in God (1) as the omnipotent Creator of heaven and earth, i.e., morally as holy Legislator, (2) as Preserver of the human race, its benevolent Ruler and moral Guardian, (3) as Administrator of His own holy laws, i.e., as righteous Judge."[185] Taken with his Christological views, these are some of the essential theological views that seem to inform his theological anthropology.

Finally, turning to his views of human change, Kant sees our journey as one that is rooted in rationality and oriented towards moral perfection. Referring to Christ, he writes, "Now it is our common duty as men to elevate ourselves to this ideal of moral perfection, that it, to this archetype of the moral disposition in all its purity."[186] Following Jesus as our model, we are called to set aside the doing of evil and instead pursue the good.[187] The essence of the spiritual journey, for Kant, is therefore one of moral perfection and the doing/being of goodness.

This journey, which is not easy, requires a number of components. Kant begins from the location of affirming the inherent goodness of our dispositions and inherent maxims, for, as he writes, "[Man] is created for good and the original predisposition in man is good."[188] Closely related to this is his assertion of the presence of "a practical knowledge," a "law," in each person that is accessible via our rational faculties and which we universally share with all people.[189] Based upon this, Kant argues for a religion of pure reason, or a natural religion, which "alone is authentic and valid for the whole world," and needs no "documentary authentication" as do historical religions such as Christianity and Judaism, but rather stands on its own on the basis of reason.[190] The spiritual journey is therefore conceived of as our coming to discovery these maxims, via reason and with Jesus as our archetype, and then freely working to live in

---

184. Ibid., 54–55, 77.

185. Ibid., 131.

186. Ibid., 54.

187. Ibid., 60, 68–69, 135.

188. Ibid., 40, 43, 62, 106.

189. Ibid., 156, 169.

190. Ibid., 105–6, 120, 123, 143, 155–56.

accordance with them via a long and gradual cultivation of virtuous liv-ing.[191] So central is Kant's view of virtuous living, that he asserts it as be-ing more important than "reverence for God," which has the potential to become a form of idolatry.[192] The journey of moral perfection is therefore one of continual struggle against evil maxims and principles and one that should be made both in a virtuous community and for the virtuousness and well-being of society.[193]

With such an emphasis on free-moral choice and self-determina-tion, we might expect Luther to ask of Kant what role God has in this scheme; for indeed it seems to be one of the kinds of "works right-eousness" religions that Luther so deplored. Kant does hold a place for supernatural intervention as he distinguishes between nature, "whatever good man is able to do through his own efforts, under laws of freedom," and grace.[194] Such interventions, for him, seem to mostly come in the form of augmenting and providing that which nature cannot or does not provide. God's intervening work in the spiritual journey is depicted as: (1) providing "a confidence in its own permanence and stability, and is our Comforter (Paraclete) whenever our lapses make us apprehensive of its constancy,"[195] (2) as one that "opens the portals of freedom to all,"[196] and (3) "breaking of [the evil principle's] power to hold against [our] will."[197] God's acting grace is therefore conceived of as "supplementing" our journeys when we need it, providing for us what nature cannot.[198] However, Kant is quick to point out, such intervening grace only comes when we adequately prepare ourselves for it and only when we have made "the maximum use of our own powers."[199] God's interventions are there-fore conceived as augmenting the intentional work of moral perfection that we are invited to grow in.

Immanuel Kant's theological anthropology is one that is thoroughly rooted in the morally perfecting life. Being inherently good, and having the components of free-willed choice and predispositions, our spiritual

191. Ibid., 42–43, 46, 148, 156, 171.

192. Ibid., 173.

193. Ibid., 42, 85, 86, 161.

194. Ibid., 179.

195. Ibid., 65.

196. Ibid., 77.

197. Ibid.

198. Ibid., 134, 179–80.

199. Ibid., 40, 179–80.

forming journeys are conceived of in direct relation to our rational faculties. Our journey is therefore one that is to be rooted in the quest for virtuous living, with Christ as the ultimate maxim towards which we are to continuously aim. Though community and augmenting grace have important parts to play, it is our self-determined efforts that compose the bulk of our transformative life according to Kant. Ultimately, he asserts, we are to come to discover and live in accordance with the inherent maxims deep within us all that are fully accessible by our rationality. It is, as his title asserts, truly a religion and spiritual quest within the limits of reason (though not alone, as grace is also considered to be a part of it as we have seen).

## KARL BARTH (1886–1968)

Transitioning now to the final three sets of contemporary theological anthropologies, we first turn to Protestant Theologian Karl Barth as his views are captured in part of his own *Church Dogmatics* as well as in Adam Neder's *Participation in Christ* and Daniel J. Price's *Karl Barth's Anthropology in Light of Modern Thought*.[200] From Barth's work, I have focused on Volume III, Part 2, Chapter X, Paragraph 46, entitled "Man as Soul and Body," which, in Barth's own words, sets out to "prove that man is to be understood as "soul and body," that this constitutes his being," especially in relation to God.[201] Neder's book focuses on Barth's work and the questions, "How can Jesus Christ be both the giver of grace and grace itself? . . . How can the being of humanity be both objectively included in Christ and subjectively realized in him?"[202] Finally, Price seeks to understand Barth's anthropology in light of modern object relations psychology in the hopes of enlightening both theology and science in both of these works.[203] Taken together, they provide a brief overview of Barth's thought in this arena.

Barth's theological anthropology is generally conceived of in relational terms. Seeking common ground between Barth's views and object relations theory, Price argues that such relationality is at the core of Barth's

200. Barth, *Church Dogmatics*; Neder, *Participation in Christ*; Price, *Karl Barth's Anthropology*.

201. Barth, *Church Dogmatics*, 326.

202. Neder, *Participation in Christ*, xi–xii.

203. Price, *Karl Barth's Anthropology*, 5, 9, 11.

anthropology, and this view is echoed by Barth himself.[204] While "human life is independent life,"[205] it is also a life that is related to others and to God.[206] More precisely, human relationality is conceived, for Barth, in terms of our relationship with Christ, who is the restoring image of God to whom we are called to cleave.[207] Such relationality also extends to the historicity of our lives as well as to our relationship with ourselves via self-knowledge; though even these are spoken of in relation to God.[208] Humanity is also asserted to be unique from other creatures because we can consciously respond to God's grace,[209] and Neder emphasizes the individual actions of persons as being central to what makes us who we are.[210] Hence, these concepts of relationality, especially with Christ, are central features of Barth's general views of human nature.

As to some of the specific components of our nature, three are explicitly addressed: spirit, soul, and body. As it relates to spirit, Barth seems to distinguish between the spirit that a creature has and the Spirit of God. For instance, he writes, "Even the animal has spirit. But we do not know how it has Spirit, i.e., what it means for the animal that through the Spirit it is the soul of a body."[211] The Spirit of God is viewed as sustaining and ordering body and soul,[212] while the spirit of a person means that one is "grounded, constituted and maintained by God," comes from God, and it is seen as "superior, determining and limiting" the body and soul, unifying them both.[213] Elaborating on this relation between humanity and God, he writes, "When we say 'man' or 'soul and body,' then wittingly or unwittingly we have first said 'God.'"[214]

204. Barth, *Church Dogmatics*, 325; Price, *Karl Barth's Anthropology*, 13, 117, 146, 153, 163.

205. Barth, *Church Dogmatics*, 397.

206. Ibid., 406, 417; Neder, *Participation in Christ*, 31; Price, *Karl Barth's Anthropology*, 97, 99, 120, 136.

207. Barth, *Church Dogmatics*, 327; Neder, *Participation in Christ*, 12, 21–22, 31, 75; Price, *Karl Barth's Anthropology*, 18, 98, 118, 123, 144, 162.

208. Barth, *Church Dogmatics*, 395, 399; Neder, *Participation in Christ*, 37; Price, *Karl Barth's Anthropology*, 121, 256.

209. Price, *Karl Barth's Anthropology*, 122.

210. Neder, *Participation in Christ*, 12, 35–37.

211. Barth, *Church Dogmatics*, 395.

212. Ibid., 347, 356, 359, 362–63, 394; Price, *Karl Barth's Anthropology*, 256–57.

213. Barth, *Church Dogmatics*, 344, 348, 353–54, 356, 365, 393, 419.

214. Ibid., 345.

In this relationship, the soul is then conceived of as being "inner," affording the freedom of a person, as well as providing "a rational and volitional structure for the animating force of the human body."[215] While body and soul are not considered to be synonymous with one another,[216] they are seen as being intimately related and they must be "integrated into a unitary human being who is an embodied soul and an ensouled body," for a person is both body and soul taken together.[217] In Barth's own words, "Man's being exists, and is therefore soul; and it exists in a certain form, and is therefore body"; we must therefore always speak of both, for both live and suffer together.[218] Body, soul, and Spirit therefore stand in an intimate and mutually unified relationship with one another in Barth's scheme, thereby rounding out the relational focus of his theological anthropology.

In this relational matrix, sin is therefore likewise conceived of by Price in terms of being a break in such relationships. Whether this break comes with others, with God, or ourselves, the effects of sins are always the same: a distortion and blinding of our abilities to see reality as it is; it is, in the words of Neder, "to cease to be human."[219] The road to recovery, as we shall see below, is therefore partly a quest to grow in our relationality in all its various forms.

---

215. Ibid., 365, 418; Price, *Karl Barth's Anthropology*, 248–49, 251.

216. Barth, *Church Dogmatics*, 397–98.

217. Ibid., 325, 350, 368, 370, 380, 396, 401; Price, *Karl Barth's Anthropology*, 21, 161, 245, 248–49.

218. Barth, *Church Dogmatics*, 325, 373, 375, 392, 432; Price, *Karl Barth's Anthropology*, 247.

219. Neder, *Participation in Christ*, 36; see also Price, *Karl Barth's Anthropology*, 98, 117, 124, 127, 129, 261.

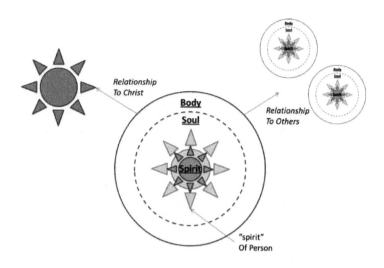

**Figure 7. Barth's Relational Human Being.**

Theologically, Barth follows Luther in giving central role and place to the person of Christ. Jesus is viewed as the core foundation for all of humanity in God.[220] "Since Jesus Christ is the origin of all things," Neder writes, "nothing exists apart from him. He is not accidentally related to all creaturely things, but is their most fundamental presupposition."[221] As such, Christ is seen as the divine mediator who saves all by freely and unconditionally giving of Himself to all, and thereby pardons all our sins for us.[222]

Given this high position, human nature is therefore to be fully and totally understood in relation to the historical person of Jesus.[223] God is therefore seen as expressing God's interaction and Divinity in creation through Christ as He participates in our fallen nature with us.[224] Such interactions, Neder asserts of Barth, are never intermingled or "confused with each other," for God must always remain God.[225] In Barth's own

220. Barth, *Church Dogmatics*, 342; Neder, *Participation in Christ*, xi; Price, *Karl Barth's Anthropology*, 154.

221. Neder, *Participation in Christ*, 17.

222. Ibid., 23, 42, 45–46, 52, 63; Price, *Karl Barth's Anthropology*, 130.

223. Barth, *Church Dogmatics*, 327, 332, 340; Price, *Karl Barth's Anthropology*, 125, 131.

224. Neder, *Participation in Christ*, 72; Price, *Karl Barth's Anthropology*, 126.

225. Neder, *Participation in Christ*, 7, 19, 62.

words, "God does not in any sense belong to the constitution of man. God is neither a part nor the whole of human nature . . . But the whole which we are in this unity and order is not without God."[226] God is therefore always revealed only under a veil of mystery and is always given as a gift "from above" that is accomplished only "by making himself the Lord of humanity."[227] Despite such separation, Barth still asserts, "In so far as [all God's creatures] live at all, they live by the Spirit."[228] Barth's theology is therefore one of a sort of transcending immanence that places Christ at the very center of the divine-human relationship.

Turning lastly to Barth's views of human change, we find many of the above assertions to carry over. According to Neder, the nature of final human transformation for Barth is conceived of as a "mutual indwelling . . . the liberation of human action by God's sovereign grace, which energizes human creatures to freely do that which by nature is impossible for them," thereby maintaining the infinite distance between creature and Creator.[229] In this union, the "sinner" dies and "a new creature appears on the scene that did not exist before the event."[230] "Discipleship," Neder writes of Barth's views, "is a transition from death to life, an event altogether grounded in the objective conversion of humanity to God in Jesus Christ."[231] Unity of our relationship to God is therefore emphasized, bringing the relationality of Barth's anthropology to completion in Christ.[232]

Such transformations are prompted by our response to God's call, via Jesus the Word, as God's elect.[233] Much of our journey is therefore a path of growing in conformity to this Word of God, by our humble participation in this historical covenant.[234] With Christ as the center, He affects all that is necessary for our salvation and sanctification; we are to become who we fully are in Him alone.[235] Barth's views of human change are therefore as Christologically centered as Luther's were, placing the

226. Barth, *Church Dogmatics*, 345.

227. Neder, *Participation in Christ*, 3, 8, 19.

228. Barth, *Church Dogmatics*, 334.

229. Neder, *Participation in Christ*, 11, 14, 54, 65.

230. Ibid., 11, 52.

231. Ibid., 82.

232. Ibid., 79.

233. Ibid., xi, 25; Price, *Karl Barth's Anthropology*, 127–28.

234. Neder, *Participation in Christ*, xiv, 9, 26, 38.

235. Ibid., 12, 23, 28, 52, 77.

whole of our salvation and redemptive journeys solely in the hands of the Person of Jesus.

Barth's theological anthropology was found to emphasize the relationality of the individual to oneself, others, and ultimately God. Sin is therefore to be at least partly understood as a break in such relationality. He also conceives of a tripartite view of human nature in which Spirit, soul, and body are distinct, yet interdependent and hierarchically ordered. Theologically, as well as anthropologically, Barth holds a very central place to Christology. Christ is God's interaction with creation, though God is also infinitely transcendent to creation as well. Despite such transcendence, humanity will find the beginning, middle, and end of its spiritual journey in Jesus.

## KARL RAHNER (1904–1984)

Moving again from what seems like one polar opposite to another, we turn next from our last three Protestant authors back to a Roman Catholic theologian with Karl Rahner's *Foundations of Christian Faith*.[236] In this text, Rahner proclaims to pursue the following question: "What is Christianity, and why can one live this Christian existence today with intellectual honesty?"[237] Set "within the framework of intellectual reflection," Rahner hopes to offer an updated version of the Christian message for today.[238] In this piece, we learn something more of his views of human nature, God's relationship to it, and something of what the spiritual journey consists of.

For Rahner, human nature is bounded in history and is whole, transcendent, free, dependent, and oriented towards God. As we shall see, his views seem to be characterized by such paradoxes and polar opposites. That humanity is bounded in time and historical experience is a central assertion for Rahner.[239] We are creatures who are constrained by "spatial extension and temporal duration," and such constraints play a fundamental part in shaping us to be who we are.[240] We are also dependent persons, "being at the disposal of other things" and partly shaped by

236. Rahner, *Foundations of Christian Faith*.

237. Ibid., 2.

238. Ibid., xi, 1.

239. Ibid., 25, 40, 138.

240. Ibid., 94, 107, 160.

the feedback we receive from others.[241] Yet, given these constraints, we are also free and responsible beings who can choose our direction and courses of action.[242] With this freedom, however, comes responsibility to actualize ourselves and to act morally, for we can choose to either say "yes" or "no" to God.[243] This freedom, when under the influence of "original guilt," can result in sinful actions in the world.[244] For Rahner, guilt is one of the primary influences that has been handed down from Adam, and is therefore an on-going tension in our lives.[245]

In light of all of these tensions and influences, Rahner emphasizes the human in their wholeness; their entirety.[246] Like the intimate and inseparable connection between spirit and matter, individuals are neither reducible nor dividable)[247]. However, given this wholeness, Rahner goes on to assert, the core of who we are is a sort of transcendent and ultimately unknowable essence or "ground," through which we experience the "absolute closeness and immediacy" of God.[248] "Man is and remains a transcendent being," he writes, "that is, he is that existent to whom the silent and uncontrollable infinity of reality is always present as mystery."[249] Given this "transcendentality," humanity is ultimately oriented towards God, as God "makes himself the innermost constitutive element of man"[250] However, given God's own transcendence, humanity is at one and the same time "radically different and distant from God" and "absolutely close to this mystery."[251] Given these polar opposites of dependence and freedom, wholeness and mystery, and closeness and distance from the God who makes us, Rahner's anthropology might be characterized as one of tensions and paradoxes.

241. Ibid., 42, 160.

242. Ibid., 35–36, 93–94, 407.

243. Ibid., 92, 100, 102, 104, 403.

244. Ibid., 109.

245. Ibid., 110, 114, 133.

246. Ibid., 28, 435–36.

247. Ibid., 31, 94, 182, 184.

248. Ibid., 75, 138.

249. Ibid., 35.

250. Ibid., 44, 116, 127.

251. Ibid., 162.

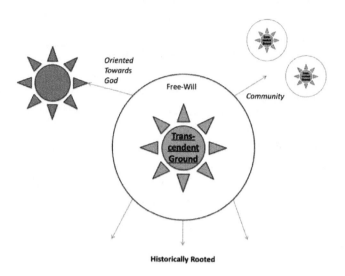

**Figure 8. Rahner's Transcendental Personality.**

Theologically, Rahner's conceptions of God mirror the paradoxes of human nature. Noting that concepts of God and the Trinity are difficult to conceive,[252] and also that words are our best attempts to grasp at such mysteries,[253] Rahner highlights the simultaneous transcendence and immanence of the Divine who can be experienced as sort of a "hidden closeness . . . something familiar which he can approach and turn to from the estrangement of his own perilous and empty life."[254] Rahner ensures that the concept of God as transcendent is firmly adhered to, referring to the Sacred as "holy mystery"; or "the ontologically silent horizon of every intellectual and spiritual encounter."[255] It is this mystery that is the ground of all being in every moment, but who is not dependent on creation for it transcends all that is.[256]

Given this transcendence, however, Rahner also emphasizes the immanence of God as well, particularly as it relates to Jesus.[257] God is therefore also conceived of as being fully present to and active within the

252. Ibid., 134.
253. Ibid., 50.
254. Ibid., 12, 131.
255. Ibid., 66, 77.
256. Ibid., 77–78, 81.
257. Ibid., 85.

world, having a "salvific will" for creation.[258] Through this immanence, God "self-communicates" with creation and especially humankind, being "the ultimate and highest dynamism of this world and its history."[259] Such self-communication happens most fully "in the fundamental unity of knowledge and love" and "to the extent that subjectivity and transcendentality are actualized."[260] Such transcendentality is most fully seen in the historical person of Jesus, who "lived in and was part of the religious milieu of his people and the historical situation in which he found himself."[261] Jesus is therefore understood as a reformer who was fully conversant and interactive with the events of his day as one who was fully human, just like us, biologically and historically located and fully alive.[262] For Rahner, Jesus is therefore presented as a model and climax of human potentiality and hypostatic union with God's self-communication.[263] In Jesus, then, do we find Rahner's paradoxes of God's transcendence and immanence coming into fully harmonization and unification, thereby synthesizing his theology into a coherent whole.[264]

Finally, Rahner's views of human transformation follow directly from what he has asserted anthropologically and theologically. Being historically located and unique to each person, our spiritual journey is presented as a journey towards both wholeness and self-transcendence.[265] Integration and wholeness are considered by him to be part and parcel of this journey; the permeating of God in the entirety of one's being and history.[266] Such unity includes self-awareness and self-actualization as well as a love which extends to one's neighbors.[267] Through this unity, one eventually and ultimately comes to a place where they must embrace the transcendentality that is the essence of who they are and is the source of their freedom; something that can only be worked out in history, both one's own and that of the larger community.[268] Through this self-tran-

258. Ibid., 87, 313.

259. Ibid., 137, 261.

260. Ibid., 118–19, 122, 151.

261. Ibid., 157, 232–33, 236–38, 247.

262. Ibid., 195, 220, 247–48.

263. Ibid., 114, 174, 176, 254, 303, 306.

264. Ibid., 181.

265. Ibid., 141, 143, 145, 154, 167, 193, 307.

266. Ibid., 172, 306–7, 411.

267. Ibid., 183, 309.

268. Ibid., 39, 40–41, 98, 139, 181, 184.

scendence, humanity is enabled with the ability "to hear something like a message from the one God-Man"; it enables God's self-communication.[269] However, these goals are, Rahner asserts, not possible in the realm of time and space, but rather will be achieved elsewhere.[270] Transcendence and unity, something which has permeated both his anthropology and theology, are therefore found to be central to his views of human change.

In order to be a part of affecting such changes, there are a number of factors and components that he touches upon. Humans must be open, oriented towards God, and fully actualizing of their freedom and decision-making faculties.[271] Each person must also exercise a certain amount of faith in their journey, which is necessary in order for God to enact God's salvific plans and in order for the individual to receive revelation.[272] However, he notes, faith itself is a horizon towards which one travels.[273] Such transformations are therefore never made in complete isolation, as the whole of the cosmos likewise needs to be transformed.[274] We need guidance, and we need the community and practices of church to help us on our journey, as all of these are asserted to mediate the grace of God in our lives.[275]

As Christians, we also need Jesus, for in Him do we find the ability to discern what is a true understanding of "the transcendental experience of God."[276] Christ is, however, not just a model for us, but also a salvific participation in His life.[277] "This discipleship is not imitation," writes Rahner, "but rather an ever unique call from out of one's own concrete life, and into participation in the mystery of the life of Jesus from his birth until his death."[278] Known and criticized for this concept, Rahner also asserts that even non-Christians, as "anonymous Christians," participate in Christ's salvation through His Spirit.[279] Human change is therefore characterized by Rahner as a historical journey towards unity

---

269. Ibid., 178, 198.

270. Ibid., 273.

271. Ibid., 149, 282, 297.

272. Ibid., 142, 240, 291.

273. Ibid., 240, 242–45, 269.

274. Ibid., 190.

275. Ibid., 159, 306–7, 330, 347, 370, 390, 427–29.

276. Ibid., 157.

277. Ibid., 299, 308.

278. Ibid., 310–11.

279. Ibid., 316, 318.

and self-transcendence and one that is facilitated and made possible by our co-participatory actions with the grace and Spirit of God in Christ.

Rahner's theological anthropology might therefore be generally characterized as a paradoxical tension between polar opposites, particularly transcendence and immanence. Not only are people understood to be historically rooted in time and space with dependencies and responsibilities, but they are also conceived of as having a fully transcendent core, essence, and ground and are free to act in creation. Such paradoxes, it was asserted, are also noted in his theological views, as God's immanence and transcendence were highlighted. In this scheme, Jesus becomes the unity of these opposites and therefore a model for the whole of humanity, which is to be ultimately oriented within and expressive of God's transcending self-communications. Human change was therefore found to be a journey towards such transcendence, though fully located historically. By turning within ourselves and to one another, we ultimately find our salvation in the Person and Spirit of Christ.

## THEOLOGICAL ANTHROPOLOGIES IN LIGHT OF MODERN SCIENCE

There have also been attempts to synthesize more classical Christian views of human nature with modern scientific finds, particularly those found in psychological and neuroscientific fields. We finally round out this Western Christian historical journey by turning to a collection of essays that explore human nature in light of both modern science and contemporary theology. Edited by Robert John Russell, Nancey Murphy, Theo C. Meyering, and Michael A. Arbib, *Neuroscience and the Person: Scientific Perspective on Divine Action*,[280] presents a series of articles that resulted from a Vatican-hosted conference whose "purpose was to explore relations between the cognitive neurosciences and Christian theology."[281] These authors, then, are interested in seeking "a fruitful concord between science and religion," with a particular interest in exploring the place and role of divine action in creation in light of contemporary scientific findings.[282] It is through these writings that we hope to come to some kind of synthesis for what a "theological anthropology in light of

280. Russell et al., *Neuroscience and the Person*.

281. Ibid., i.

282. Ibid., i–iii, 216.

modern science" might look like according to these authors. Many of the concepts discussed in this section will also be reviewed in the next part of this book. This last set of explorations therefore stands as a transition into the second part where we consider contemporary science-based views of human nature.

In general, the human person is conceived of as a multi-layered, hierarchically arranged unity, that may have an unknowable core. A number of these authors conceived of the "person" as a unified, single entity.[283] Such unity is considered to be inclusive of everything that makes up our lives, including "conscious and unconscious, rational and emotional, active and passive, individual and social, etc."[284] This unity, or the "self," as one author asserts, is considered to be "the highest level in which all of the lower levels are integrated."[285] The person is therefore also viewed as having multiple layers that are hierarchically ordered.[286] Exploring the relationships between the mind and the body and the body and the soul, these layers are also considered by some to be irreducibly dependent on and unified with one another, yet not in a dualistic way.[287] Instead, their relationship is conceived of by a few authors in a "supervenient" or "emergent" fashion in which each layer both constrains and is influenced by the layers above and below it.[288] One author also asserts that the "self" is unknowable and "totally impenetrable to anyone else," recognizing the similarities in our concepts of the person with classical views of God;[289] a microcosm/mirror reflection that we have noted of other authors above.

Given these general views of human nature, several components of our being were discussed among these essays, comprising the bulk of their anthropological reflections. Firstly, consciousness and personal subjectivity was discussed in a number of ways. Clearly, it was noted, there is a "thinking thing," an inner conscious reality of subjective experience, that each of us has as a part of our being, though to varying degrees.[290] Conceived by one author as an integrating factor,[291] this sub-

283. Ibid., 86, 323.

284. Ibid., 231, 252, 254, 261.

285. Ibid., 276.

286. Ibid., 198, 249, 265, 269.

287. Ibid., 92, 129, 153, 183, 190, 210.

288. Ibid., 150, 184, 196, 199, 201, 219, 221, 228, 230, 296–97, 450–51.

289. Ibid., 34, 37.

290. Ibid., 24, 197, 260, 452.

291. Ibid., 302.

jectivity of higher consciousness is a part of identity formation, planning, evaluating, and execution, and the freedom and responsibility we demonstrate in our actions.[292] Somewhat related to this are our memories, without which, one author asserts, we are not who we are.[293] Being linked to various brain regions, memories are active occurrences that enable us to make comparisons between past and present and are therefore intrinsic to how we operate.[294]

Following on this concept, several authors also discussed the role of schemas as a part of our nature. In short, schemas are basically internal models of our world that we may automatically use, in conscious and unconscious ways, to live, decide, and act in the world; we are even asserted to have "a total model of the universe" within us that is based on these schemeas.[295] With various schemas, which can also be considered to be a conceptual framework for describing the world, being both locatable to specific regions of the brain as well as distributed across the brain, they are activated by both internal and external stimulations.[296] Though schemas are asserted to play a major role in influencing our lives, it must also be noted that they are not fixed entities, but can be changed via learning and reconditioning.[297]

Another set of influences include emotions, feelings, and the soul. Distinguishing between emotions (which are biological reactions to a stimulus) and feelings (which are our conscious awareness and evaluations of emotions), both are asserted to have a central impact on who we are and how we live in the world.[298] Closely related to these affective dimensions, some of the authors also discussed the place of a "soul" as sort of "personal inner calling" that is linked in a unifying way with both affect and the meaning or significance we give to things.[299]

Finally, many of these authors also discussed the centrality that relationships have on oneself, not just with others, but also to the environments in which they find themselves. Having its roots in our evolutionary

292. Ibid., 24, 32, 58, 73, 113–14, 258.

293. Ibid., 323.

294. Ibid., 116, 182–83, 300–301, 465.

295. Ibid., 57–58, 60, 88, 98, 162, 297–98.

296. Ibid., 85, 89, 95–98, 106, 108, 194.

297. Ibid., 91, 104, 159.

298. Ibid., 101, 117, 252, 254, 261, 465.

299. Ibid., 81, 84, 144–45, 312.

history,[300] our need for relationships is biologically rooted as our brains give shape to and are shaped by others.[301] Being biological organisms, we humans are therefore also shaped by our environments and such physical and social relationships are integral to who we are and how we act.[302] In light of all of this, the human person is therefore generally depicted as being a unified and emergent whole of complex, interrelated parts, which include subjectivity, biology, memory, schemas, affects, and relationships.

Turning now to the theological assertions made by some of these authors, we find a diverse range of viewpoints. Many of the classical views of God were touched upon by many of these authors. God can, even in a purely "physicalist's" scheme, still be asserted as a non-physical entity.[303] God is also presented as being all-knowing and everywhere present.[304] God is also presented by some as having person-like qualities such as a will and memory.[305] Yet, God is also conceived of as being transcendent to creation.[306]

As it relates to God's actions in creation, which is part of the main focus of this text, there were a range of possibilities presented. God is presented as being self-limiting and self-giving, or "kenotic."[307] Though self-limiting, God is fully active in the events and history of creation.[308] These interventions, in light of modern science, are not viewed as violating the "laws" of creation, but rather is God's action seen as acting through them.[309] Yet, one author holds, God could still be asserted to intervene in more direct ways as well.[310] Summarizing the forms God's actions can take, Peacocke writes, "This interaction has been variously classified in the history of Christian thought: (1) the creative active of God; (2) the sustaining activity of God; (3) God's action as final cause; (4) general providence; (5) special providence; (6) miracles."[311] In light of

---

300. Ibid., 67, 72.

301. Ibid., 68, 145, 296.

302. Ibid., 73, 110, 157, 195, 240, 252, 254, 261.

303. Ibid., 184.

304. Ibid., 236, 280.

305. Ibid., 237, 323.

306. Ibid., 235, 280.

307. Ibid., 244, 454, 459.

308. Ibid., i, 235.

309. Ibid., 236, 460–61, 470, 472.

310. Ibid., 472.

311. Ibid., 233.

modern science, these authors are therefore found to depict God's nature and role in creation in both classical and novel ways.

Lastly, we find human change being discussed by some of these authors, though not directly. Overall, these views reflect the scientific location from which many of these authors come. Change is therefore discussed in terms of evolutionary history and chaos theory.[312] As discussed above, schema change/conditioning theories are also highlighted as way of fostering human transformation[313]. Environmental, social, and internal feedback loops are also seen as being an integral part of whether a person changes or not.[314] One author also asserts the need for us to be an active part of all of these changes through such interventions as "meditation, prayer, or spiritual reading."[315] Such change, however, is ultimately beyond our control and we must actively seek the "revelations" of God within and through the world around us to find meaning and direction.[316] Human transformation is therefore largely presented as occurring through the natural processes of creation, though Divine intervention can be sought in and amongst them.

The theological anthropology found in this collection of essays is therefore quite varied and complex. Human nature, while understood as a unified emergent whole, is comprised of a number of elements which different sciences take as their object of study. Including consciousness, schemas, relationships, memory, affects, et cetera, the human person is presented as being quite complex. The theologies which were briefly presented provide us with further ideas for conceiving of God's presence and role within and through the so-called "natural" processes of creation. Human change, like anthropology, was also found to be presented in terms of the various processes and components of the person in these various authors.

312. Ibid., 73, 268.

313. Ibid., 91, 104, 112.

314. Ibid., 157, 161, 302, 465.

315. Ibid., 463.

316. Ibid., 241, 243–44, 463.

## COMMON ELEMENTS FOR A CHRISTIAN-BASED THEOLOGICAL ANTHROPOLOGY

This first part of this book has sought to briefly explore and present the theological anthropologies of nine different perspectives from across Western Christian History. There are several general commonalities, trends, and differences across these varying perspectives that may be noted. From these, we can extract some of the essential elements that a Christian-based theological anthropology should address in relation to its view of human nature, the Divine, and human transformation according to these authors. Each of these will then become foundational as we seek to synthesize a theological anthropology in light of modern science. Throughout this section, the reader is referred to the Appendix A, wherein summaries of each of these authors are provided in a table. As we continue on, noting these will be important as we seek a synthesis of these common elements with those propounded by the fields of modern science that we will review in the next section.

### Human Nature

As it relates to views of human nature, there are seven common elements that are generally upheld across these authors. The first is the *physicality of humans*. Each of these authors assert, in one way or another, that we are inherently embodied creatures. Whether our physical aspects were associated with our sensing self, as it was with authors such as Augustine, or whether they were conceived as merely being the form of the soul, as Aquinas claimed, each of these authors affirmed the physical nature as human beings. As a result, a Christian theological anthropology needs to take this common element into account.

A second element included the *affective* parts of our lives as humans. These were discussed as passions by those such as Maximus or as emotions by our contemporary authors. For our Neoplatonists, such desires and movements were viewed negatively while for others like Aquinas, such desires may work either for one's good or bad. Overall, these affirm that there are affective or feeling movements that comprise part of our lived experience as human beings.

*Cognitive aspects* compose yet a third common element in this set of writers. I have combined the concepts intellect, will, rationality, consciousness, memory, understanding, mind, et cetera. In essence, this aspect is primarily concerned with the conscious intentionality that we have as humans. We are able to perceive, think, and reason about things as well as to act with conscious deliberation. It is the part of ourselves that consciously discerns and for many of our authors, such as Augustine, Maximus, Kant, and Rahner, it is one of the primary means by which liberation and perfection come. Kant, in particular, asserts the use of reason as the primary means by which achievement of the "ultimate maxim," or Jesus' ideal life, comes. As a result, the conscious or cognitive component of human nature is perhaps one of the more primary aspects found in these texts.

In addition to these, which we will find repeated when we review our modern science authors, there is an aspect that is more unique to these texts and that is the *Divine connection* that most of these authors (4) upheld. With a core affirmation that humans are made in the Image of God, this aspect fundamentally asserts that there is some direct connection that we inherently and/or ultimately have with the Divine. However, the nature of this relationship does vary across these texts. In particular, there seem to be at least three ways that such a connection is conceived, ones which closely parallel the collective theologies discussed below.

The first way that some of these authors conceive of our connection with the Divine is via transcendence. This view was seen most clear 4a with Rahner, Maximus, and even Augustine and Kant. For Rahner, this connection was seen as being in a relationship with Ultimate Mystery. It is one where we come to connect with our "transcendentality"; the ultimately unknowable Ground of our being. In Maximus' anthropology, such transcendent Divine connections were viewed as being the pinnacle of spiritual development wherein we attain the "vita mystica" through which we come to know the Unknowable God. Even Augustine, at the end of his text, was found to discuss deeper places of inner and sometimes wordless kinds of knowing. Similarly, Kant asserted that each of us possesses the capacity to access Mystery. For each of these thinkers, our connection with the Divine is one of self-transcendence where the unknowable God of Mystery is attained to some degree.

A second mode of connection with the Divine found amongst these 4b authors is one of a personal relationship. Divine connection conceived in this way is seen most clearly with Augustine, Luther, Maximus, Barth, and even Kant. Particularly as it relates to the person of Christ, for most of these authors, He is conceived of a Heavenly Mediator who personally affects transformation within one's life and soul. For Augustine and

Barth, Jesus is a saving sacrament and relationship for our inner person who fashions us in the image of God. Similarly, Maximus asserts that Christ is the Divine Mediator who unites our soul and makes our human and divine natures become one. In Luther's scheme, Jesus wins our battles by becoming present within us through faith thereby transforming us into a new person in God. Finally, Kant conceives of Grace as providing that which nature cannot, including comfort, freedom, and strength for the journey when we need it most. For each of these writers, I assert, such Divine connections are conceived of as more of a direct and personified type of relationship.

A final mode of connection with the Divine is one that is less obvious but nevertheless present. It is one where God's life is experienced immanently within and through our growing spiritual life. Allusions to this mode of connection may be found most clearly in Green, Maximus, Aquinas, Luther, Barth, and even Kant to a limited degree. In Green's model, Divine Wisdom and/or Christ become more present within and through us as we proceed along the gradual journey of repatterning our lives in God. Similarly, for Maximus and Aquinas, as we come to be more like God, God comes to be more in and through us; all that we are and do. Furthermore, for Luther and Barth, an analogous process of deification occurs wherein the Divine becomes more fully present within and through us as we grow in faith and our life with God. Even in Kant's thought, which so emphasized the need for living a rationally guided and virtuous lifestyle, we can hear the emphasis that is placed on pursuing a life in God through these ethical efforts. Of course, Kant does not seem to discuss such ethical living in relation to direct connections with the Divine other than those discussed above. Nevertheless, it is this understanding that our connection to the Divine occurs immanently, within and through our thoughts, feelings, motives, actions, et cetera, as we grow in our life with God. Taken collectively, regardless of how each of these three modes is specifically conceived, these authors unanimously affirm that a more direct connection with the Divine is an essential common element of human nature.

Fifth, given these various parts above, *integration* is yet another common element found in these Western Christian theological anthropologies. Seen most clearly in Maximus' framework, humans are internally interconnected beings who have the capacity for more complete levels of unity and wholeness. For Augustine, such unity comes in sets of trinities while for some of our contemporary authors this unity materializes as greater and greater levels of integration emerge. Green's understanding of the biblical concept of the "soul" was conceived as an undivided wholeness of self. Integrative wholeness or unity is therefore a common element among these authors.

With these first five elements focusing primarily on the internal aspects of the human being, this sixth one turns to the external *relationships* that we have with other people, creation, and beings from other realms (i.e., angels, saints, demons, et cetera). In addition to one's direct relationship with God, these relationships are considered to be central to these theories of human nature propounded by many of these authors. The importance of context is seen most clearly in Rahner's system where in human beings, and even Jesus Himself, are historically located. Aquinas similarly asserts the need for supportive communities in growing spiritual life. Barth, according to Price, goes so far as to assert that sin itself is fundamentally a break in relationships. We also saw the role of non-material beings in the growing, or degrading, spiritual life with authors such as Augustine and Maximus who held a central place to the influences of the Devil in their frameworks. Who we are as an individual, claim many of these authors, is therefore very much linked to our context and the relationships that we have both in this realm and beyond. As we shall hear more in the next section, it is both nature and nurture that shapes us.

Across the board, with the exception of some of our contemporary authors, a core part of our lived experiences as humans are *distortions*.  For Green, Maximus, Aquinas, and Kant, human nature was asserted to be fundamentally and inherently good; seen as being made in the image of God and as sort of a microcosm of the macrocosm. For others, particularly Augustine and Luther, human nature was viewed more from the perspective of being trapped in "sinful flesh" and therefore in need of liberation. Each of these specifically Christian authors, whether they affirm humanity as being inherently good or evil, assert that we are not, in our current state, perfect; that there are distortions or even sinfulness that is an integral element of our nature. For some, such as Augustine and Luther, these distortions are asserted to arise from our fleshy or carnal self; or inner dispositions that we have according to Kant. For others, such as Maximus and Aquinas, these arise as a result of poor choices that one makes in their life. While still for others, as is the case with Maximus and Augustine, sinfulness is partly the result of external influences such as the Devil or society itself. Regardless of the sources, any theological anthropology based on Western Christian authors such as these needs to find a place for such distortions to human nature.

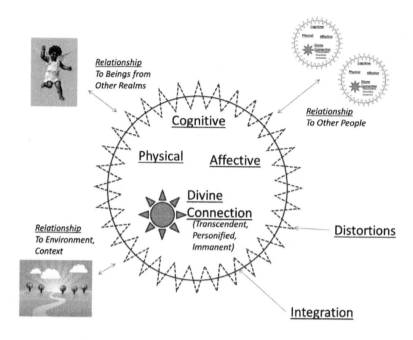

**Figure 9. A Synthesized Western Christian Theological Anthropology.**

These seven common elements of human nature can be taken to comprise foundational components that one will need in developing their own theological anthropology. In reflecting on each of these, however, it should be noted that the concept of the "soul" is not included as an explicit element here. This is because this concept seemed to vary widely among the authors that used this term. For instance, we found Green's biblical understanding of the soul to be an undivided wholeness or integration of the human person. In Maximus' and Aquinas' anthropologies, conversely, soul was conceived of more as a separate component of human nature that is intimately connected with the body and God. In their frameworks, the soul has many of the characteristics that are outlined above. In Barth's scheme, the soul seems to be more related to "rational and volitional" parts of one's self. Finally, a few of our contemporary authors asserted the soul to be more related to the affective or unifying feeling parts of our being. It is due to these wide variations that this concept has been excluded here as an explicit component. It is also because

I assert that the seven common elements above capture how the soul is understood by these very different frameworks. In other words, my claim is that this concept is collectively covered by the common elements above, just not in an explicit way. Of course, Christians may then immediately raise the question of what survives death, as the soul is sometimes understood to be the eternally enduring part of our existence. Indeed, any Christian-based theological anthropology will need to address this question as well. Nevertheless, these are the seven common elements that I assert any theory of human nature needs to explicitly address.

## Theologies of Theological Anthropologies

Given these, we now turn briefly to some of the theological views that were sketched out above. Again the reader is referred to the summary table in the appendix. Since this is not a *Summa Theologica*, our task here is not a comprehensive treatise on theology but rather to better understand how these authors were found to conceive of God in relation to human transformation. In doing so, we hope to extract some of the common theological underpinnings that have informed these authors in the formulation of their own theological anthropologies. Our hopes are to better understand what some of the possible implications of these theological views for personal spiritual formation. With this said, I find there are a number of common elements that are addressed as it relates to God and Jesus. Overall, the distinctions between these two terms are not always clear as there is much overlap for the characteristics named for each. Of course, this is to be expected given Christianity's views of the Trinity as being inseparable and indistinguishable aspects of a greater unified whole. For the purposes of our discussions here, then, I shall highlight those common elements for Christ that are used specifically for Him and reserve the more general ones for God or the Trinity as a unified whole.

As it relates to God, more generally, there are three common elements or characteristics addressed across these writings. The first two are more explicitly addressed while the third one seems to be more implicit, but commonly present nonetheless. The first is related to God's *transcendence*. Many of these authors held that God in some way is utterly beyond all creation. Being in Rahner's words an "ontologically silent horizon," God is conceived of as an invisible, pure non-physical, unknowable, unchangeable Reality. For some, particularly Augustine, Rahner, and Maximus, this aspect of God's nature is directly related to their views of human nature as union with this Transcendent reality is viewed as being the pinnacle of human transformation. For those that hold this element as a central part of their theology, then, it should have some direct implications for their theological anthropology and the personal spiritual formation programs that are based upon it.

Aquinas, our *Summa* champion, holds God's transcendence to be an essential element of his theology. However, as we heard above, Aquinas also asserts that it is from a transcendent Love that creation arises directly out of God's ultimate "no-thingness" at every instance in time. In other words, with as utterly transcendent as God is, God is also simultaneously, and paradoxically, *immanent* within and through all of creation. Many of these authors view God as being the creator and sustainer of all that is. God is upheld as everywhere present and all-knowing, the ultimate source of life and grace, and God is therefore asserted to work through the natural laws of creation, claim some of our contemporary authors.

Of course, this view is consistently with the divinity element above which claims that each individual contains something of God within them. Beyond this, the implications of such views for a theological anthropology may be seen most clearly in the writings of Green, Maximus, Aquinas, Kant, and some of our contemporary authors. These thinkers assert a view of spiritual formation that focused more on the transformation of one's complete life rather than only the attaining of transcendence. In Green's and Aquinas' views, as well as some of the contemporary authors, spiritual formation must be focused on the gradual re-patterning of the whole of one's life; "thinking, feeling, believing, and behaving" in the words of Green. Maximus conceived of the spiritual journey, not just for humans but for all of creation, as a series of mediations whereby the whole of creation is reconciled with God. Finally, Kant was found to assert a quest for virtuous living wherein one's life is reoriented in line with these ultimate maxims. In short, based upon a theology of immanence and the views of these authors, personal transformation may be conceived of as a journey of coming to live more in tune and harmony with the ever manifesting life of God within and through every part of creation.

A third common element that is addressed in one way or another by most of these authors is the *powerfulness* of God, or God's abilities to influence change in creation. Many of these writers seem to assert a classical Christian understanding of God as being all-powerful, able to influence and enact change as God sees fit. Among these include Augustine, Luther, and Barth. For these authors, therefore, human transformation is viewed as happening as a direct result of God's (or Christ's) direct and liberating interventions in our lives. As we saw most explicitly with Luther, it is Christ alone who wins our battle for salvation. Paradoxically, however, these same authors also still hold some place for the necessity of one's free will or faith in allowing God to effect such changes. If this is the case, then one might ask if God is really all-powerful. At least a couple of our contemporary authors asserted that God is self-limiting, choosing not to exert the fullness of God's power in every situation but instead allowing for the expression of free will.

Such theological discussions are relevant for spiritual formation because such doctrines can greatly influence not only our views of personal transformation but also how we go about engaging them. In Luther's Barth's systems, for instance, a much heavier emphasis is given to the role of faith in Christ than to the role of works as it is with our more monastic authors such as Maximus and Aquinas. This is not to say that any of these writers assert an extreme view of one to the complete neglect of the other. However, particularly with Luther, their writings about spiritual formation may more heavily favor one than the other. In the end, the point may be irrelevant as each of these authors claim that both faith and works are necessary for the journey. Nevertheless, how their systems are articulated is still influenced by their theology of the powerfulness of God in the unfolding spiritual journey.

As mentioned previously, the terms "God" and "Jesus" are often used interchangeably when discussing these three common elements of theology. However, many of our authors additionally address attributes that are more specifically and directly related to Christ. There are three in particular that are relevant for our purposes here.

The first is related to the view of Jesus as being a *mediator* between God and creation, particularly humanity. This understanding was most clearly seen with Augustine, Maximus, Luther, and Barth. Here, Christ is asserted to be the One through whom salvation comes, the One who pays our debts, bears our sins, and restores us to right relationship with God. In essence, Jesus is viewed as the Divine mediating bridge between humanity and God. The formation foci of these authors, and contemporary communities who hold similar views,[317] is very centered on a personal relationship with Christ; they would be considered to have a very high Christology.

 A second view related to Jesus is one where He is asserted to be a *model* for humanity. For Kant, Jesus is the "ultimate maxim" or archetype to which we are to conform. For Luther, Christ is the "maxima persona," or greatest person, who is the Divine example. Asserted by Aquinas as being the visible manifestation of God, Jesus therefore becomes the perfect model for humans to imitate. Clearly, such views have immediate and concrete ramifications for spiritual formation as we can seek to incorporate not only the values and maxims by which He lived, but also the practices, prayers, and even lifestyle of His as depicted in the Gospels.

The final common element found in some of these authors relates to the *humanness* of Jesus. With Rahner being the most explicit on this point, Jesus is recognized as being both biologically and historically located. For Maximus, an emphasis is given to the two united natures of Christ: human and divine. Aquinas conceived in part of Jesus as being a close and intimate friend with humanity. Finally, Barth asserts that Christ participates fully in our suffering and fallen natures. Overall, very much consistent with both a theology of immanence and with the view of Jesus as a mediator, this common element sees Christ not as a distant "Other" but rather as One who has and continues to participate in the very humanness of our daily lives. From a formative perspective such a view is relevant particularly for fostering close and personal relationships with Christ.

Collectively, these are some of common elements of theology found among these authors. As we can see, the theologies that we hold can fundamentally influence not only how we conceive of our theological anthropologies but also in how the spiritual formation systems we create or sustain. Related to this, we can also see that there seem to be at least three fundamental theological bases for these systems: God as being Transcendent, Immanent, and a Deity in Christ. Some systems give greater emphasis to one of these aspects of God than the others, as we heard. It is therefore important that we identify where the focus of ourselves and our communities lie in formulating our own theological anthropologies and the programs of personal transformation that are connected to these.

---

317. For example, see such texts as Hull, *Complete Book of Discipleship*; Lawrenz, *Dynamics of Spiritual Formation*; Willard, *Renovation of the Heart*.

## Theories of Change

Finally, some level of consistency in three broad areas was found in relation to the views of human change depicted by these authors. Overall, these authors repeatedly addressed two of these three broad categories as it relates to their theories of change. The third category or common element, however, is significant enough to include for our discussions here. Combined with the components of human nature and the theologies discussed above, these three areas are a necessary part of any Christian-based theological anthropology according to these authors. Once again, the appendix provides a tabular summary of these claims.

The first common element, or broad category, of their views here relates to their assertions about the *nature of change*. Within this category, there are three aspects addressed. Many of these authors asserted that such transformations are primarily ones of coming to be ever more fully united with the Divine. For Augustine, this was conceived of as our soul coming to cleave to God. In Aquinas' writings, there was a twofold movement wherein we become more like God as God becomes more fully in us. For others, such as Luther and Barth, the nature of the journey is viewed of as a battle with sin and our older self as we gradually come to embrace our newer and more inner life in Christ. Overall, then, the nature of the Christian journey of personal transformation for many of these authors is one of uniting with the Divine.

This journey is also understood as happening gradually, over extended periods of time. Often times we may want our growth in God to happen instantaneously, but these writers instead admonish patience and perseverance throughout. In Kant's writings, there is an emphasis placed on the habitual cultivation of virtuous living as one seeks after the ultimate maxims of their life. For some of our contemporary authors, schema change happens mostly via a conditioning process over time and with experience. Green similarly asserts a repatterning process of one's entire being, happening day-by-day. The nature of change is therefore further understood to be one of a gradual unfolding.

Finally, such transformation is intended to be holistic for many of these authors as well. For Green, this includes one's "thinking, feeling, believing, behaving." In Aquinas' thought, a harmonizing with the Divine is needed across the whole of one's entire life. No part of our life can be weighed down by sin, asserts Augustine, and such wholeness in God is foundational for our quest for self-transcendence in Rahner's system. The nature of change purported by many of these authors therefore includes a holistic approach. In other words, our personal spiritual formation programs need to address each of the aspects of human nature outlined above.

A second broad category, or common element, found among these writers is related to their discussion of the *necessary supports* that they highlight are needed for personal transformation. As we might expect, the specific supports recommended varied widely across these authors. Our monastic writers, Augustine, Maximus, and Aquinas, assert contemplation as a central support or practice that is needed. Luther, on the other hand, gives a great emphasis to hearing the word of God as it is depicted in the Bible. With a focus on ethical living, Kant asserts the need for the cultivation and practice of the virtues. In addition to these, the use of reason, self-knowledge, supportive communities, and general education were also expounded upon. Common across most of these authors, however, was the central role that God/Christ plays being the author, sustainer, and finisher of the unfolding spiritual journey. Regardless of the specific supports that each author asserts, common to all was the claim that we need them. In other words, transformation does not happen of its own accord without our active and intentional participation in it. On the contrary, it is our willful participation and the environments in which we live that greatly support or hinder our growing personal life in God.

The third broad category, or element, found in relation to their theories of change is one that was actually not addressed by most of these thinkers. It is related to the *stages of the journey* and how these stages are asserted to unfold, and it is only explicitly found among five of our writers. For Augustine, Luther, and Barth, the journey is viewed as a gradual transition that happens from old to new person, from earth to heaven, and from outer to inner life. While these transitions are not given a great amount of detail, they nevertheless help us to better understand some of the possible stages that might unfold along our journey.

For Maximus and Aquinas, on the other hand, the stages are outlined more definitely and with much greater detail. For Maximus, we can recall, the journey moves through vita practica, vita contemplativa, and vita mystica stages. They move from the practice and acquisition of the virtues, to contemplation of the true nature of things, finally to an intimate knowledge of the Unknowable God. For Aquinas, similarly, our voyage to God moves from an aptitude to know and love God, to our habitually doing so, finally to a perfection in this knowing and loving.

While these authors do differ in their formulations of these stages, both in content and in amount of detail, they nevertheless call to our attention the idea of stage development. For our own theological anthropology and the theories of change associated with them, we might therefore choose to articulate what we perceive the stages of the spiritual life are. Not only can such stages help us to anticipate our future journey, but they can also empower us to move through them more harmoniously with God's Life in and through them. They therefore comprise a third broad category, or common element, of the theories of change found among these authors.

## Summary

Overall, these comprise some of the essential common elements of a Christian-based theological anthropology found in these authors. They can therefore be used as a strong foundation in the formulation of our own theories and models of human nature and transformation. In fact, some may be so inclined as to stop at this juncture and develop their own model. One could use these common elements as an outline and turn to one or more of the specific thinkers explored thus far to further inform the details. Or, one can more simply choose one of these theorists and fully adapt their model with minimal change.

For the purposes of this book, however, our goal is to further expand on this rich history of views about human nature that have been found in the Western Christian tradition. As we moved towards these "modern" times in history, there have been different insights into human nature that are being offered by the physical and social sciences. Some of our contemporary authors, as we saw, have therefore sought to better understand humans in light of these insights. However, they did not do so in any sort of coherent and fully synthesized way. The question at hand for us now, then, is to explore whether or not this rich history of Christian theological anthropologies might be further augmented and refined in light of the findings and assertions of some of the modern scientific fields. In the next part of this book, we will therefore turn our attention to some of these fields to briefly review some of the primary claims that they are making in relation to human nature. Overall, the goal is to continue to seek greater knowledge and insight so that our own Christian-based theological anthropologies might better enable us to partner more fully with the Life of God that is ever at work in our lives and our communities.

# CHAPTER 2

# Modern Science Views of Human Nature

GENETICS, CULTURE, "ID-EGO-SUPEREGO," MOTIVATION, and self-determination; there are so many factors that are said to influence our lives and our behavior according to modern science. In this chapter, we will be exploring some of the common views held by various fields of modern scientific researchers whose work provides insights into human nature. Similar to the previous chapter, we will be briefly visiting these various views. For many of these, we will not only explore the area more generally, but we will also be considering specific historical and representative thinkers. These general and specific views should help us to better understand the nature of the specific area.

We will then step back and reflect on whether a more unified model of human nature might be synthesized in light of these disciplines. In the end, such a model will be presented as will some of the possible implications of this model for spiritual formation. This model, in addition to the one asserted in the last chapter, will be compared and contrasted and ultimately become the basis for the synthesized model that will be presented in the next section. Overall, this chapter is intended to help broaden our understanding of some of the various dynamics of human nature so that we might engage in our spiritually forming work in more informed ways.

## TRAIT-DISPOSITION VIEWS

This set of views primarily has to do with the study of broad and stable traits that are operative in an individual's life over the course of their lifetime. Such enduring traits are seen as being a central and guiding aspect of human nature. Broadly conceived, traits are an attempt to capture stable qualities of a person that are enduring across many situations, in many different contexts, and over long periods of time.[1] These traits are considered to be "deeper psychological entities that can only be inferred from behavior and experience"[2] and are posited as being integral to one's personality structure.[3] From a layperson's, or commonsense perspective, trait theories attempt to verify the conviction that how we behave throughout our lives has some sense of stability to it;[4] i.e., "that individuals can be characterized in terms of relatively enduring patterns of thoughts, feelings, and actions."[5] Such traits are considered to be hierarchically ordered within the personality system and, while there is relative stability to them, life experiences do seem to alter these enduring traits.[6] Using various qualitative and quantitative techniques (such as peer rating scales, self-reports, measures of needs and motives, expert rating systems, and personality disorder symptoms), trait theorists find that such stability can be seen more readily as the number of test samples increases and are combined together thereby supporting the assertion that traits are an integral and influential part of human nature.[7]

A contemporary example of such trait-disposition models comes with what is known as the Five-Factor Theory (FFT). Based upon psycholexical research methods, which analyze language looking for common patterns related to personality traits,[8] this model asserts that there are five dominant traits in each individual's personality structure: *Neu-*

---

1. McCrae and Costa, "The Five-Factor Theory of Personality"; Mischel et al., *Introduction to Personality*, 43, 46, 56.

2. McCrae and Costa, "The Five-Factor Theory of Personality."

3. Mischel et al., *Introduction to Personality*, 51.

4. Ibid., 48–49.

5. McCrae and Costa, "The Five-Factor Theory of Personality."

6. Eysenck, "Genetic and Environmental Contributions to Individual Differences"; Mischel et al., *Introduction to Personality*, 64.

7. McCrae and Costa, "The Five-Factor Theory of Personality"; Mischel et al., *Introduction to Personality*, 57, 68.

8. Mischel et al., *Introduction to Personality*, 58.

*roticism* (e.g., anxiety, angry hostility, depression, impulsiveness, vulner-ability); *Extraversion* (e.g., warmth, gregariousness, assertiveness, activity, excitement-seeking positive emotions); *Openness to Experience* (e.g., fantasy, aesthetics, feelings, actions, ideas, values); *Agreeableness* (e.g., trust, straightforwardness, altruism, compliance, modesty, tender-mind-edness); and *Conscientiousness* (e.g., competence, order, dutifulness, achievement, striving, self-discipline, deliberation).[9] While other trait-disposition theorists have argued that there are actually only three (e.g., Eysenck), these five traits have been demonstrated to show considerable stability over time.[10] While these traits, which are viewed as evolutionary adaptations, are seen as being central for any model of human nature, some FFT proponents still assert that a fuller model of the personality system is needed.[11] The trait-dispositional level, then, is primarily con-cerned with studying those characteristics that stably endure for an indi-vidual across many contexts and over the course of one's lifetime.

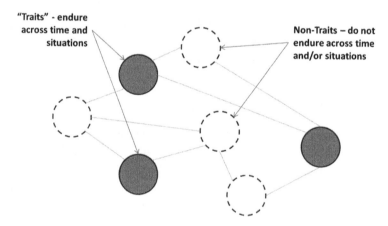

Figure 10. A Trait-Disposition Model.

One historical representative of this view is Gordon Allport. In two of his books, *Personality* (1937) and *The Nature of Prejudice* (1954), he captures some of the trait-disposition theorist's perspectives and ways of viewing human nature. For Allport, traits are not viewed in rigid, fixed terms, but are rather seen as being more flexible, malleable, and

9. McCrae and Costa, "The Five-Factor Theory of Personality"; Mischel et al., *Introduction to Personality*, 61.

10. McCrae and Costa, "The Five-Factor Theory of Personality"; Mischel et al., *Introduction to Personality*, 61.

11. McCrae and Costa, "The Five-Factor Theory of Personality."

changing.[12] Traits are seen as arising from the coalescing of a set of habits, life experiences, and neural functions within the human person that have adaptive significance.[13] In essence, Allport views traits as focal points in one's personality that are relatively enduring over time and across situations and therefore contribute to the relative consistency that is commonly observed in a person's behaviors.[14] While flexible and varying among individuals, such dispositions do represent "a limited number of basic interests, shared by all men, and presumably innate."[15]

An example of these given by Allport are "ethnic traits," such as prejudice.[16] Like other dispositions, Allport asserts that the prejudice trait is formed from the in-group cultures, life experiences (such as racism), and habits that one has been and is exposed to throughout their childhood and over the course of their entire life.[17] As a result of these influences, he writes, "prejudice may become part of one's life tissue, suffusing character because it is essential to the economy of a life."[18] Prejudice is therefore viewed as an enduring disposition that one comes to be formed in over the course of their lives.

As we can see from all of this, Allport's views of traits are that while they are relatively enduring nuclei, they are also flexible, formable, and changeable across one's lifetime. Allport therefore sees the larger personality system as a highly dynamic and integrated organism which continually adapts and changes based on one's conditioning, habits, traits, perceptions, and inner subsystems.[19] Traits are therefore conceived of as being only one part of human nature that helps to account for both the commonalities and differences among individuals across time and situations.[20]

12. Allport, *Personality*, 331–32.

13. Ibid., 292, 319.

14. Ibid., 286, 295, 327, 330.

15. Ibid., 193, 252.

16. Allport, *The Nature of Prejudice*, 68.

17. Ibid., 45, 112, 139, 202, 233, 277, 283–86.

18. Ibid., 371.

19. Allport, *Personality*, 102, 139–40, 365; Allport, *The Nature of Prejudice*, 19, 410–11.

20. Allport, *Personality*, 313, 330, 562.

## BIOLOGICAL VIEWS

Biological views of human nature are associated with three closely inter-twined influences: Evolution, Genetics, and the Biological Brain. Each one of these influences is considered to play a significant role in the similarities and differences among individuals. Evolutionary approaches to studying the personality system "focuses on the processes that have shaped the genes over the long course of the species' development."[21] Based on analyzing processes of natural selection, which occur over gen-erations of species' development, the goal is to understand why individu-als behave in the ways that they do in light of evolutionary principles.[22] One of the core principles of evolutionary theorists is not so much on the commonly known "survival of the fittest" principle, but more on "the fate of the gene pool that is distributed in groups across a population."[23] In other words, personality characteristics and behaviors are analyzed in light of the evolution-based question, "How is this or that behavior related to the genes' efforts to both endure and spread?" Evolutionary theory is therefore one way of reflecting the personality system.

Closely related to this are genetic-based views of human nature. As we've already seen, genes are thought of as being by-products of evo-lutionary history and have a significant impact on human development and expression.[24] Genetic influences are asserted to influence such re-lated factors as physiology, temperaments, traits, as well as attitudes and beliefs.[25] These genetic influences, it is asserted, may account for as much as half of the effects related to human nature.[26] A central and on-going debate for genetic researchers in personality science is related to "the age-old question: how much of personality reflects nature, and how much nurture—and how do these two sources of influence interact in shaping

21. Mischel et al., *Introduction to Personality*, 140.

22. Ibid., 140–41.

23. Ibid., 141.

24. Canli, "Toward a 'Molecular Psychology' of Personality"; Krueger, "Behav-ioral Genetics and Personality"; Mischel, "Personality Coherence and Dispositions"; Mischel and Shoda, "Toward a Unified Theory of Personality"; Mischel et al., *Introduc-tion to Personality*, 99, 110, 119.

25. Canli, "Toward a 'Molecular Psychology' of Personality"; Mischel et al., *Intro-duction to Personality*, 99, 101–4.

26. Krueger, "Behavioral Genetics and Personality"; Mischel et al., *Introduction to Personality*, 101, 103, 105, 107, 108.

human characteristics?"[27] While there is growing consensus that both of these factors play a major role, what is still being contested is the extent to which each one has an influence and what those influences are more specifically.[28] Regardless of where one falls in this debate, the message is clear: genetic factors are a significant influence for the development of human nature.

A final influence that is considered at this level is related to the biological brain. The brain is closely connected with gene expression[29] and its functioning plays a foundational role in human nature.[30] Neurophysiologically, certain areas of brain activation have been observed to coincide with certain forms of behavior and emotional experiences.[31] For instance, a region in the brain known as the amygdala has been noted for its role in preparing an individual for the fight or flight response.[32] Similarly, people with predominantly positive emotional reactions seem to demonstrate higher activation levels in the left-side of their brain whereas those with negative reactions are more associated with right-sided activity.[33] All of this is saying that biological brain functioning plays a very central role in human nature along with evolutionary and genetic influences. Further discussions are given in the next section where we will learn more extensively about neurophysiology and its relationships to human behavior and development. For our purposes here, what is important to note is the intimate interconnection between the brain, evolutionary history, and gene expression.

27. Canli, "Toward a 'Molecular Psychology' of Personality"; Krueger, "Behavioral Genetics and Personality"; Mischel et al., *Introduction to Personality*, 93.

28. Canli, "Toward a 'Molecular Psychology' of Personality"; Krueger, "Behavioral Genetics and Personality"; Mischel et al., *Introduction to Personality*, 105, 111, 114–15, 119, 121, 149.

29. Canli, "Toward a 'Molecular Psychology' of Personality"; Krueger, "Behavioral Genetics and Personality"; Mischel and Shoda, "Toward a Unified Theory of Personality"; Mischel et al., *Introduction to Personality*, 125.

30. Mischel and Shoda, "Toward a Unified Theory of Personality"; Mischel et al., *Introduction to Personality*, 116, 125, 487.

31. Mischel et al., *Introduction to Personality*, 135.

32. Ibid., 137, 458.

33. Ibid., 129.

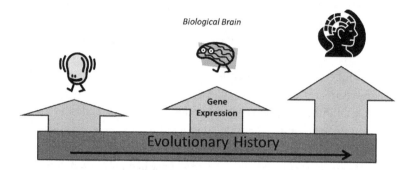

Figure 11. Bio-Genetic Expression Across Evolutionary History.

With these overall understandings of this level of analysis in place, I now turn to one historically representative theorist, Edward Wilson, and his Pulitzer Prize Winning book, *On Human Nature* (1978). Wilson's purposes for this book are two-fold: to offer a non-scientific (i.e., philosophical) view of human nature based on sociobiology and evolutionary theory, and to try and offer hope to our species by asserting that we, as humans, have the ability to change the course of evolution through the acquisition of knowledge of its principles and laws.[34] Following the biological categories above, Wilson goes on to discuss aspects of human nature related to evolution, genetics, and brain biology. Evolutionarily, significant aspects of human nature, such as culture, altruism, and religion, are the result of evolution's work to continually improve upon and propagate its genes.[35] Again, from these evolutionary influences, genes (in relation to the environment) are cultivated across many generations giving rise to various adaptive behaviors and characteristics.[36] Some of these behaviors, he asserts, can be considered to be traits, or particular patterns of behavior that are not easily modifiable, and these traits can be found not just in individuals but also in entire societies of species.[37] Such enduring behavior patterns, which arise from our genetic heritage, include the extreme forms of aggressiveness found particularly in the human species.[38] Finally, being one of the results of these genetic expressions, the biological brain (which then gives rise to the psychological

34. Wilson, *On Human Nature*, x, 6, 13, 97, 196, 201, 208–9.

35. Ibid., 153, 162–63, 177, 188.

36. Ibid., 16, 43, 71.

37. Ibid., 16, 19, 31, 57.

38. Ibid., 100, 106.

mind) is viewed as sort of a pre-programmed machine that is evolutionarily designed to guide us through the course of our lives.[39] Following
this line of philosophizing, he even goes so far as to refer to a new born
infant as "a marvelous robot."[40] The mind ultimately is, he asserts, "a de-
vice for survival and reproduction."[41] For Wilson, then, human nature is
almost entirely conceived of in terms of evolutionary, genetic, and biological brain influences.

## NEUROSCIENTIFIC VIEWS

Beyond being related to evolutionary history and genetic expression,
the biological brain plays a crucial role in human nature. As mentioned
above, correlations have been noted between neurophysiology and behavior and it behooves us to further understand some of the key findings from neuroscientific fields. Towards these ends, I will give a brief
overview of neural anatomy and brain transformation. More specifically,
we will briefly explore the basic building blocks of the brain, its three
"meta-regions," and how biological change is understood to occur neurophysiologically. Rather than focusing on a representative theorist, we
will simply be reviewing some of the common basics known about the
brain. This section is therefore intended to provide us with only a very
basic introduction to brain physiology.

　　Some of the key fundamental building blocks of the brain are: neurons, axons and dendrites, and glial cells.[42] Neurons are the primary cells
in the brain "that sense changes in the environment" and communicate
these changes to other neurons via the axons and dendrites that connect
neurons with one another. Glial cells, which are still largely a mystery to
neuroscientists,[43] essentially play a supportive role to the neurons.[44] From
these basic building blocks, the larger neural networks and architecture of
the brain is developed. With there being more than one hundred billion
neurons and each of these being about twice as small as an average cell

---

39. Ibid., 67, 195.
40. Ibid., 55.
41. Ibid., 2.
42. Bear et al., *Neuroscience*, 24, 26.
43. Ibid., 46.
44. Ibid., 24.

in the body,[45] the brain's architecture is extremely complex, having many different possible states of activation. In fact, neuro-psychiatrist Daniel Siegel writes, "This number [of possible states of activation] is thought to be larger than the number of atoms in the known universe."[46] That is a lot considering that the average adult brain weighs only about three pounds![47]

Within this very complex biological structure, certain areas of brain activation have been observed to coincide with certain forms of behavior, functioning, and internal experience.[48] Overall, some authors assert that there are three major systems, or meta-regions, of the brain to which many of these functions can be mapped: the brainstem and cerebellum; the limbic system; and the cortex.[49] As a part of these three systems, the brain is—as is commonly known—also noted to have left and right hemispheres, each of which has their own specialized functions.[50] It must also be noted that the "brain," contrary to how it is being presented here, really entails the entire body as there are neural networks distributed throughout.[51]

Beginning with the brainstem and cerebellum, known as the "reptilian brain,"[52] this system is commonly associated with stimulus-response actions. It is responsible for such functions as movement control, breath and body temperature regulation, as well as controlling our wakefulness and sleeping.[53] It is also responsible for balance and coordination in addition to storing, in the words of neuroscience author Joe Dispenza, "learned, coordinated, [and] memorized" action-response behaviors.[54]

---

45. Ibid.

46. Siegel, *Mindsight*, 38.

47. Chudler, "Brain Facts and Figures."

48. Mischel et al., *Introduction to Personality*, 135.

49. Dispenza, *Evolve Your Brain*, 106–8; Carter and Frith, *Mapping the Mind*, 33; Siegel, *Mindsight*, 15. Also note, however, that some neuroscientists have pointed out that, while there is some correlation between behavioral functions and brain structures, there is also much difficulty in clearly defining coherent "systems" within the brain because of its immense complexity and the observed fact that there does not always seem to be "a one-to-one relationship between structure and function" (see Bear et al., *Neuroscience*, 571.). The meta-regions presented herein are therefore only intended as an introductory overview of the brain's architecture and some of the functions therein.

50. Bear et al., *Neuroscience*, 628; Siegel, *Mindsight*, 108, 113.

51. Bear et al., *Neuroscience*, 172–73.

52. Dispenza, *Evolve Your Brain*, 109; Siegel, *Mindsight*, 15.

53. Bear et al., *Neuroscience*, 171; Dispenza, *Evolve Your Brain*, 108–9.

54. Dispenza, *Evolve Your Brain*, 109.

These include, Dispenza asserts, such stimulus-response actions as "attitudes, emotional reactions, repeated actions, habits, conditioned behaviors, unconscious reflexes, and skills that we have mastered."[55] Finally, this system is asserted to also control basic motivational mechanisms such as our drives for "food, shelter, reproduction, and safety."[56] This first system is therefore primarily composed of stimulus-response mechanisms.

Alternatively, the limbic system is noted to be the affective and emotional center of the brain and is sometimes called the "old mammalian brain."[57] This region works very closely with the first system and therefore helps in the regulation of many of the functions listed above. It also, however, works to generate the emotions that we feel.[58] It is therefore central for the formation of relationships. As Siegel writes, "The limbic area is also crucial of how we form relationships and become emotionally attached to one another."[59] This part of the brain is therefore primarily associated with our emotional and relational functioning, in addition to the body regulations and mechanisms of the brain stem and cerebellum.

Finally, the cortex system is generally understood as those regions of the brain that wrap or fold around the top and outer portions of the brain.[60] We can think of it as a "thinking cap" as this system includes many of the cognitive functions that humans have such as developing ideas and concepts as well as the ability to consciously construct and process mental representations of such abstracts as time, self, and morality.[61] This system, which is highly interconnected with the two discussed above, is also implicated in many other functions as well, such as memories, feelings, response flexibility, fear modulation, empathy, insight, moral awareness, pattern recognition, and intuition to name a few.[62] It is, therefore, the most complex and dynamic of the three systems and is sometimes seen

55. Ibid., 110.

56. Siegel, *Mindsight*, 17.

57. Bear et al., *Neuroscience*, 568; Dispenza, *Evolve Your Brain*, 110; Siegel, *Mindsight*, 17.

58. Bear et al., *Neuroscience*, 568–71; Carter and Frith, *Mapping the Mind*, 81–82; Siegel, *Mindsight*, 17–18. Note, however, that some neural researchers distinguish between an emotion, our feeling of that emotion, and our consciousness of that feeling; see Damasio, *Feeling of What Happens*, 8, 37.

59. Siegel, *Mindsight*, 17.

60. Ibid., 19.

61. Dispenza, *Evolve Your Brain*, 141; Siegel, *Mindsight*, 19.

62. Dispenza, *Evolve Your Brain*, 129, 135, 173, 261; Siegel, *Mindsight*, 26.

by some as being what distinguishes humans from many other animal species.[63] This system, which is also involved in the functioning of the other two systems, is therefore often associated with the more complex cognitive and affective abilities.

As it relates to human growth, it has been noted that the development of the brain occurs in spurts and continues across the lifespan.[64] It has also been observed that brain development occurs in a cyclical fashion with parts of the frontal cortex maturing only later in life after a prolonged period of time.[65] Such development is also related to the well-documented "plasticity" of the brain.[66] At the level of the most basic building blocks, neuroplasticity is asserted to proceed in accordance with the often cited "Hebbian Principle" which asserts, "neurons that fire together, wire together."[67] In essence, this means that under the right conditions connections between different parts of the brain can be strengthened and/or modified by repeated use, or neuron firing.[68] Such conditions include, but are not limited to: experiencing different external stimuli, emotional arousal, repetition of actions, internal reflections and mental rehearsals, and focused attention.[69] From the perspective of spiritual formation, knowing these basics about the brain is important because it can help us to better understand how to better work with people in our programs.

## PSYCHODYNAMIC-MOTIVATIONAL VIEWS

In the early 1900s, Sigmund Freud turned the then contemporary science-based views of human nature upside down by formulating a theory that the conscious, rational mind is but only the "tip of the iceberg" and that most of what drives and guides one's motivations lies in what he came to

---

63. Carter and Frith, *Mapping the Mind*, 181–82; Damasio, *Feeling of What Happens*, 16; Dispenza, *Evolve Your Brain*, 346; Siegel, *Mindsight*, 19.

64. Dispenza, *Evolve Your Brain*, 147–54; Morra et al., *Cognitive development*, 351, 355.

65. Matlin, *Cognition*, 461; Morra et al., *Cognitive development*, 354, 355–56; Siegel, *Mindsight*, 41.

66. Bear et al., *Neuroscience*, 4, 14, 56; Nelson et al., *Neuroscience of cognitive development*, 38–39.

67. Bear et al., *Neuroscience*, 710; Dispenza, *Evolve Your Brain*, 184, 192, 238; Siegel, *Mindsight*, 40, 185.

68. Dispenza, *Evolve Your Brain*, 238; Siegel, *Mindsight*, 40.

69. Dispenza, *Evolve Your Brain*, 4, 44, 238, 241, 424; Siegel, *Mindsight*, 40.

describe as the unconscious. Thus, modern psychodynamic and motivational theory, it is asserted, was born.[70] Psychoanalysis was therefore an attempt to investigate the unconsciousness and understand how a person is motivated and influenced by it.[71] Put in comical and metaphoric terms, specifically because of its fundamental focus on that which is not readily apparent to the conscious mind, psychoanalysis has been described as "looking for a black cat in a dark room where there is no black cat—and finding one anyway."[72]

Freud's conceptions of psychodynamics are quite complex and involve several components such as: 1) its general understanding of the human nature as being inherently conflict-driven, 2) his views of three levels of consciousness, 3) the id-ego-superego constructs, and 4) the centrality of motivation in human nature. Each of these is relevant for this level of analysis and I shall briefly discuss each of them in turn. Following these discussions, we will briefly touch upon the contributions of Neo-Freudians before reviewing the works of two representative historical authors at this level.

Generally speaking, psychodynamics conceives of the personality system as being driven by a number of impulses and motives that are beyond the realm of conscious, rational control.[73] As a result, people are not the rational, calm personalities that Freud's contemporary Victorian society of the late 1800s and early 1900s wanted them to be. Rather, people are "torn by unconscious conflicts and wishes that pushes them in seemingly puzzling ways."[74] Psychoanalysis therefore views the personality as being one fundamentally in conflict with itself.

From this general view, Freud went on to develop his conceptual views of consciousness. According to him, there are three levels consciousness and these include the preconscious, the unconscious, and the conscious.[75] The conscious realm comprises that which we have

---

70. Mischel et al., *Introduction to Personality*, 152, 156. Of course, as we saw in the previous section, probing the unconscious did not originate with Freud but has been a central part of many of the world's major religious/spiritual traditions.

71. Westen et al., "Psychoanalytic Approaches to Personality."

72. Ibid.

73. Freud, *The Ego and the Id*, 9; Mischel et al., *Introduction to Personality*, 156–57.

74. Freud, *The Ego and the Id*, 40, 73; Mischel et al., *Introduction to Personality*, 174.

75. Freud, *The Ego and the Id*, 9; Mischel et al., *Introduction to Personality*, 157.

immediate and direct access to,[76] whereas the pre- and unconscious levels are not readily "responsive to our deliberate efforts at recall."[77] Modern social psychological (and other) studies are corroborating these claims as it has been observed that much of our social processing seems to happen completely outside of our conscious awareness.[78] Freud was primarily concerned with the unconscious and many of the psychodynamic approaches he used, such as dream work and free association, were aimed at attempting to access this realm.[79] One of Freud's core convictions, therefore, was that many of our behaviors are influenced by the unconscious.[80]

From these views of the different levels of consciousness, Freud further conceived of the psyche as having three different influential structures: id, ego, and superego.[81] In its essence, id is an inherited, biological structure in the psyche that is the source of instincts, passions, and energy for human nature.[82] Ego, for Freud, was that part of our minds that exhibits conscious control on the psyche. It "represents what we call reason and sanity" and it is what creates internal "objects" of the external world.[83] While ego emerges out of the id, Freud asserts, it ultimately seeks to bring the id into subjugation to itself resulting in such phenomena as fixation, transference, suppression, and projections.[84] Finally, the superego is conceived of as being an "ego-ideal," a "conscience" or "morality judge," and it is the embodiment of all that a person "ought" and "ought not" to do and can be dictated by society as well as by one's own inner representations.[85] Its origins, Freud asserts, lie in both the ego and the id, in the internal and the external worlds, and it

76. Freud, *The Ego and the Id*, 10.

77. Ibid., 9, 12; Mischel et al., *Introduction to Personality*, 157.

78. Mischel et al., *Introduction to Personality*, 199; Westen et al., "Psychoanalytic Approaches to Personality."

79. Freud, *The Ego and the Id*, 11–12, 19; Mischel et al., *Introduction to Personality*, 158.

80. Freud, *The Ego and the Id*, 11–12; Mischel et al., *Introduction to Personality*, 240.

81. Westen et al., "Psychoanalytic Approaches to Personality."

82. Freud, *The Ego and the Id*, 30, 52; Mischel et al., *Introduction to Personality*, 159.

83. Freud, *The Ego and the Id*, 15–16, 30, 37, 48; Mischel et al., *Introduction to Personality*, 161, 167.

84. Freud, *The Ego and the Id*, 28, 68, 82; Mischel et al., *Introduction to Personality*, 164, 172, 175, 193, 202, 206, 213.

85. Freud, *The Ego and the Id*, 44–45; Mischel et al., *Introduction to Personality*, 162.

is the tensions between these sources that ego is attempting to resolve.[86] The id-ego-superego was therefore a central component for Freud.

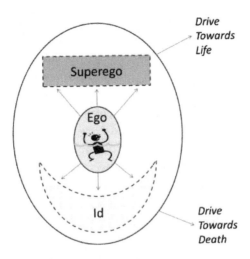

*Figure 12. A Freudian Psychodynamic Model.*

Finally, from these three intrapsychic phenomena come various motivations that influence the human nature as a whole. As it is assumed that "all behavior is motivated" by this level of analysis,[87] motivation is therefore a central component for understanding human nature.[88] Freud conceived of there being at least two fundamental and interrelated instincts that were "active in every particle of living substance": the death and life instincts.[89] The former is more concerned with the decay of life while the latter, also called 'Eros,' is concerned with the uniting and sustaining of life.[90] Since Freud, motives have continued to be seen by theorists in this field as an influential part of human nature at conscious and unconscious levels. They are also seen as acting to move us either towards

86. Freud, *The Ego and the Id*, 46, 48, 69–70, 73; Mischel et al., *Introduction to Personality*, 167.

87. Freud, *The Ego and the Id*, 56; Mischel et al., *Introduction to Personality*, 170.

88. Schultheiss, "Implicit Motives"; Westen et al., "Psychoanalytic Approaches to Personality."

89. Freud, *The Ego and the Id*, 56, 59; Mischel et al., *Introduction to Personality*, 160.

90. Freud, *The Ego and the Id*, 55, 64, 66, 77; Mischel et al., *Introduction to Personality*, 160.

or away from events and experiences.[91] Motives are therefore a central component to this field of study.

Since Freud, there have been many others who have carried psychodynamic-motivational theories and practices forward, modifying and elaborating on them along the way.[92] Known as "Neo-Freudians," they have sought to broaden these theories to include contemporary research and findings from other fields of study such as: cognitive and affective processes, genetics and biological factors, attachment and inter-relationship theories, self-esteem and alternative motivational models, et cetera.[93] Notable Neo-Freudians and Neo-Freudian Schools include the works of Attachment theorists, Adler, Anna Freud, Fromm, Erikson, Horney, Jung, Kohut, Murray, and Object-Relations Theorists.[94] This level of analysis, it is clear, continues to make an on-going contribution to our understandings of the human nature.

Given these extensive contributions, there are two representative historical theorists from this level that we will now briefly review the works of. The first is Alfred Adler and his book, *The Practice and Theory of Individual Psychology* (1927/1955). Adler's main contribution to the field of psychodynamics was his theory that one of the primary motivational drives in a person's life is their attempts to overcome feelings of inferiority.[95] In this book, Adler begins by asserting that the most fundamental "law" of all psychic happenings is that "we cannot think, feel, will, or act without the perception of some goal."[96] Goals are therefore seen as being what drives and guides every part of our lives and they result in the formulation of a life-plan by which an individual lives either consciously or unconsciously.[97] Such life-plans, he further claims, go back to one's childhood and it is this period of life that is considered to give rise to all of one's attitudes and motivations.[98] It is therefore in childhood that we are fundamentally formed, and the most central drive that we have is

---

91. Ryan and Deci, "Self-Determination Theory"; Schultheiss, "Implicit Motives"; Westen et al., "Psychoanalytic Approaches to Personality."

92. Mischel et al., *Introduction to Personality*, 412–13.

93. Ibid., 210, 412–13; Westen et al., "Psychoanalytic Approaches to Personality."

94. Mischel et al., *Introduction to Personality*, 186–91, 216–35; Westen et al., "Psychoanalytic Approaches to Personality."

95. Mischel et al., *Introduction to Personality*, 219.

96. Adler, *The Practice and Theory of Individual Psychology*, 3.

97. Ibid., 4, 6, 12, 62, 108, 229.

98. Ibid., 10, 18, 61, 69.

our need to come to terms with our helplessness and inferiority, part of which is inherited and part of which comes from our early experiences.[99] It is this fundamental inferiority that therefore characterizes and deeply influences our goals and life-plans. We can therefore see in Adler's work some of the core psychodynamic components at work such as his emphasis on motivations, unconscious influences, and stages of development.

A second representative theorist is Karen Horney and her influential book, *Our Inner Conflicts* (1945). Horney begins by both questioning and criticizing Freud's claims that all inner conflicts are fundamentally rooted in his sex/instinct drive theories.[100] Rejecting these claims, Horney instead turns to feminist psychological models and alternatively asserts that all inner conflicts and "neuroses are generated by disturbances in human relationships" and they are further influenced by the cultural dynamics that surround us.[101] Viewing conflicts as an opposition of incompatible attitudes within one's self, she posits three different ways that we try to resolve them: by moving towards people, against them, or away from them.[102] We can move towards others by needing to be dependent on them, against them in aggressive or competitive ways, or away from them by being detached and autonomous from them.[103]

While each of these are ways that people try to deal with conflicts in their lives, Horney asserts that they can really only be resolved by dealing directly with them, "by changing those conditions within the personality that brought them into being."[104] She then goes on to discuss some of the many defenses to conflict as well as their effects on our lives.[105] In the end, Horney's stated goal is to help others to achieve "wholeheartedness: to be without pretense, to be emotionally sincere, to be able to put the whole of oneself into one's feelings, one's work, one's beliefs," something that she asserts is only possible after their inner conflicts are resolved.[106] Horney is therefore also representative of the assertions and findings of this field

99. Ibid., 23, 25, 32, 35, 37, 80, 100, 141, 228, 240, 268, 308, 312–13, 350.

100. Ibid., 11, 13, 199.

101. Ibid., 11, 12, 19, 24.

102. Ibid., 18, 47, 73–74, 96.

103. Ibid., 50, 54, 63, 65, 74–80.

104. Ibid., 73–74, 217.

105. Ibid., 135–40; see also chaps. 9–12.

106. Ibid., 242.

as she seeks to directly address some of the inner conflicts and struggles that influence human nature.

## BEHAVIORAL-CONDITIONING VIEWS

For the Behavioral-Conditioning views, a primary emphasis is given on exploring the relationship between an individual's behaviors and the external conditions that appear to give rise to them. Its contributions, while critically questioned by many, are nonetheless viewed as being a central part of the history and field of psychology. Research experiments from this perspective, such as those conducted by Russian psychologist Ivan Pavlov, have found that certain behaviors can become conditioned in relation to specific stimuli.[107] For instance, people in relationships have been observed to have "often unintentionally reinforced and strength-ened in each other the very behaviors that they were trying to control," and knowing about such condition-prompted dynamics can therefore be helpful for fostering human development.[108]

In order to study such stimulus-behavior connections, behaviorists have historically turned to the study of animals (something which has been questioned by others as to the applicability of their findings to hu-mans) as well as to direct observations of people under certain conditions and stimuli.[109] Proponents of these methods, such as Skinner, Dollard, and Miller, "deliberately avoided asking questions about anything that they felt they could not test experimentally" in hopes of achieving an objective view of human nature with little or no implicit inferences.[110] In other words, behaviorism was partly an effort to adhere more rigorously to empirical scientific standards than is sometimes found in psychody-namic theory. The result of such approaches were findings that people can be conditioned towards certain behaviors when under the influence of certain stimuli and that behavioral learning principles can be used to help them to find more adaptive ways of living their lives.[111] By using both positive and negative reinforcements in direct relation to specific behav-iors, this view asserts, people can be gradually conditioned to behave in

---

107. Mischel et al., *Introduction to Personality*, 248, 254.

108. Ibid., 241, 261.

109. Ibid., 245–46, 252, 254, 262, 275, 413.

110. Ibid., 245–46, 259, 262, 271.

111. Ibid., 242, 257, 259, 264, 277.

certain ways.[112] In light of these claims, however, behaviorism has been criticized for ignoring deeper issues that underlie behavior, overlooking the wider complexities of an individual's behaviors, and questions have been raised as to whether such reconditioning actually endures for long periods of time or not.[113] Nevertheless, behavior-conditioning views are considered to be another important way of understanding human nature.

One historical representative text of these views is *Personality and Psychotherapy: An Analysis in Terms of Learning, Thinking, and Culture* (1950), written by John Dollard and Neal Miller. Fascinated by Freud's findings, but skeptical about the methods of psychodynamic inferences, Dollard and Miller sought to "rethink psychodynamic conflicts in the language of learning" using controlled experiments with rats; an approach that they felt was a more objective way of experimenting.[114] In this book, they posit that there are four primary factors for learning: drive, response, cue, and reinforcement.[115] Drives are those things that compel us to act, cues initiate the drives, responses are our resulting actions, and reinforcements ensure that this entire behavioral pattern either continues or is discouraged.[116]

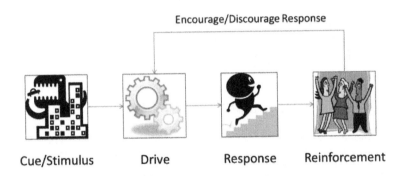

Figure 13. Dollard and Miller's Four Primary Factors for Learning.

112. Ibid., 283–84, 288.

113. Ibid., 288–89.

114. Dollard and Miller, *Personality and Psychotherapy*, 3, 8, 25, 63, 181; see also Mischel et al., *Introduction to Personality*, 246–47, 252.

115. Dollard and Miller, *Personality and Psychotherapy*, 25–26; see also Mischel et al., *Introduction to Personality*, 249.

116. Dollard and Miller, *Personality and Psychotherapy*, 30, 32, 35, 39, 48, 62, 88, 93, 100.

As an example of these principles, they offer an explanation for why lower-class children perform worse in school than middle-class children.[117] They assert that it is not so much because they have a "mental inferiority," as was commonly assumed at the time, but rather it is the result of how both the teachers and society views and rewards them (or not) and their behaviors. In other words, they assert that lower-class children are actually being conditioned to perform at lower levels than are middle-class children.

Turning next to the realm of psychodynamics, Dollard and Miller begin by hypothesizing that "all the laws that have been discovered for learned responses to external cues also apply to internal response-produced cues."[118] This means that inner fears, drives, repressions, and even the use of reason, can be learned in similar ways as external behavioral-response stimuli are learned.[119] With this conceptual framework in place, they go on to discuss therapeutic approaches, which include psychodynamic techniques such as free association and dream work, to help people to overcome their inhibitions.[120] Throughout these discussions, their main thesis is that the road to recovery, and a fully healthy life, comes primarily through the use of discrimination, reasoning, and planned activity via gradual conditioning techniques.[121] Despite their use of and engagement with psychodynamic theory, they are representative of Behavioral-Conditioning views because of their emphasis on conditioned learning principles and their applications to one's inner life as well as outer life.

## PHENOMENOLOGICAL-HUMANISTIC VIEWS

In response to what was considered by Phenomenological-Humanistic researchers to be a too narrowed view of psychodynamics' focus on pathology and behaviorism's work with animal behavior, proponents of this view instead sought to intentionally take a different approach to studying human nature.[122] The primary focus of researchers at this level is to

---

117. Ibid., 45.

118. Ibid., 100.

119. Ibid., 68, 75, 120, 157–58, 187, 192–93, 204; see also chaps. 8 and 9; see also Mischel et al., *Introduction to Personality*, 252.

120. Dollard and Miller, *Personality and Psychotherapy*, 241, 256, part V.

121. Ibid., 229–31, 279–80, 303, 320, 347–48, 444.

122. Mischel et al., *Introduction to Personality*, 296.

understand how people view and understand themselves and how they consciously and subjectively construe the world and their personal experiences of it.[123] The goal, then, is to better understand how people construct their views of themselves and their life based on the assertion that each person is a proactive participant and co-creator of their experiences.[124] As George Kelly is credited with saying, "Every person is a scientist," meaning that each person is viewed as actively and continually interpreting, judging, categorizing, et cetera the experiences of their own lives.[125]

Based on these assertions, such views place a central role on the study of the constructs that people create about themselves and their world. Starting from the perspective that humans are whole and integrated organisms,[126] this level asserts that within this organism there are self-created theories, or "constructs," that are intended to help us to make better sense of the world.[127] These constructs not only help us to better understand life, but they also act as guides for our future actions.[128]

For researchers at this level, the most important construct is the one that people generate about themselves.[129] Such "self-constructs" are vitally important because they help guide how one views and treats themselves as well as how they react to and internalize their life experiences.[130] The basic claim here is that we try to live in accordance with these self-constructs and that we are continually modifying them in light of the experiences we have.[131] Therapy at this level is therefore primarily concerned with helping clients to uncover and modify these constructs and the maladaptive effects they might be having on their behaviors.[132] One of the key contributions of these views of human nature, then, is that a person's subjective perceptions

---

123. Ibid., 295–297, 319, 320, 326, 345; Ryan and Deci, "Self-Determination Theory."

124. Mischel et al., *Introduction to Personality*, 299–300, 304, 312, 341.

125. Ibid., 317.

126. Maslow, *Motivation and personality*, 19; Mischel et al., *Introduction to Personality*, 298, 304; Rogers, *Client-Centered Therapy*, 486–87; Ryan and Deci, "Self-Determination Theory."

127. Mischel et al., *Introduction to Personality*, 313; Ryan and Deci, "Self-Determination Theory."

128. Mischel et al., *Introduction to Personality*, 317, 319; Ryan and Deci, "Self-Determination Theory."

129. Mischel et al., *Introduction to Personality*, 326.

130. Ibid., 307, 332, 413.

131. Ibid., 307, 313, 324, 341.

132. Ibid., 312, 333–39; Rogers, *Client-Centered Therapy*, 139.

of themselves and the world do matter, and that they sometimes provide more accurate predictions of behavior than do sophisticated assessment tools created and used by others; a claim and possibility that was discounted by psychologists for many years.[133]

A final assertion of Phenomenological-Humanistic views is that people can be and are actively influential participants in the direction of their lives.[134] Stemming from Existentialist views related to the totally free and responsible human being, proponents of this level, such as Ryan and Deci's theory of Self-Determination, hold that human beings are autonomous and can do much to alter and direct the course of their lives.[135] As Mischel, Shoda, and Ayduk write, "individuals don't have to be the victims of their biology and their biography but can do much to change both their life course and their internal states and experiences by altering how they construe or interpret them."[136] Not only is self-actualization possible, then, but one's health and well-being, it is asserted, depends upon our being intrinsically motivated in pursuit of the goals we construct and choose to attain.[137] These views therefore hold that the active, subjective experiences and constructs of each individual are vitally important for the personality system.

There are two key representative theorists that we will now consider. The first is Abraham Maslow and his well-known book, *Motivation and Personality* (1970). Somewhat similar to other theorists, Maslow views human nature as an integrated organism that is greater than the sum of its individual parts, and is comprised of clusters, or "syndromes," that are organized into interrelated hierarchies.[138] He also conceives of this system as having a series of various and diverse kinds of drives and needs, most of which are unconscious, that are fundamental to the human condition.[139] These drives serve to organize and prompt the organism towards their fulfillment and therefore serve as a means to an ends.[140]

---

133. Mischel et al., *Introduction to Personality*, 326, 328, 336.

134. Ibid., 312.

135. Ibid., 299, 309; Ryan and Deci, "Self-Determination Theory."

136. Mischel et al., *Introduction to Personality*, 413.

137. Ibid., 339; Ryan and Deci, "Self-Determination Theory."

138. Maslow, *Motivation and personality*, 19, 29, 303, 305–6, 315, 321.

139. Ibid., 20, 54.

140. Ibid., 21, 26, 57.

Maslow conceives of these needs, particularly the fundamental or "Basic Needs," as being organized into the following well-known hierarchy: Physiological, Safety, Belongingness and Love, Esteem, and Self-Actualization.[141] The basic idea here is that lower needs are more important for survival purposes, and therefore dominate when the organism is unsatisfied, but as they are satisfied a person can move on to focus on the higher ones.[142] As one is able to consistently do this, not only will they become more stably rooted in the higher needs, independent of the lower ones, but they will also be better able to achieve what Maslow refers to as a healthy personality: one who is more accepting, spontaneous, stable, empathetic, loving, and less-dichotomous.[143] Given these views of the autonomy and the potential for self-realization, Maslow is firmly representative of these views.

A second representative historical theorist is Carl Rogers and his 1951 book, *Client-Centered Therapy*. As with Maslow and others, Rogers also fundamentally views the personality system as a sort of integrated and holistic organism that reacts to the "phenomenal field" that it finds itself currently within.[144] "The organism," Rogers claims, "has one basic tendency and striving—to actualize, maintain and enhance the experiencing organism."[145] An integral part of this organism are the "self-concepts" that are created or emerge in an effort to help people to move towards these ends and meet the challenges and necessities of life.[146] In essence, Rogers asserts, these self-constructs are the inner perceptions we create of ourselves in relation to the experiences of our lives.[147] Our ways of behaving and responding at least partly stem from them as we actively strive to live in accordance with them.[148] Rogerian "Client-Centered Therapy," with its heavy emphasis on seeing life through the eyes of the client, is therefore primarily focused on helping individuals to uncover and continually work

---

141. Ibid., 36, 39, 43, 45, 46.

142. Ibid., 47, 59, 97–98, 101.

143. Ibid., 58, 62, 67–68, 72, 155–79, 185.

144. Rogers, *Client-Centered Therapy*, 486–87; see also Mischel et al., *Introduction to Personality*, 304.

145. Rogers, *Client-Centered Therapy*, 487, 491.

146. Ibid., 191, 497–98; see also Mischel et al., *Introduction to Personality*, 304, 307.

147. Rogers, *Client-Centered Therapy*, 136–37, 503.

148. Ibid., 503, 507, 517; see also Mischel et al., *Introduction to Personality*, 307.

with these self-concepts so that they are better able to live a more open and constructively adaptive life in relation to their environments.[149]

## SOCIAL COGNITIVE VIEWS

These views of human nature primarily have to do with attempting to link external situations with "what goes on in the mind of the person—their thoughts or cognitions, emotions, goals, and motivations."[150] Drawing directly from behaviorism, phenomenological-humanistic, and social cognition studies, the hopes of proponents of this view are that researchers will be able to better connect one's internal happenings to specific and particular types of situations, thereby gaining greater insights into how people "process and use information about themselves and their social worlds."[151] Following on the work of the previous Phenomenological-Humanistic views and the "cognitive revolution" that has come since then, central to these views is the notion of constructs or "schemas" and how they give shape to our perceptions and guide our lives, particularly in relation to our social world.[152] Also relevant are the "self-schemas" that people have about themselves and how these impact coping and adaptation for them.[153] These schemas, like the personal constructs discussed above, not only influence such factors as one's self-esteem and how one relates to others, but they also have been shown to exhibit "a good deal of stability."[154]

What is of particular importance to these views, however, is the extent to which such schemas are situationally and culturally influenced.[155] One of the core assumptions is that "the self is essentially social and interpersonal."[156] The basic idea here is that who we are and how we learn

---

149. Rogers, *Client-Centered Therapy*, 26, 34, 48, 53–54, 77, 139, 178, 192, 494, 520; see also Mischel et al., *Introduction to Personality*, 309.

150. Bandura, *Social Learning Theory*, vii, 194; Mischel et al., *Introduction to Personality*, 347–48.

151. Bandura, *Social Learning Theory*, 11–12; Mischel et al., *Introduction to Personality*, 366, 375, 414.

152. Mischel et al., *Introduction to Personality*, 355, 371–74, 380, 382, 392, 398, 414.

153. Ibid., 383, 390–91.

154. Ibid., 387–89, 391–98.

155. Benet-Martinez, "Handbook of Personality"; Mischel et al., *Introduction to Personality*, 388.

156. Benet-Martinez, "Handbook of Personality"; Mischel et al., *Introduction to*

is heavily influenced by the particular situations, contexts, and cultures of which we are a part.[157] These views of human nature are therefore primarily focused on understanding the relationship between one's internal dynamics and the specific situations that they find themselves in.

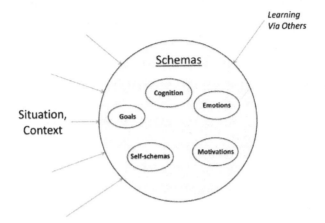

Figure 14. Social-Cognitive Elements of the Psyche.

One historical theorist representative of this level is Albert Bandura and his book, *Social Learning Theory* (1977). Having the social cognitive focus articulated above, Bandura sets out to explore a learning theory that considers the social environment as a central component in the learning process.[158] His central assertion is that "virtually all learning phenomena resulting from direct experience occur on a vicarious basis by observing other people's behavior and its consequences for them."[159] The basic idea here is that learning primarily happens by observing what others around us do and the consequences that come with those actions.[160] Doing so enables us to adopt new patterns of behavior without our having to personally experiment with and experience each new behavioral pattern.[161] Instead, we cognitively and emotionally (i.e., "vicariously") learn by observing others.[162]

*Personality*, 390–91.

157. Benet-Martinez, "Handbook of Personality"; Mischel et al., *Introduction to Personality*, 352, 355.

158. Bandura, *Social Learning Theory*, 11–12.

159. Ibid., 12; see also Mischel et al., *Introduction to Personality*, 352, 354–55.

160. Bandura, *Social Learning Theory*, 22, 35, 50, 96.

161. Ibid., 12, 35; Mischel et al., *Introduction to Personality*, 353.

162. Bandura, *Social Learning Theory*, 13, 22–29, 60, 160.

Such learning is fostered through antecedent (or predictive) occurrences, through rewards and self-reinforcement, and via cognitive control.[163] Bandura also asserts that such social learning processes then generate useful constructs that "serve as guides for future behavior."[164] With these links between internal cognitive-affective elements and external situations, we can therefore see in Bandura some of the key claims of these views of human nature.

## TRANSPERSONAL-PARAPSYCHOLOGICAL VIEWS

Finally, Transpersonal-Parapsychological views of human nature are related to those aspects that involve either fostering a deeper unitive relationship with some other part of creation or experiences that seem to be beyond the five physical senses.[165] In the words of transpersonal researcher Rosemarie Anderson these aspects are "beyond or through the personally identified aspects of self."[166] Anderson goes on to identify the arena of transpersonal studies as they strive "to delve deeply into the most profound aspect of human experience, such as mystical and unitive experiences, personal transformation, meditative awareness, experiences of wonder and ecstasy, and alternative and expansive states of consciousness."[167] Transpersonal studies therefore focus on better understanding and helping people to both deepen and expand their normal experiences and consciousness of self in relation to creation.

In addition to transpersonal researchers, parapsychologists study phenomenon that seem to be beyond experiences that are connected to the five physical senses. In particular, extrasensory perception (ESP), psychokinesis (PK), and near-death (NDEs) or out-of-body experiences (OBEs) are the main focus of this field,[168] though some parapsychologists also study encounters with ghosts and/or beings from other realms.[169]

163. Ibid., 48, 59–60, 96, 130, 147, 160, 171, 180.

164. Ibid., 13, 22, 58, 60, 160–61; see also Mischel et al., *Introduction to Personality*, 355.

165. Bourgeault, *Wisdom Way of Knowing*, 88; Huebner, "Spirituality and Knowing," 163–64; Radin, *Conscious Universe*, 13.

166. Anderson, "Introduction," xxi.

167. Ibid.

168. Griffin, *Parapsychology, Philosophy, and Spirituality*, 11; Irwin and Watt, "An Introduction to Parapsychology," Kindle Locations 95–96; Radin, *Conscious Universe*, 2.

169. Irwin and Watt, "An Introduction to Parapsychology," Kindle Locations

ESP experiences include the ability to see into another's mind (telepathy) or to see objects at a distance (clairvoyance).[170] PK experiences involve one being able to influence physical as well as animate objects using only one's mind; i.e., they deal with mind-matter interactions.[171] Finally, NDEs and OBEs are those experiences that appear to the individual as being detached from or outside of one's physical body.[172] Parapsychological views of human nature therefore pursue claims that who we are extends beyond our physical selves and seems to support the assertion that we are connected to creation in ways that are beyond the five physical senses.[173]

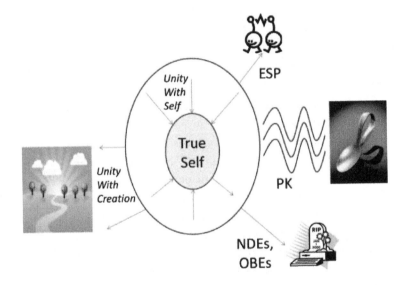

Figure 15. Transpersonal Influences of the Human Person.

196–99.

170. Griffin, *Parapsychology, Philosophy, and Spirituality*, 11; Irwin and Watt, "An Introduction to Parapsychology," Kindle Locations 195–96; Radin, *Conscious Universe*, 14.

171. Griffin, *Parapsychology, Philosophy, and Spirituality*, 11; Irwin and Watt, "An Introduction to Parapsychology," Kindle Locations 2336–37; Radin, *Conscious Universe*, 15.

172. Griffin, *Parapsychology, Philosophy, and Spirituality*, 11; Irwin and Watt, "An Introduction to Parapsychology," Kindle Locations 3814–16, 4212–14; Radin, *Conscious Universe*, 15.

173. Bourgeault, *Wisdom Way of Knowing*, 5, 10, 27, 88; Braud and Anderson, *Transpersonal Research Methods*, 51, 53, 64, 173; Radin, *Conscious Universe*, 2, 14, 158, 290.

While it is has been statistically noted that as much as 70–75 percent of the population in the United States believes in possibility and authenticity of such experiences,[174] there is still much skepticism related to these views of human nature particularly from conventional scientific fields as well as among some religious communities. Among conventional scientists, some of the core criticisms noted are that such phenomena are not repeatable under controlled conditions, the methods of study used are not truly "scientific," reports of such experiences involve fraud or delusions of some kind, or that they fundamentally challenge modern and materialist worldviews.[175] Nevertheless, several notable individuals and communities, both scientific and non-scientific, have agreed with either the philosophical possibility or scientific basis for such phenomena including Carl Sagan, the Congressional Research Service, the Army Research Institute, William James, Sigmund Freud, Carl Jung, Thomas Edison, William Blake, Arthur Conan Doyle, and Mark Twain.[176]

On the side with religion, particularly in the Christian tradition, concerns have been raised that transpersonal and parapsychological explanations challenge classical doctrines related to healings, miracles, and supernatural Divine intervention.[177] Nevertheless, many Christian communities, particularly charismatic ones, hold a place in their worldviews for similar kinds of phenomena such as prophecy (i.e., seeing through time), healing through laying hands on a person and/or mental prayer (i.e., mind-matter interactions), interacting with beings from other realms (e.g., angels and demons), and seeing into the mind/heart of another person.[178] Regardless of the interpretations given to such occur-

174. Irwin and Watt, "An Introduction to Parapsychology," Kindle Locations 5416–20; Radin, *Conscious Universe*, 301.

175. Braud and Anderson, "Conventional and Expanded Views of Research," 3; Griffin, *Parapsychology, Philosophy, and Spirituality*, 17, 30, 42; Irwin and Watt, "An Introduction to Parapsychology," Kindle Locations 115–16; Radin, *Conscious Universe*, xii; chap. 13.

176. Griffin, *Parapsychology, Philosophy, and Spirituality*, 13; Radin, *Conscious Universe*, 3.

177. Griffin, *Parapsychology, Philosophy, and Spirituality*, 21; Radin, *Conscious Universe*, 19.

178. For examples, see such texts as Hunter and Hunter, *How to Heal the Sick*, chaps. 3, 7, 10, 14; Osborn, *Healing the Sick*, chaps. 8, 15, 19, 28; Palmer, *Way of Holiness*, 47, 156–57; Parker, *Led by the Spirit*, 74–77, 82, 85, 98–99; Rasmussen, *Modern African Spirituality*, 68, 70, 75, 83–87; Torrey, *The Power of Prayer and the Prayer of Power*, 21–22.

rences, the phenomenon studied by transpersonal and parapsychological fields seems to be affirmed by the religious experiences of individuals and communities in traditions such as Christianity.

One representative theorist for these views is Robert Assagioli and his book *Psychosynthesis*. In it, Assagioli presents psychosynthesis as an attempt at unifying many of the then contemporary views of and approaches to psychology ranging from psychosomatic to Eastern views.[179] Based upon this foundation, he then presents an anthropology that includes such elements as lower, middle, higher, and super-consciousness (which includes some of the transpersonal and parapsychic abilities discussed above), a conscious and higher Self, and connections with the collective unconsciousness of creation (which contributes to some of our parapsychic abilities).[180] The primary aim of psychosynthesis is then defined to be the work of seeking to synthesize and integrate these various parts with one's higher Self. In Assagioli's words, it seeks "the harmonization and integration into one functioning whole of all the qualities and functions of the individual."[181]

The journey towards such integration, Assagioli claims, unfolds along four stages or phases. In the first leg of this journey, it is asserted that we must spend an extensive amount of time to better understand and open ourselves up to the unconscious depths of our psyche.[182] Part of the goal here is to find and work for greater liberation from the fears, patterns, and influences that keep us from our higher and truer Self. A second set of processes then includes our coming to control and dominate the unconscious influences with which we so often identify ourselves.[183] As this work unfolds, our unifying Center will then begin to emerge and will be as unique as is each individual in the third stage of our journey.[184] Here, integration of the lower with the higher Self begins to happen much more fully and intentionally. Finally, in the fourth stage, the more extensive work of psychosynthesis progresses wherein "we are in a position to build around [our unifying Center] a new personality—coherent, organized, and unified."[185]

179. Assagioli, *Psychosynthesis*, 14–16.

180. Ibid., 17–19.

181. Ibid., 7; see also 37.

182. Ibid., 21.

183. Ibid., 22–23.

184. Ibid., 24–25.

185. Ibid., 26.

Such is the pinnacle of psychosynthesis work according to Assagioli. It is one that seeks to attend to the integration of the whole person with their core or higher Self; i.e., self-realization. Much of this journey involves the transmutation of inner physical and psychical energies with the higher and super-conscious levels of awareness and/or energies.[186] In support of this work, Assagioli also presents a series of techniques that can be used to aid one, usually in consultation with a pscyhosynthesis therapist, in each stage of this unfolding journey.[187]

Due to his emphasis on the integration of one's whole being, Assagioli's material might be considered to be somewhat of a holistic representation of many of the previous views above. However, since he does give a central place to the development of super-consciousness, or what he terms "spiritual development," he is also representative of the transpersonal-parapsychological views discussed in this section.[188] Assagioli also provides a number of imaginative and intuitive-based techniques to help foster such super-consciousness further demonstrating the principles of these transpersonal-parapsychological views of human nature.

## ESSENTIAL MODERN SCIENCE ELEMENTS

Unlike with our Western Christian writers, some of these different views of human nature come from different fields of scientific study, which have their own focus. For instance, neuroscientists primarily study the physiological dynamics of the brain whereas many of our psychological-based fields are more interested in the movements of the mind. Of course, as it has been noted above, there is still much overlap and even some correlations between such studies. Nevertheless, there are significant differences in the primary foci of these different disciplines which must also be respected.

As a result, our purpose in this section is somewhat different than it was for our Christian writers. In the last chapter, we were primarily looking for commonalities, themes, and patterns across these various authors. While we will still be doing this here, we will also be looking for the dominant themes that each view highlights as they may focus more intentionally on an essential part of human nature that some of the others

186. Ibid., 56–57, 65, 87.

187. Ibid., part II.

188. Ibid., 192–97.

do not because of their very different foci. However, since all of these do have the same general focus (i.e., human nature) we expect there to be many elements that are common among them.

One caution that we must enter into such reflections with is related to the nature of scientific methods. As we briefly saw above, transpersonal-parapsychological views have been neglected or outright rejected based upon claims that such phenomenon, if they truly exist, are not accessible via the repeatable and empirically observable methods of science. While the fields reviewed above do not use exactly the same sets of research methods, they each are still primarily interested in those aspects of human nature that appear across the general population and can therefore provide insights into the personalities and behaviors of a wide range of people.

The caution that therefore emerges from this is related to the limits or narrowness of the elements of human nature identified by each field. In other words, they will have primarily identified those elements that seem to be common from one person to the next, rather than those that might only appear for one single person or even a smaller group of people. In addition, we must also note that all of our modern science authors/communities, like their Christian counterparts, are Western, basing their claims mostly on European and U.S. populations. In short, what we must keep in mind for this entire exploration is the very real and narrow limits of these sources.

With this said, we may find the following to be some of the essential elements of human nature and change found across these views. The reader is referred to Appendix B for a summary table of each of these modern science views and the essential elements which we will now address. As we shall see, and might expect, many of these views of human nature and transformation closely parallel and align with many of the common elements found among our Western Christian writers, though with some noted differences.

## Human Nature

A few of these authors discuss at least three basic characteristics of human nature in a general way. First, *people are asserted to have physical, psychological, and even transpersonal aspects that are enduring.* Found most centrally with Trait-Disposition views, humans are asserted to include structures that are stable across time and with varied contexts. In addition, Neuroscientists and our Social-Cognitive writers also asserted such enduring phenomena with their concepts of brain structure and schema theory. Indeed, as discussed above, each of these views claims that the dynamics that they study are enduring to some degree for people across their lifetime, with the possible exception of parapsychological phenomena. As a result, human nature is found to consist of characteristics that are enduring. While this point seems rather obvious, it is an important one to make for the following reasons: 1) Without such enduring characteristics, there could be no scientific study of human nature; and 2) The enduringness of human nature must be held in tension with its flexibility and changeableness, which will be discussed below.

With these enduring structures, a few of these modern science fields go on to assert that *parts of human nature are also well-ordered.* The observed fact that the brain itself seems to have different regions associated with different functions (though it also has been observed to operate in a distributed fashion as well) supports this claim. Our Behavioral-Conditioning authors also asserted the presence of stimulus-response mechanisms that essentially locate behavior actions in relation to external events. Phenomenological-Humanistic views claim that there are "self-constructs" by which people partly live their life in accordance with. All of this is to say that human nature is at least partly well-ordered and organized.

Given this enduring and partly ordered system, however, it was also noted as the third and final basic characteristic that *human nature is flexible, malleable, and potentially ever-changing.* Asserted by Allport as being organism-like, human nature is not entirely a fixed entity or system. Indeed, even at the more enduring physical level, the biological brain can and does structurally change in response to repeated firings. Similarly, Psychodynamic-Motivational views conceive of human nature as a system that is in constantly changing conflicts and tensions with the many fears, drives, motives, et cetera that seek to compel us this way or that in any given moment. Finally, Bandura's social learning theory fundamentally held that who we are and how we behave will be partly influenced by the actions and resulting consequences of others around us on a daily basis. In short, human nature is therefore very malleable and in a constant state of change.

Given these basic characteristics, there were also at least three distinctive parts of human nature that can be identified across these various views. Clearly, *physiology* is a central element of human nature according  to these authors. Ranging from genes which give rise to physical development to the biological brain to Freud's Id, the physiological aspects are considered to be a strong component of consideration for any model of human nature. Even from a Transpersonal perspective, the transmutation of physical and sexual energies was considered to be of central importance to Assagioli's framework.

More broadly than this is the second essential part of human nature found in this part of the book, which we might be tempted to further subdivide but is not always clear as to where and how to do this. As we might expect, with so many of our authors being in this field, *psychological dynamics* were considered vital to their models of human nature. These dynamics included a wide range of phenomena. For the Trait-Disposition views, aspects of one's personality structure are asserted to influence how one behaves and governs their life. Central to both the Neuroscientific and Psychodynamic-Motivational views were the emotions and *affective* movements that influence and even dominate our lives. Fears, instincts, drives towards life and/or death, et cetera all affect the choices we make according to these writers. For Phenomenological-Humanistic and Social-Cognitive researchers, the more *cognitive* self-constructs and conscious decision-making processes that we engage in also help to determine our nature as human beings. Such dynamics, it is noted, are so closely intertwined with one another that it is not always clear where more purely "affective" influences end and more purely "cognitive" ones begin. As a result, I label these joint cognitive-affective dynamics as the psychological part according to these authors.

A third and final essential part of human nature is *super-consciousness*. Noted almost solely by our Transpersonal-Parapsychological authors (though it may also be found in some Humanistic writers such as Maslow), this part of human nature is concerned with creation connections that appear to be beyond the five physical senses. As discussed above, this may involve seeing through time and/or space, influencing other people and/or matter with one's mind, OBEs and NDEs, or interacting with beings from other realms. While this aspect was not discussed across most of these authors, I hold a place for these phenomena partly because of the substantial evidence that exists in support of these dynamics and partly because such views are in accordance with the religious experiences of many Christians (though a different explanation is given for such experiences than the one offered by researchers in this modern science field as discussed above in the Transpersonal-Parapsychological section above).

With these three essential elements of human nature in place, some of these authors also asserted the need for *integration and harmony* in their models. In the Psychodynamic-Motivational framework, the ego was asserted to have a primary function of trying to harmonize the energies of Id with the ideals of the Superego. For Phenomenological-Humanistic writers, a central goal of integration and self-actualization is asserted. Finally, for Transpersonal proponents such as Assagioli, harmonization with one's higher Self was the primary focus of their formation efforts. Central to human nature, it may therefore be asserted, is the role of and even quest for such personal integration and inner harmony.

While these factors related to the internal aspects of human nature, most of these authors assert the centrality of *context* in the development and expression of human nature. For Evolutionary researchers, the role of one's environmental context cannot be overstated as species are asserted to evolve in adaptation to where they live. Similarly, for Behavioral-Conditioning and Social-Cognitive theorists, how we behave is partly, if not largely, shaped by the social and cultural influences and reinforcements that we continually find ourselves in. Even the ideals of the Superego and the phenomenological constructs that we create are molded in part by the relationships we have and the environments we grow up in. As a result, the role and influence of context is central to any model of human nature that is based upon these fields of study.

Finally, and closely related to this but also distinct enough to consider it as being separate, is the influence of *historicity* on human nature. Addressed most directly by the Biological, Psychodynamic-Motivational, Behavior-Conditioning, and Social-Cognitive views, it is the basic claim that who we are is significantly influenced by the histories that have worked to shape us: genetically, culturally, socially, et cetera. The enduring patterns of human nature, and perhaps even the non-enduring ones, are partly the product of these past experiences. Our histories, it is claimed, influences not only which genes we have and how they are expressed, which then help to give rise to the inner personality structures (traits, constructs, schemas, et cetera) that we have, but also the cognitive-affective processes by which we often live our lives. Historical influences, in both evolutionary and contemporary forms, are therefore a final essential influence on human nature found in these modern scientific fields of study.

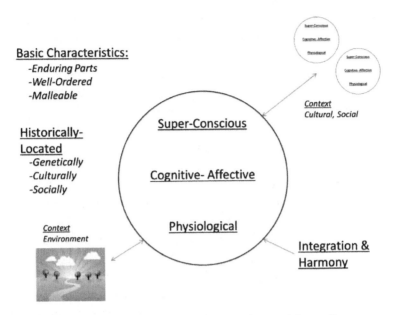

Figure 16. A Synthesized Modern Science-Based View of Human Nature.

## The Nature of Change

As it relates to the common themes across these views on the nature of change, some general observations and principles may be made. The first relates to the *aims* that are noted by some of these authors. Goals such as the Ego's balancing of Superego and Id, psychosynthesis' quest for integration in the higher Self, and Humanistic ideals of self-actualization are examples of such aims. Overall, a self that is more harmonized, balanced, and well-integrated appears to be a goal that is shared by many of these authors.

Secondly, human transformation is commonly asserted to come primarily via the work of *repatterning*. As we might expect, what is repatterned is articulated in terms of each field's more primary focus of study. For Trait-Disposition writers, this entails working with the enduring dispositions that one has. In the Neuroscience framework, this means seeking to intentionally repattern the neuron connections and firing patterns that one has neurophysiologically. Clearly, this is inherent to the Behavioral-Conditioning views as one strives to continually reshape the stimulus-response habits that one has. In the Social-Cognitive and Phe-nomenological systems, we are expected to work with the schemas and self-constructs that partly influence and guide our lives. In addition, our Biological authors asserted that such repatterning requires knowledge of the laws and principles of evolution and gene expression in addition to the long-term work of habit reforming. Again and again, do we here these authors emphasize the need for repatterning the enduring struc-tures, processes, et cetera of our lives.

As discussed above, these authors also noted influences that affect human nature, many of which are also asserted to guide transformation as well. Clearly, one's evolutionary history was claimed by our Biological thinkers to be a significant factor in how we develop as a species. Brain-wise, genetic expression in connection with environmental factors also guides how we grow as human beings. Interpersonal and cultural factors are also a commonly asserted influence for human change, being as-serted most forcefully by Social-Cognitive and Behavioral-Conditioning authors. Many internal factors help to drive and guide our growth as well, with emotional arousal, fears, imagination, and cognitive processes be-ing a few that were named by Psychodynamic, Phenomenological, and Transpersonal thinkers. Paralleling the essential elements of human na-ture outlined above, the factors that influence human transformation are numerous.

Given all of this, however, there are some questions as to *what can be changed* in human nature *and to what extent.* In the Trait-Disposition views, for instance, a trait is determined to be those characteristics that endure across time and contexts. If these enduring personality structures really do endure then questions can be raised as to what extent human transformation is really possible. Similarly, from a neuroscience perspec-tive, while it may be possible to alter some of the neuronal connections that one has to some extent, we can ask questions of whether this can be done on a larger scale. In other words, if development of the biological brain is partly influenced by gene expression that has been established across the long scale of evolutionary history, then how much can a person alter these historically inherited neural pathways in a single lifetime? It is questions such as these that can be raised as we read across them in relation to human transformation. Nevertheless, these are some of the themes that emerge regarding the nature of change.

## Comparisons with Western Christian Common Elements

With these essential elements of these modern science views identified, we are now in a position to take a step back and compare it with the common elements found among our Western Christian writers. As we lay the two compiled models of human nature side-by-side, a number of commonalities and differences may be noted. However, some of the differences are not as divergent as they might first seem to be. In this section, we will therefore note some of these comparisons as such reflections will help us to move towards a more unified model in the next part of this book.

Beginning with the commonalities, we can immediately note how similar both of these compiled models are to one another. Clearly, the physical-physiological and cognitive-affective components directly correspond to each other. However, how these were viewed did differ across these authors. For instance, Augustine viewed the body as being of lower importance particularly in relation to neuroscientists who give its study a central priority. At the psychological levels, many of the drives, passions, instincts, et cetera dynamics were also fairly similar for both sets of writers. Indeed, what is hopefully apparent at this stage is that study and exploration of the psyche did not begin with Freud but has been part and parcel of the Christian religious tradition (as well as many of the other major religious traditions) for thousands of years.

Similarly, both sets of theorists viewed integration as being a central part of human experience. Both generally affirmed the wholeness of human nature. This is say that each part of one's personhood does not exist in complete isolation from the greater whole of which it is a part. The human being is essentially an interconnected system where each element contributes, to some degree at least, to the overall health and functioning of this system. Wholeness and integration, as Green so loudly emphasized, is therefore affirmed by most of these authors to be an integral characteristic of human nature.

A final obvious commonality is the importance of the relationships that one has. For our modern science authors, such relationships were asserted to include the genetic, cultural, and social ties that one has. For our Western Christian thinkers, these relationships similarly include those we have with one another, and even beings from other realms, as well as to the environments and contexts which we find ourselves within. Of course, the major differences between these are genetics and contact with beings from other realms, something which will be discussed further below. Despite this, these authors collectively assert the inherent relationality of the human species.

Based upon these identified commonalities, we can begin to assert a more unified model. If each of these elements really are common across this vastly diverse range of thinkers and theorists, then any model of human nature must address them to some degree. To neglect any of these would seem to deny an element of human nature that is integral to our existence. In other words, it would be a denial of reality as it is lived and observed by many people. These commonalities therefore begin to form a broad structural basis for the more specific unified model that I will be attempting to construct in the next part of this book.

Turning back to these two compiled models, we can also note that there are also some seemingly significant differences between them. However, some of the differences are not as disparate as it might seem at first glance. Beginning with the compiled modern science model, we note that Super-consciousness does not appear in the Western Christian one. Already a controversial one among conventional/contemporary fields of science, we will recall that it is one that is intended to capture the parapsychological dynamics that humans have been observed to be had by some. These included the ESP, PK, and NDE-OBEs that people reportedly have. As we have already noted in the Transpersonal-Parapsychological section above, there are many similar kinds of religious experiences found within the Christian tradition that seem to closely parallel these phenomena. Indeed, the argument could be made that the Super-Conscious component is akin to the relationship with beings from other realms as well as to some aspects of Divine Connection that appear in the Western Christian model. In fact, in Assagioli's own framework, he equates "spiritual development" with the growth of Super-consciousness.[189] Hence, while there are some significant differences between these that would need to be clarified in a more unified model, the differences are not as divergent as we might have first thought.

A second difference that the modern science model has from the Western Christian one is its discussion of the Basic Characteristics of human nature. These included the assertions that human nature has enduring parts, is well-ordered, and is malleable. Given that scientific method primarily focuses on studying enduring, empirically observable

189. Assagioli, *Psychosynthesis*, 192–93.

phenomena and their interrelationships with one another, it is no wonder that these characteristics surfaced.

Turning to our Western Christian writers, I do not think that any of these authors would outright disagree with these claims. Since they have asserted an explicit theological anthropology, which is understood to be representative of the general population, I believe that they would not argue with the statement that there are parts of human nature that are enduring. Many of these Christian writers also articulated a well-structured and highly hierarchical model of human nature, so I do not think that they would contest this point as well. Finally, given that these authors also collectively asserted that we are distorted and in need of transformation to some degree, leads me to assert that they would likewise support the malleableness of human beings as well. In short, I assert that these Basic Characteristics are affirmed by the totality of these authors and may therefore be considered to be yet another common element that any theological anthropology needs to incorporate along with those named above. One of the benefits of conducting pluralistic and diverse studies such as this one is that sometimes one community of theorists helps another to more clearly see that which is already in their midst but overlooked to some degree.

A final difference that we see on the modern science side is the emphasis that is given to the historically located nature of human beings. While we did hear something of this in Rahner's thought, it appears that many of the other Western Christian authors do not overtly discuss this. One could assert that such a view is inherently present in these writers since some of them noted the "Fall of Man/Adam" as being the basis for sin and distortion in the world which is subsequently passed on or present from one generation to the next. Such a view was particularly found with Augustine and Maximus.

However, I believe that these are genuine contributions and challenges that the modern sciences are bringing to the world's religious traditions, in this case Western Christianity. The basic contribution here is that who we are as human beings is partly determined by enduring and traceable cause-and-effect relationships across generations. Such a view could be taken to augment (or even replace depending on one's theological position) the classical Christian doctrine of Original Sin to assert that the distortions/sins of one generation are passed on to the next via genetic, cultural, and social learning/conditioning patterns. Nevertheless, this difference is a significant one for Western Christian theorists as it can potentially modify our understanding of some of the core influences that shape human beings across contexts and even generations.

Turning next to the Western Christian model, there are two significant differences not already discussed. The first is the Distortions element. Many of these authors asserted that humans are somehow flawed or incomplete and therefore in need of further and/or on-going transformation. Such a claim is the foundational basis the existence of the field of Christian spiritual formation. On the modern science side, such views can be found, but not to the same extent as it is in Western Christianity. Freud, for instance, was found to assert that human nature is fundamentally conflict-ridden and has two fundamental competing drives towards life or death. Much of Freud's psychodynamic theories and approaches subsequently focused on pathology, or the distortions and struggles of humanity. The majority of the other fields, however, did not seem to have such a focus. Instead, they sought to identify enduring dynamics and patterns related to their specific areas of focus, be that the biological brain, interpersonal interactions, or the self-constructs that we have. In other words, their work seemed to be more descriptive than evaluative as it was for most of our Western Christian authors.

Noting this, challenges can be raised for both communities. For our Christians writers, we might ask whether human nature is as distorted as it is made out to be. Is the nature of "sinfulness" in humanity really as deep and extensive as these writers collectively seem to claim it is? Looking at our world today, with its widespread violence, some might answer a resounding "yes." Nevertheless, it is a question that one must grapple with in the construction of their own theological anthropology. On the science side, especially given the ideals of harmony and integration that were asserted as aims for human transformation, we might ask whether there is a place for asserting more explicitly the need for continual human growth. While science seeks non-evaluative "objectivity" as a part of its methods, we might still challenge these fields to encourage positive human development that is not only well-integrated and balanced, but also ethical, compassionate, serving, et cetera. These are common ethical guidelines and aims found across religious traditions.

A second and final difference between these two compiled models is the obvious one related to Divine Connection. Being secular humanistic in nature, most of the scientific disciplines we reviewed did not explicitly address theology or humanity's relation to it in any explicit ways. Clearly, such claims are not a part of their worldviews as a field. Given this, there again are challenges that can be lodged in both directions. For modern scientists, caution is rightly held in not wanting to assert personified Divine intervention as a cause of specific phenomena (i.e., God directly intervening outside of or in addition to the already scientifically identified cause-and-effect relationships, or "laws," of the physical world). The concern here is that one may claim that Deity is the primary cause when alternative explanations may be given.

However, and this is where the challenge to modern science comes, we must remember that such secular scientific explanations are also not the only plausible explanations that are possible, even for the laws they have identified. As we saw in the theologies of some of our Western Christian writers, God can also be conceived of as acting within and through these enduring cause-and-effect relationships, as is asserted by Panentheists.[190] The challenge, then, is that we do not necessarily need to except the secular science claims as "facts," for they are merely secular interpretations and explanations given to certain sets of data. One could look at the same sets of data and offer alternative theories and explanations that are more theistic in nature, as the Panentheists have done.

On the Christian side, there has long been the tendency to ascribe phenomena to the direct intervention of God, as personified Deity. For instance, volcanic eruptions were once commonly considered to be the actions of an angry god. What must be remembered, therefore, is that while God might be asserted to be the Sustainer of all that is, God does not seem to explicitly act as an external Deity in every occurrence of creation. Immanently, it can be claimed that God is an inherent part of every manifestation. However, such theological conceptions differ markedly from the assertions that God (again as explicit, external, personified Deity) directly intervenes always and everywhere in a creation that is dualistically distinct from God's personified Self. The challenge for formulating one's theological anthropology, then, is that one must be clear as to what the enduring cause-and-effect relationships are in relation to human nature and how God relates to this model immanently, transcendently, and as personified Deity.

Given these various commonalities and differences, and their associated challenges to both modern secular scientists and Western Christians, we are now in a position to begin developing our own more unified

190. For further discussion, see panentheism writers such as Clayton, *Adventures in the Spirit*; Clayton and Peacocke, *In Whom We Live and Move and Have Our Being*; Peacocke, *Paths from Science towards God*; Smith, *God, Energy and the Field*.

model in light of both of these sets of contributors. Even if we used a blended version of these two models, much more work still needs to be done to fill in the details in relation not only to the components of human nature but also to their associated theologies and theories of change. It is in the next chapter of this book that we will now set about working towards this more detailed and rigorous task.

CHAPTER 3

# Seeking Synthesis
## *Toward a General Theory of Human Nature*

WE HAVE NOW COMPLETED the first of our three goals. We have completed a diverse survey of some of the many different views of human nature found in both Western Christianity and contemporary modern science. We are now in a position to begin constructing our own theological anthropologies in light of this exploration for use in spiritual formation. As we shall see, doing this is quite extensive. In fact, to build a completely comprehensive model of human nature, with all of the intricate details and dynamics for each part, would be a formidable task. It is much more of an advisable endeavor to sketch a broad structure or framework for our theological anthropology and then fill in the necessary specifics for each of its parts as our spiritual formation programs require us to do so. It is in this third part, then, that we will be learning how to sketch such a broader framework that may then be used to generally guide our formative efforts. Almost like creating a map that contains only the general outlines and regions. In the final part of this book later on, we will then follow one case example where more specific details (i.e., a street-level kind of map) will be needed for the concrete application that is presented.

## CONSTRUCTING AN ANTHROPOLOGY: LIMITS & CHALLENGES

One significant critique that needs to be highlighted for this work so far is the lack of depth that was presented for each of the views of human nature that we have reviewed. Choosing breadth over depth provided us with a broad view of the range of such views but at the expense of exploring each one in greater detail. Choose any of these views, Western Christian or modern scientific, and much more could be said in relation to it. Aquinas' collected works, for instance, comprise volumes and volumes of reflections and insights. The scholarship on his thought is a complete field unto itself and one could spend an entire career immersed in these writings alone. Similarly, each one of the science-based views is a discipline that requires extensive education and training. In short, we really have not done full justice to each of these views but merely skimmed the ideological surface of only some of their insights into human nature. While we have learned much along the way, and have picked up on some of the general elements of human nature, there is still much more to be gleaned from these many thinkers and fields of study.

A second limitation, which directly follows from this first one, is that human nature is far more complex than the synthesized models that we have compiled thus far suggest. For instance, as we learned in our section on neuroscience, the biological brain is composed of more than one hundred billion neurons each of which is capable of making connections with as many as 10,000 other neurons. The very complex firing patterns and neurophysiological dynamics which have emerged over evolution's long history are still not well understood, though much progress has been made over the last thirty years. To make things even more complex, each single neuron is a universe unto itself. Complete with their own nucleus, energy producing mitochondrion, and many other intracellular structures and processes.[1] Indeed, the physiological level of human nature alone reveals itself to be extremely complex.

Paralleling the limitations discussed above, now translate this immense complexity to each of the other levels that were identified by the two compiled models. The cognitive-affective part, the super-conscious element, and the relationships that we have and how they influence us, for example, may all be taken to be just as complex as the neurophysiological dynamics of the human person. The limitation that emerges,

---

1. Bear et al., *Neuroscience*, 28–35.

therefore, is the immense challenge of generating a detailed model for any one of these areas, much less a fully comprehensive one for the whole of human nature.

The challenges that therefore lie ahead are related to the following. First, should we even attempt to develop such a comprehensive model of human nature? If the dynamics of each part are so complicated and detailed, can we really create a broad model that captures them with enough accuracy? Secondly, if we were to create a more generalized model, how much detail needs to be included in order to help ensure that the model is useful enough for our purposes? Do we, for instance, really need to include the physiological mechanisms of each neuron in order to have a model that helps us to better understand the teenagers that we are working with in our youth ministry programs or would a much less detailed model suffice? In other words, where do we draw the line on what to include and what to leave out?

These are some of the primary limits to our explorations thus far and challenges that lie ahead for us. From the outset, we must recognize that we have only touched upon some of the brief details of what are much more extensive and complex views of human nature. Each part of our compiled models are, therefore, much more complex and detailed than what has been depicted. In constructing our own theological anthropologies, then, we must continually wrestle with how many features to include and whether our models are sufficiently detailed enough to guide our program development without being too detailed as to so overwhelm us that they are rendered useless due to their complexity.

## APPROACHES TO CREATING OUR OWN MODEL

With so many complexities to consider, there are a number of steps that one can go through in order to create their own theological anthropology. From knowing what the basis of discerning which models to use, to knowing what approaches are available to us in working with these models, some of these can be quite complex. Nevertheless, knowing the range of these approaches can help us in our quest to create our own model of human nature.

## Discerning Which Models to Draw From

The first set of steps to creating our own model involves deciding what sources to base our theological anthropologies on. In actual practice, one of the primary sources for such models must include one's experiential knowledge of the people and communities that they are working with. This is because if we are attempting to create a model that gives us greater insights into their lives so that we may better work with them, then we absolutely must include what we know about them. The methods for gathering such data and incorporating them into model-building, however, are well beyond the scope of this text though there are some resources for guiding these efforts.[2] As a result, this section will refer solely to the range of models that we have considered herein.

The first step in this process, then, is to decide which model or set of models to begin working with. Part of this discernment is primarily dependent on at least two sets of considerations. The first is our own preferences in relation to the models we reviewed: which of these seem most accurate, comprehensible, and appealing for us? Does one model seem to stand out more than any of the others? Or do different parts of different models seem to make the most sense for the context we are working in? If we are going to be adapting one or more of these models as the basis for our own theological anthropology, then one of the primary considerations needs to be our intuitive sense of which of these models seems most accurate, appropriate, et cetera for the purposes that we are intending to use them for. Indeed, such considerations are essentially a discernment process where we are asking God to guide us towards those models that we will need to help us to better partner with and support the work that God is doing with our communities. This first consideration therefore entails us prayerfully seeking to focus in on those models, or parts of models, that will aid this work.

Another part of this discernment can be based upon the models that our own community currently uses. Which of the views presented herein is closest to the ones of our local church or denomination? How do the people we work with think about themselves? Which of the models that we have considered most closely matches these views? Such considerations are important because if we are going to use a theological anthropology as the basis for our spiritual formation programs with this community, then there should be some connections between these

---

2. Britt, *Conceptual Introduction to Modeling.*

models and the ones that our community currently utilizes (implicitly or explicitly). Having identified this, however, we may still critically reflect on these by asking questions such as whether they seem most accurate to the kinds of human transformation that we are seeing in our communities; with whether they more accurately capture the actual dynamics of our context. For instance, if members of our community regularly view and speak of themselves as "poor wretched sinners" and such views appear to having a detrimental effect on their lives, then we might seek to discourage such damaging self-images.

Overall, the goal is for these models to help us to better partner with what God is formatively doing in our midst. If the theological anthropology that is being used does not aid or provide us with an accurate picture of such transformations, then it needs to be altered. In our own discernment, then, two primary considerations include our own discernment processes as well as reflecting on what the views of human nature are that are held by our community.

## Choosing How to Work with These Models

Once we have begun to discern which models appeal to us and fit well with the views of our communities, we are in a position to begin to construct our own model. There are a number of ways to going about such endeavors and the following are some of the primary ways to work towards synthesizing a model.[3] The hopes are these will help to guide us in our efforts to draw from the range of models we have considered in the generation of our own generalized version.

First, we can simply pick one of the models we have reviewed and use it without modification. If one of the Western Christian anthropologies particularly appealed to us, we might simply decide to accept it as is. For instance, Luther's views of inner and outer person and moving from old to new life may particularly appeal to us and our community. If such a model seemed to accurately capture the kind of journey that parishioners in our congregation go through, then it may very well provide the kinds of insights that we need to better understand and more effectively work with our community. Accepting such a model as is, then, may serve our needs very well if it provides us with such accurate insights into their

---

3. For a more complete discussion of these, see Kyle, *Living Spiritual Praxis.*

unfolding spiritual journey. If this is indeed the case, then Luther's model might be adopted without modifications.

Secondly, we might also choose one model as foundational and then modify it based upon input from one or more of the other theological anthropologies, or based upon what we personally know of our communities. For example, we might select Freud's Id-Ego-Superego framework as the basis for our theological anthropology. However, being that it is articulated from a secular worldview, we might also decide to augment it by adding Rahner's "transcendentality" views. In this approach, Freud's model comprises the primary basis for our model while Rahner's model augments it slightly.

Next, we might choose two or more models and seek to synthesize these by giving more equal weight to each of them. In this approach, one model does not just slightly augment another model. Rather, it fundamentally alters the resulting theological anthropology in significant ways. There are at least two ways that such significant augmentation can occur. First, these models might simply complement one another. Such a relationship is one in which the models being considered do not overlap in any significant ways so that no major modifications are necessary between them. The models are simply linked together like a jig-saw puzzle. An example of this might be to take Kant's virtuous model and link it together with the Transpersonal-Parapsychological views. Doing so in a complementary way would mean that we more simply added these views onto Kant's anthropology without fundamentally altering either one.

A second obvious way is for the models to fundamentally and mutually alter each other in significant ways. If we were to take the schemas theories of the Social-Cognitive view and merge these with Maximus' anthropology of the parts of the soul, a new model might emerge. In such an integration, perhaps, the various parts of Maximus' soul might be seen as psychic schemas that we might work to reshape according to some of the principles outlined by Social-Cognitive researchers as well as by Maximus. In doing so, if such an endeavor were indeed successful, a new and significantly different model will have emerged as result of these more extensive synthesizing efforts. These two ways therefore are indicative of considering two or more models on an equal scale and either merging or modifying them accordingly.

Finally, we can also create our own theological anthropology from scratch, using one or more of these theories as a source of inspiration. It might very well be in reflecting on these various views of human nature in light of our own context, that none of them—or any combination of them—accurately captures the dynamics that we find in our community. We might therefore seek to create our own version. While such a theological anthropology will no doubt contain resonances with these other varied views, the resulting model may nonetheless be different enough to represent a new model altogether.

As stated many times now, the goal is to create a model that will provide us with helpful insights and a deeper understanding of the people that we are working with so that we might more closely partner with God for their spiritual transformation. If setting all of these alternative views aside to create our own version helps us towards these ends, then we must not be afraid to venture off into new and seemingly uncharted waters, discerning along the way.

## MERGING SCIENCE & RELIGION: PROPOSING A UNIFIED THEORY OF HUMAN NATURE

With these general approaches to combining models of human nature briefly sketched out, we now turn to one concrete example of what some of these processes looks like. In this section, I will be proposing my own version of a general theological anthropology. To do this, I will be addressing each of the major components that I see as being central to my own views. For each of these elements, I will then turn to the various authors we have considered to further explore and outline each one with some level of detail.

This approach is therefore a two-step process. First, it entails looking back at the two compiled models from the previous parts of this book and deciding which components are most relevant/significant for my own theological anthropology. Then, it involves providing more details as it relates to each component based upon the views that we explored above. From these two movements, I will therefore be sketching a general unified model that not only seeks to synthesize these various thinkers and communities, but one that is also relevant for my own ministerial contexts. As noted above, however, such a model will only be a generalized one for which further details will need to be filled in before it may be used for specific spiritual formation programs. This we will be doing in the final part of this book. For now, our goal is to synthesize this basic framework.

Once these major components are identified and given some sketchy details, we will next be stepping back to reflect across these components. In particular, we will be reflecting on how these various components might be related to one another, something which is essential for our formation efforts. As we heard many of our authors assert, which I agree with, human nature is a high interconnected system. This means that making a change in one area will affect each of the others to some extent. For instance, if one takes drugs which alter the physiology of the bio-logical brain, there may be psychological and relational changes as well. As a result, we must also give some consideration to how these various components are connected and mutually influence one another. This we will be doing in the next part of this book as I propose a more generalized model for spiritual formation work that is intended to not only address these interconnections, but also the theologies and theories of change that are associated with them.

## Major Components of This Unified Theological Anthropology

As noted, the first step involves choosing which components of the two compiled models seem most relevant for my own theological anthropol-ogy. In discerning this, as we saw above, there are two primary consid-erations in these efforts: reflecting on my own preferences and looking to the communities that I work with. As we move through each of the components that I have chosen for my own view of human nature, I will be addressing each of these. The goal of this section is not only to offer an additional theological anthropology for the reader to draw from, one that has been intentionally synthesized in light of the various views we have explored, but to also offer insights into some of the underlying processes that go into such considerations.

It will also be noted that I will address theologies, theories of change, and distortions for each one of these components individually. Part of the complexity of human beings is that each of these components, as was noted particularly of our modern science authors, can be formatively worked with separately. For examples, doctors work with the health and vitality of the physical body while counselors and psychologists focus more exclusively on the psychic dynamics of a person. Of course, each change to one area then affects the other components as just discussed. Nevertheless, we can formulate a theory of change and discuss the theology and distortions commonly associated with each component. In addition to these separate discussions, however, we will take up a general theory of change and return to theology again when we explore the more generalized theory in the next chapter.

Given all of this, we will therefore address each of the following topics for each component: 1) Why is this component important? Why was it chosen based on my own preferences and ministerial location?; 2) A brief description of the component's essential elements and dynamics based upon our historical and contemporary explorations in the two previous parts of the book; 3) The theory of change that is related to this component; 4) The theology that I associate with it; and 5) Examples of the kinds of distortions sometimes found. Such reflections will hopefully provide the reader with insights as you work to construct your own theological anthropology.

Overall, there are nine essential components to this proposed model, which may seem quite complex at first. However, the model is really divided into three sets of three, paralleling Augustine's affinity for trinities (though not intentionally). The three major categories of components are the Intrapersonal, Interpersonal, and Transpersonal Aspects. As we shall see, the second two emerge directly from the Intrapersonal thereby providing us with a simpler view of what is a very complex system. Let us now take each of these in turn.

### *Theological Foundations: A Trinitarian Theology of Spiritual Formation*

For each component, we will be addressing the theology that is relevant for that aspect. Overall, however, we can articulate the general theology out of which these reflections emerge. As we may recall from the compiled Western Christian theological anthropology, there were three primary aspects of Divine Connection that were noted: transcendent, personified, and immanent. Collectively, they comprise a Trinitarian theology upon which the theological reflections for this section are based.

The transcendent aspect was related to God being mysterious and utterly transcendent, the unknowable Ground of all creation according to Rahner, Aquinas, Maximus, and Augustine in particular. The personified aspect of this Trinitarian theology had more to do with the person-like attributes and relationship that one can have with God. Often associated with Christ, as seen particularly in the writings of Luther and Barth, this Deity-like aspect is also concerned with how God interacts "externally" on creation, as one person would with another. Finally, the immanent aspect asserts that God is present within and acting through the "natural" laws and dynamics of creation. Noted more clearly in Maximus and Aquinas, this aspect of God is the one which emerges more fully in our lives and our world as we become more like God, more "spiritualized" if you will (i.e., in the views of Maximus and Aquinas, "God becomes in us as we become in God").

Beyond their individual characteristics, these three aspects may also be related to one another. As was briefly mentioned when we reviewed Augustine, some parts of our being seem to materialize out of a wordless nothingness, or "no-thingness" to be more precise. Similarly, Rahner was found to assert that we have a transcendent core out of which our being emerges. Theologically, I therefore assert (or hypothesize) that if the ground of God is utter transcendence, as Maximus most clearly asserted, then maybe material creation manifests out of this Ground that is "nothing." In other words, maybe the immanent aspect of God literally materializes and creation is both made and sustained by this living Ground of no-thingness that is continually within and through and beyond all that is, ever working for its on-going transformation.

Of course, we would still need to wrestle with the question of why there are distortions in the world if God is present within and through it. In response, for my own theology, I hold in congruence with many of our Christian authors that free will is an inherent part of existence at this material level of creation and that such free will is partly the source of such distortions in and amongst humanity. However, I also extend such free will beyond the human species even beyond animals and plants. In fact, it is my theological-cosmological position that such free will is an inherent part, a gift of God if you like, for every part of this material creation. This view is precisely the position of Process Theologians to whom I am indebted for these insights and will be discussed in greater in the next chapter.[4] As we proceed through the sections below, this view will be important for describing some of the distortions found for each aspect.

So, the theological picture thus far is that out of the transcendent aspect of God emerges the immanent aspect; i.e., all that is manifest in creation. We might think of the immanent aspect as the fabric of creation,

4. For examples of such Process views, see Cobb and Griffin, *Process Theology*; Suchocki, *God, Christ, Church*; Whitehead, *Adventures of Ideas*.

the "stuff" or stuffing out of which creation is composed. If there really are multiple universes or realms, which many of our Christian authors held in line with classical doctrines of Heaven and Hell, then clearly God's immanence emerges in a myriad of ways. Such diversely immanent manifestations could therefore be seen as a theological-cosmological basis for a personified Deity. If God really does want to help creation, particularly the free willed material realm of which we are a part, then it stands to reason that God might manifest God's Self as Deity partly to aid such formative endeavors.

When many of the Christian writers spoke of humans being made in the image of God, it was often to this personified aspect of God that they were referring; a God with a will, one who acts in creation, one to whom we can personally relate—and/or vice versa. The views of Barth, Luther, and the biblical model, which asserted the presence of more purely personified spiritual and divine spark within human nature, might be interpreted in light of this personified aspect of God. In other words, as Deity, God may be asserted to relate to each and every human being in deeply intimate and very personal ways as an inner companion, friend, savior, et cetera. As Trinity, then, it might be claimed that as we grow in our spiritual life, God truly does become within, to, and beyond us with increasing intimacy, through to the very core of our being.

Of course, unlike humans, this personified aspect of God in creation is not distorted, but rather is the pure manifestation of God as Deity. Such a view might therefore also become the basis for a Christology: Jesus living a fully human life, manifested out of the same "stuff" as humans are, but doing so fully as God, undefiled and undistorted, though tempted and free to choose just as we are nonetheless. As this is not intended to be a theological treatise, I will leave the more detailed discussions of this topic to the systematic theologians who continue to debate the validity and details of such a theology.

These three aspects are therefore inexplicably intertwined. Each one is fully a part of the other as the totality and complete unification of God's Trinitarian life—transcendentally, immanently, and personified as Deity—fully One as God. Taken together, then, I assert that these provide a comprehensive Trinitarian theology upon which to base our spiritually formative efforts. If spiritual formation is thought of as forming people and communities (and all of creation, thinking more broadly) in the Spirit, then this Trinitarian theology provides guidance in how to think about such formative endeavors. In other words, our task is to help people and communities to grow in each of these three aspects of God: transcendence, immanence, and personified. This theology of spiritual formation is therefore the foundation for my theological reflections in the sections that now follow and our goal will be to relate each anthropological component to this Trinity.

## Intrapersonal: Three Core Components

Now turning to first of three levels for the theological anthropology that I am proposing, the intrapersonal aspects essentially have to do with the internal dynamics and influences of a person that help to shape who we are and what we do. While these, as we saw in the two previous parts of this book, are quite varied and diverse, I assert for my own model that they may be divided into three core components: physiological, psychological, and integrative-transcendent. My own experiences in pastoral ministry and now as an educator, supports this view. A common theological anthropology that has been often asserted by the people that I have worked with is the "mind-body-spirit" model that is common in our culture.[5] While views of what the "spirit" component is vary widely, this unified model of mine is therefore very much in line with the views of the communities that I regularly work with so let us now explore each of these sub-components in turn.

### PHYSIOLOGICAL ASPECTS

The first intrapersonal sub-component of my own theological anthropology is one that was common to both compiled models as well as the majority of the authors we have considered. The physical level is inherent to our existence as beings living a life on this material planet. I agree with Green that who we are is inextricably linked to our embodiedness. Again and again, the vast majority of these authors give a central place to our body and its role in our life. It is the most concrete and enduring part of our existence while on Earth. Not only does it entail the wonderfully complex dynamics of the brain and central nervous system, but also the vast array of other physiological phenomena that comprise the various

---

5. For examples of such a model, see Hauser, *Moving in the Spirit*; Van Kaam, *Fundamental Formation*, 60; Wilber, *Integral Spirituality*, 203.

parts of our bodies, with all of its diverse organs, tissues, homeostatic processes, genetic expressions, et cetera.

For me, it also includes at least part of the stimulus-response and instinctual mechanisms highlighted by the Behavioralists and by Freud's concept of Id. Some (or even most) of these, in my own framework, are shared by other animals thereby linking the human species in with the long and continually unfolding evolutionary history of our planet. As we saw, formators who focus more exclusively on this aspect are neuroscientists but also doctors, physical trainers and therapists, nutritionist, and the like. The physiological aspect is therefore held as one of the foundational sub-components in my own theological anthropology entails at this intrapersonal level. As a result, I assert that we must intentionally and continually work to nurture the health and vitality of our physical being in our spiritual formation systems.

As we look back over our authors, particularly our modern science thinkers, we might note that the theories of change for this aspect were quite consistent. In neuroscience, a central principle of change was the Hebbian rule of "neurons that fire together, wire together." For our Behavioral-Conditioning writers, there was a similar idea that change at this level comes via a repeated conditioning of our stimulus-response mechanisms. For some of our Western Christian theorists, particularly Augustine, Maximus, Aquinas, Luther, and Kant, working with one's bodily passions, appetites, and dispositions requires an intentional and long-term engagement in order to hone and refine, if not overcome altogether. The primary theory of change for this aspect therefore is one of sustained, intentional, and concrete repatterning of our physiological processes to the extent that this is possible.

A metaphor that I would like to introduce, which we will come back to again for the next two sub-components, is regarding the phases of a substance: solid, liquid, and gas. Human transformation at this level appears to be more like working to reshape a malleable solid. Since the molecules of solid are so tightly connected, reshaping it requires far more energy and effort than does pouring a glass of water. Change at this level, like a reshaping solid, therefore requires much more sustained pressure and energy, much more long-term work and intentionality, and even then there are very real limits to the transformations that we can enact.

Turning now to theological considerations for this component, we find possibilities for how each aspect of the Trinity might relate. For the transcendent aspect, as noted above, the physical is understood as emerging out of the no-thingness of God. In every moment, our physical being is sustained by the ever outpouring of God's immanent life within and through creation. This immanent aspect continually works for body's redemption, health, vitality, and full functioning of each part. In concert with these immanent efforts, God as Deity further works for each part of our body's greater good, perhaps providing additional strength and energy as Kant was found to assert and that our parapsychological and transpersonal thinkers might agree with. In line with this, our spiritually formative efforts must therefore seek to partner with these efforts of the "Trinitarian Spirit" as God seeks the liberation and enrichment of our physiological being. A spirituality of the body is one where we work to discern how God is seeking to manifest God's vital life through each part. Having a healthy diet and active lifestyle are therefore central for such a theology.

Finally, as we heard particularly among our Christian authors and even some of our modern science researchers, there are a number of distortions that we may need to contend with at this level. At their heart, a distortion is any tendency to act/manifest contrary to God. As noted above, my cosmological position holds that every part of this material realm in which we live has the free will to do so. From electrons to plants, to human beings, and even to societies as a whole, each part (or collection of parts) has the freedom to manifest in ways that are contrary to God's pure Trinitarian life. Such is therefore a theological-cosmological foundation and reason for the presence of distortions in the material realm at all levels of existence.

For example, at this physiological level, as our Biological theorists pointed out, there may be genetic predispositions which do not help the flourishing of the gene pool. For our Behavioral-Conditioning writers, there may be stimulus-response mechanisms that need to be repatterned because of their detrimental effects on our lives. A few of our Christian thinkers, particularly Augustine and Luther, asserted that the "flesh" can and often does have passions that tempt us away from living a more healthy life in God. Looking at our world, we see physiological addictions such as drug abuse that deteriorates the body. We see cancers and illness that destroy tissue and decimate entire species of plants and animals, including itself. These, in my framework, are examples of distortions at this physical level. They are not fully manifesting of God's vital life nor, I assert, are they in line with God's desires and work for the physical realm. As a result, any work that is done to repattern these distortions—from doctors to occupational therapists to addiction counselors—are inherently doing spiritually formative work.

The physiological aspect is therefore one of the core components of the theological anthropology that I am asserting herein. It is comprised of the foundational physical and biological processes that make up our bodies. While transformation needs to be very intentional and rigorous, and distortions abound at this level, God's Trinitarian life is asserted to work continually for its health and vitality. Along with the nutritionists, neuroscientists, and many others who formatively work at this level, our spiritual formation programs must seek to partner more closely with the life of the Spirit within, to, and beyond our physiological being.

## PSYCHOLOGICAL (COGNITIVE-AFFECTIVE) ASPECTS

Out of the physiological emerges the psychological.[6] This aspect probably requires the least overview and explanation because it is the most widely acknowledged one among all that we will be considering here. However, and perhaps because of this, the psychological aspect is also one of the most complex ones as well.

Clearly, this aspect includes the intellect, rationality, mind, consciousness, and free will of our Western Christian authors. It also comprises the cognitive constructs of our Social-Cognitive and Phenomenological-Humanistic researchers. Freud's Ego also lies well within these bounds as does his Superego with all of its "oughts" and "shoulds." The psyche is also composed of schemas and traits that are of a psychological nature. In short, the psychological aspect entails the cognitive components that this range of writers has covered.

Similarly, the psychological aspects include the affective movements of our lives as well. Though these have their origins and bases in the body's physiology (such as with hormones), the psychological influences that we have are significant. Augustine's passions can motivate people to make decisions that go against God's will. Emotions can influence the self-constructs that we have therefore hindering or aiding the development of one's self-esteem and identity. And, as some of our contemporary authors in Western Christianity noted, the soul was even conceived as the

---

6. The topic of Emergence Theories will be taken up in the next part of this book when we discuss the interconnections between these various levels.

deeper feeling part of one's being. The affective elements are therefore a central part of this aspect as well.

This aspect also includes the role of memories and other unconscious processes of the psyche. Being very complex indeed, I do not feel that I am in a position to offer a unified model of these psychological aspects. There are those who are working towards such a model,[7] however, their results are not only very detailed and complex but they are also still very much a work in progress. Rather, I have chosen to briefly sketch out the dominant dynamics that have been identified in relation to this aspect and leave further details to be addressed as needed based upon the needs of the application. This is something that we will be doing the final part of this book with our case example.

Here, then, what is most important to note is that there are cognitive-affective dynamics that act in both conscious and unconscious ways within us. Some of these appear to act in very structured ways, as do the schemas and traits of our lives, while others are less well-defined, such as the Id-drives and passions that might motivate us in unseen and less enduring ways. Formators who work primarily at this level are counselors, psychologists, spiritual directors, motivational speakers, and educators to name a few. Psychological balance, compassion, and wholeness therefore need to be a central part of any holistic spiritual formation programs directed towards the individual.

Regarding theories of change for this aspect, the water metaphor now turns to the liquid phase. Unlike a solid, which can be grasped and held, liquids are much more difficult to understand and even harder to direct when there is too much of it (image the work it would take to redirect a river). Nevertheless, moving water can be observed and its dynamics understood to some degree. And yes we can, as some communities have, channel the movements of water to flow in different directions.

For the Psychological aspect, this metaphor provides insights. There is a certain amount of intentionality that is required to retrain one's mind. Maximus asserted that the first stage of spiritual development entails acquiring the virtues. For Aquinas, an emphasis was given to first learning about and working to love God more and more. In Kant's framework, we are to use our rational mind to help orient us towards the good. Likewise, among our modern science writers such as Allport, we find the need to intentionally work to repattern less desirable traits such as prejudice. For

7. For one example of this kind of work, see Dietrich et al., *Simulating the Mind*; Mischel and Shoda, "Toward a Unified Theory of Personality."

Phenomenological-Humanists, an intentional effort is given to bring to the surface and work with the self-constructs that one has. Similar for Social-Cognitive thinkers, we must continually be aware of the schemas that help to shape and guide our lives.

However, such formative work with the psyche is not as concrete and clear as it appears to be for the Physiological aspect. Psychodynamicists were found to claim that much of what psychologically influences our lives lies below or beyond the surface of consciousness. We heard Wilson refer to babies as marvelous little robots who are genetically preprogrammed for life thereby further supporting this view that much of what influences us psychologically is not always available to our consciousness let alone our direct control. Such views are supported by some of our Christian writers, particularly Luther and Barth, where a heavy emphasis was given to Christ winning our battles and bringing about change because such transformations are ultimately beyond our control—though both also asserted the need for intentional spiritual practices such as hearing the Word of God and other means of grace.

Hence, the theory of change that emerges for this level is one that is similar to handling water in its liquid form. There is much that we can do to better understand the complex dynamics and liquid-like movements of the psyche via the use of spiritual practices, rationality, and other facets of our conscious mind. However, there is also much that is beyond our direct control. For Christians, this is why faith is so central to a growing psychological spiritual life as I believe Luther so rightly emphasized. We must do what we intentionally and consciously can to help foster the kinds of change that we believe God is working towards within, to, and beyond us. The rest is left up to God, the current psycho-physical dynamics of our life, and the communities to which we are attached as we shall see more below.

Theologically, we can again conceive of God's Trinitarian Life as being fully active in relation to the psyche in part and as a whole. As utter transcendence, we have already heard from Maximus and Augustine in regards to our growing abilities to directly access this Mystery and we will hear more of it next. Again, is each movement and dynamic of this psychological aspect asserted to continually emerge out of and be sustained by this transcendent Ground. However, just as it is for the physical aspect, what happens psychologically is influenced by its genetic and cultural histories. Immanently, then, is God's Life also active within and through these dynamics and processes whether they be enduring or not. God may be asserted to be immanently a part of every persona, part, complex, emotion, thought, et cetera. As Deity, we can (as many do) relate to God on a personal level. While some may reductionistically assert that such experiences are nothing more than inner psychological manifestations with no basis for reality,[8] I assert that such a relationship is to some degree genuine, though affected by our inner life as well.

As Maximus asserted, the mind is the "primary instrument of [a person's] relationship to God." As we heard with many authors, Christ acts on our behalf helping us at every step of the journey in very intimate and personal ways. In line with this tradition, I assert along with Green's biblical view the presence of a "divine spark." It is a view that God is personally present to each person's psyche in very real ways, one that asserts that God gives of God's Self to each individual to help lead, guide, inspire, et cetera our psychological lives. We can therefore expect God to be working to foster hope, love, positive self-constructs, virtuous deeds, cognitive-affective schemas that contribute to the flourishing of one's life, et cetera. As a result, a Trinitarian theology of the psychological aspect is therefore one that again finds God to be fully active within, to, and beyond the psyche.

Finally, as was also commonly discussed among our Christian writers, there are also many potential distortions. Temptations towards aggression, indulgence, unhealthy self-centeredness, negative self-images, hatred, et cetera are all examples of such intra-psychic distortions. For Psychodynamics, these would include the Ego-Ideals that drive people in harmful ways. For Trait theorists, these would be psychological traits that contribute to a person's instability such as high levels of neuroticism. In Green's framework, and many other Christian thinkers, these would be turning towards and embracing those thoughts and actions that we know are "sinful."

Psychological distortions abound and part of our spiritual formation work must therefore be oriented towards helping one another to allow God's Trinitarian Life to manifest ever more fully throughout it all. While such transformations are not completely in our control, as water in its liquid form is not always easy to direct, we can still work in many ways towards these spiritual ends. Similarly, as we have seen, the Psychological aspect is a very intricate one that is not yet even fully understood by those who rigorously study its' complexities. Nevertheless, it is a core

---

8. For an example of such a thesis, see Ostow, *Spirit, Mind, & Brain.*

component of not only the two compiled models we reviewed previously, but the one being presented here.

## INTEGRATIVE-TRANSCENDENT ASPECTS

The final intrapersonal sub-component relates to the integrative and transcendent abilities that some of our authors were found to discuss. This aspect forms a foundational part of not just Christian spirituality but other religious traditions as well.[9] Seen most prominently in Rahner's notion of "transcendentality," it entails our abilities to experience self-transcendence. This is our ability to seemingly move beyond our own limits and confines to experience something more of ourselves and our world. For Maximus, such experiences do not come until later in one's developmental life. Moving from the practice of virtues through contemplation to finally experiences of the unknowable God, Maximus conceives of this aspect emerging fully only later in life. This view is further supported by neuro-psychiatrist Dan Siegel and his book, *The Mindful Brain*, where he argues that such experiences are supported by the development of the integrative regions of the brain's middle prefrontal cortex through the long-term engagement with mindfulness practices.[10] Noting that these regions of the brain do not mature at least until one's young adult life,[11] some neurophysiological research currently seems to support this claim.

In addition, for both of our compiled models, the integration of the one's being was found to be a central ideal for many of these authors. Green's view articulated a view of wholeness as essential to the growing life in God. Maximus similarly conceived of this journey as one of various mediations that need to unfold in one's life that ultimately bring greater harmony. Our Phenomenological-Humanistic authors also held integration to be an important milestone and goal for our psychological lives.

These notions of transcendence and integration, which appear to be closely connected, are therefore taken to be an essential component of this theological anthropology. This aspect essentially captures our abilities to live an integrative life, one that not only embraces the whole of

---

9. Examples: Abe and LaFleur, *Zen and Western Thought*, xxi–xxii; Morinis, *Everyday Holiness*, 14–15; Wong, *Taoism*, 199.

10. Siegel, *Mindful Brain*, 109.

11. Matlin, *Cognition*, 461; Morra et al., *Cognitive development*, 354, 355–56.

who we are but also transcends it as well. In addition to the fields already mentioned, formators who focus more directly on such aspects of human transformation are contemplative practitioners and mindfulness-based therapists and educators.[12]

Moving on to the final phase of the solid-liquid-gas metaphor, we complete its application by reflecting on some of the qualities of gases in an effort to help us to better understand the nature of change at this level. While there are many similarities in how liquids and gases behave, gases are much more fluid and highly dynamic. We can hold water in our hands and guide and direct to some extent. Gas, on the other hand, seems to deny our efforts to trap it. Wave our hands and it spreads out and disperses in all directions. Paradoxically, it is when we are completely still that the air all around us seems to settle in its place, though even this takes time. We must wait patiently for it to come to rest.

For authors such as Maximus and Siegel who detail the journey towards integration and transcendence, there are a number of parallels with this metaphor. Achieving such development is actually not an achievement at all. In other words, we do not work for it *directly*. This is not to say that there is no intentionality. On the contrary, such levels of growth cannot come unless we work to nurture its unfolding. What differs, then, is how we are to go about nurturing this aspect. Rather than trying to directly foster it, it is instead asserted to unfold of its own accord when we intentionally and mindfully rest in stillness. Like the air around us that we wish to settle, the theory of change for this aspect is one that calls for silence and stillness within us. Only then, these authors claim, will such integrative-transcendent experiences unfold within our very being. It is indeed a journey, one that takes much time and focus, but also one that also requires much releasing stillness as it develops within us seemingly of its own accord.

Theologically, we can clearly see that the transcendence of God is most related to this aspect of human nature. In Maximus' framework, the pinnacle of the spiritual journey was to achieve such development so that we might more directly relate to God's unknowable transcendence. As we recalled previously, Augustine briefly spoke about such capabilities when he described his own experiences of thoughts that seem to emerge out of a wordless nothingness. For my own theological anthropology, which I

12. For examples, see Brice and Kourie, "Contemplation and Compassion"; Hart, "Opening the Contemplative Mind"; Langer, *The Power Of Mindful Learning*; Lichtmann, *Teacher's Way*; Rosenzweig et al., "Mindfulness-Based Stress Reduction."

shall discuss in greater detail below, the emergence of this level of our being essentially endows us with the ability to connect more intimately with the transcendent aspect of God. It may therefore be asserted, as I will in the next part of this book, that as these psychological and integrative-transcendent levels emerge in our lives, we are endowed with the capacities to know more and more of God's Trinitarian Life, particularly the transcendence aspect.

Nonetheless, the immanent and personified aspects of God are still fully operative at this level as well. Immanently, God's Life may thought of as continually working towards the integration and harmonization of one's being as Maximus, Green, and Aquinas asserted. God's personified work of grace as well as the divine spark within our lives can be asserted to further support this work. Augustine, Kant, Luther, and Barth articulated a theology of God/Christ working to further liberate us from our bondages and endow us with the strength and courage to overcome our limitations and distortions. As we partner with this transforming Life, these integrative-transcendent experiences and ways of spiritual being and becoming are able to flourish more fully. In other words, as we have been gradually seeing throughout these intrapersonal components, all three aspects of God's Life continually labor in harmony for the full development and flourishing of humanity at every level and in every way.

Nevertheless, there are still distortions that can and do emerge at this integrative-transcendent level as well. Self-transcendence can be a liberating experience, but not if it is then used to oppress one's self or others. With this stage of development, because of the focus and intentionality that is required for its' unfolding as discussed above, people often experience greater abilities for self-discipline and control. Also, because it is fundamentally one of transcendence, we can possess greater potential for detachment not only within ourselves but also towards that which surrounds us. In other words, with transcendence often comes detachment and the greater ability to separate from one's own physical and psychological parts as well as from others. If one then uses such liberation to forego empathic connections and cause more pain and suffering, this would clearly be a distorted development.

In addition, with integration comes the greater capacity to see connections among various components. Each one of these capacities is a powerful development for one's life. As with most tools, they can be used for great good or for massive destruction. One of the core distortions that can arise with this aspect is the use of its associated and enhanced capacities. Without a simultaneous cultivation of ethics and the molding of one's heart towards compassion, empathy, love, generosity, and service, these capacities may be used in oppressive and destructive ways.

The final aspect of these intrapersonal sub-components is the development of one's integrative-transcendent abilities. Found among many of our Christian writers, as well as in other religious traditions, this aspect appears to emerge only gradually and later in life—at least in its' fuller and more sustained manifestations. While this aspect is asserted to provide us with the capacity to experience God's transcendence more intentionally, both of the other two theological aspects were claimed to support the unfolding of this level of human development. Nevertheless, such capacities may be used for great evils, so this development should not be pursued without the simultaneous cultivation of the virtues.

## Interpersonal: Our Relevant Relationships

From the internal we now turn to the external and those influences that further help to shape who we are and how we develop in the world. Paralleling the core sub-components above in my own theological anthropology, I find there to be at least three sets of such direct external influences. These essentially entail the relationships and connections that we have via our physical senses. In other words, they comprise those influences that concretely and directly impact our lives. As we shall in the final set of transpersonal influences below, who we are and how we develop might also be impacted by others, yet more subtle and distant, influences. In this section, however, we are primarily dealing with those influences that we can directly observe to have a more direct and tangible effect on us.

### PHYSICAL ENVIRONMENT

Just as the majority of our authors were found to emphasize the role of the physical and body aspects in one's life, particularly among our modern science writers, so too was the physical environment given a central place for this group. Seen most clearly with the Biological and Neuroscience views, the physical world plays a central role in shaping how we develop as physical beings. The environment not only influences the human species genetically across generations but also in gene expression across the lifespan. Someone growing up in a drought stricken area with little access to proper nutrition, hygiene, and medical care will obviously not develop in the same ways as someone who has had access to all of this. Similarly, populations growing up in different environmental contexts and ecosystems have been observed to have developed different adaptive capacities. While our Western Christian authors did not emphasize the physical aspects of one's context, some such as Green did mention its importance in relation to the physical aspects of the human person.

In agreement with these authors, this theological anthropology includes the role of the physical and biological environment as a central component and there are three primary reasons for doing so. First, I agree that the historical-genetic and lifespan development of each person is fundamentally shaped by the environment as our biological and neuroscience authors assert. In addition, the theology associated with this model of human nature asserts that God is active within and through the whole of creation, including the physical world. The implications of this claim for humans is that the environment is therefore one of the primary ways that God continually works to shape and guide our lives—that is if we affirm the physical aspect of our nature, which this model does. Finally, and directly following from this second reason, is that we are therefore invited to partner with God's ever emerging Life within, to, and beyond this physical realm as it works for the flourishing and vitality of this massive ecosystem that we call "Earth." Hence, not only is the physical environment asserted to play a pivotal role in the shaping of human nature but we, as a species, are called to play a part in its health and ongoing spiritual development as well.

Theologically, then, we can again find God's Trinitarian Life to be working through the environment to shape our lives. Immanently, as just discussed, we can conceive of God as working through the foods we eat, the ecosystems we adapt to, et cetera to nurture human growth and evolution across both one's lifetime but also throughout history.[13] Of course, the cosmology described above also holds a place for the free will of every part of material creation so that God's Life may not be fully manifest always and everywhere. Transcendentally, the environment, our relationship to it, and the mutual impact that we have on one another may again be seen to emerge in each moment out of the infinite no-thingness of God's non-being. As Deity, God's grace may be seen to further augment and support such an unfolding. Of course, this view will be challenged

13. In my own framework, God is also asserted to be doing likewise for all other species as well.

by some who assert that there is no need to conceive of the presence of external and "supernatural" interventions in creation.[14] However, if such interventions are non-enduring, then they cannot by definition be studied via scientific methods as these focus exclusively on repeatable and empirically observable phenomena.[15] Contrarily, if such Deity actions are repeatable, then they will not be distinguishable by scientific tools since they focus exclusively on the empirically observable phenomena and are not privy to non-empirical influences that God—as Deity—may work through.[16] The theology of this theological anthropology therefore asserts that all three aspects of God's Life may be conceived as being part and parcel of these environmental influences on human nature and vice versa.

How we develop and change in relation to physical environments and influences is the on-going study of many fields of scientific study. In addition to geneticists and neuroscientists, the medical fields, biologists, chemists, nutritionists, and even physical trainers all study how the human body responds to external physical stimuli. Geneticists, as we heard, assert that the human species develops and evolves in ways that support its flourishing and adaption to the environments in which it continually finds itself (or creates). As living organisms, humans may be viewed as being very malleable in response to the environment. In other words, as our physical surroundings change, we must adapt by working to alter ourselves, the environment, or both. Such changes might include evolutionary and genetic adaptations and/or they might involve the development of new behaviors or tools. The theory of change that emerges here, then, is one in which our growth and development unfolds in relation to our environments and the mutual influences that we have on one another.

Finally, as with the intrapersonal aspects, there can be distortions that emerge as a result of these environmental connections. Perhaps the most obvious contemporary example of this is the massive environmental challenges that our planet is currently facing. In my own view, it seems that the human species is going too far in its quest for its own

14. Clayton, *Adventures in the Spirit*, 77, 186; Peacocke, *Paths from Science towards God*, 34, 70, 75, 83, 93, 146.

15. For more detailed descriptions scientific methods, see such writings as Allport, *Personality*, 3; Sagan, "Can We Know the Universe?"; Wynn, "Does Theory Ever Become Fact?"

16. Clayton, *Adventures in the Spirit*, 60, 89, 97, 99, 202; Griffin, *Reenchantment without Supernaturalism*, 49, 52; Peacocke, *Paths from Science towards God*, 39.

survival. We have created industries that have become so good at and fo-cused on harvesting petroleum, food, and mineral resources, that entire ecosystems have been and continue to be destroyed. As we heard from Wilson in the Biological views, aggressiveness seems to be one of the evo-lutionary adaptations that has emerged and continues to develop among our species. For me, such developments and industrial behaviors are evolutionary-based distortions because they are devastating parts of our planet and because such greed-based aggressiveness is not in accordance with my own theological views of a God who works nonviolently for bal-ance, integration, and harmony of all parts of creation. We are therefore called, as Wilson likewise asserted, to use our knowledge of evolution's principles as well as our own biological development to directly address and change such distortions in this very physical and direct relationship with the environment.

Our relationship with the physical environment, which parallels the physiological aspect above, is therefore taken to be yet another central aspect of human nature. Just as it is for other living organisms, the en-vironment shapes our development not only across the lifetime but also across generations. While God's Trinitarian Life is asserted to be fully active in this intimate physical relationship, distortions still abound with the current devastations to our planet being one example. We must there-fore, as this theological anthropology claims, work in closer partnership with God to foster a more thriving relationship with our beloved physical world, caring for its' thriving survival as well as for our own.

## SOCIAL-CULTURAL CONTEXTS

While discussions of the effects of the physical environment were most exclusively taken up by our modern science authors, particularly our biological and neuroscience researchers, this social-cultural aspect was much more widely acknowledged and addressed. Repeatedly discussed throughout were the relationships that we have and the communities that we are a part of. On the Western Christian side, Green, Maximus, Aqui-nas, and Rahner all asserted that who we are is fundamentally linked with such social-cultural influences. For Kant, an emphasis was given to the need for a virtuous society wherein each citizen can learn of the ethical "maxims" or principles that they should be working to cultivate. Barth was likewise asserted to hold relationships as central to his theological anthropology. Who we are, as children of God, is therefore intimately connected to the relationships and communities that we grow in according to these authors.

Similarly, on the modern science side, Freud was found to assert that the Ego-Ideals that the Superego compels us towards is partly shaped by the society that we are a part of. Similarly, trait-disposition theorists, such as Allport, argued that some of the traits that guide our lives are formed by the cultures we grow up in, with prejudice being the example that was given. This aspect is seen most clearly, however, by our social-cognitive researchers. The focus of their studies lies in better understanding the intimate connections between one's social environment and the schemas that make up the inner personality system. Overall, then, this interpersonal aspect is intended to capture how the close relationships and cultural dynamics that surround us directly influence us. Formators who study and work more directly with these influences include marriage and family therapists, sociologists, cultural anthropologists and psychologists, and social workers to name a few.

Regarding how we change in response to such social and cultural relationships, we can learn from the social-cognitive views, particularly Bandura's work. As we may recall, one of the primary ways that people learn, according to Bandura, is by watching the behaviors of others and observing the consequences of their actions. More broadly, the people around us become models for the kinds of behavior and values that we have, as Kant asserted. Such communities support our growth and development, claims Aquinas, and we can grow in either positive or negative ways as a result. In Freud's scheme, the Ego-Ideals that we internalize will have an effect on our behaviors to the extent that our Egos seek to pursue in balance or conflict with the propensities of Id.

One of the theories of change that therefore emerges here is that these kinds of relationships provide the models and reinforcements for the molds that we strive to live into. These interpersonal influences are not only a source for ideals, values, behaviors, et cetera, but they also shape our life by providing constant feedback on our actions. Similar to the theory of change at the environmental level above, who we are and how we behave seems to therefore develop in an organism-like fashion partly in response to the social-cultural contexts that we find ourselves in. In other words, human nature emerges as a result of a mutual tension between these external contexts and our internal psychological dynamics. Theories of social adaptation, as found in Bandura, as well as self-actualization, as found in Maslow, may therefore be asserted and equally embraced side-by-side.

Theologically, our discussions parallel the many that we have now had. God may be asserted to immanently work within and through these relationships to shape and guide our lives as well as vice versa. Here, God's life is conceived as being more fully manifested within and through those relationships and cultural influences that foster such growth as self-actualization as well as mutually loving relationships. In the Christian tradition, a widely quoted saying of Jesus is, "where two or three are gathered in my name, I am there with them."[17] It is the theological notion that Christ's Life may be partly found to be actively incarnate in our relationships as a whole and not just through the individuals that make them up. Transcendently, God may again be seen as the sustainer of such interpersonal influences. Couples might even experience something of this transcending mystery in their love for one another, though these discussions are reserved for the final aspect of these interpersonal influences. As Deity, God may be thought of as further supporting interpersonal life and vitality. Barth was asserted to view sin fundamentally as a break in relationships, with God, ourselves, and others. If this view of Barth is accurate, then we can assert that God's Trinitarian life will continually and actively work to foster healthy relationships as well as to repair broken and distorted interpersonal dynamics.

Interpersonally, distortions abound socially as well as culturally. We need to look no further than to the nightly news, or the long histories of violence, abuse, and even genocides that have and continue to plague our planet. In Kant's framework, these would constitute social dispositions and maxims that are directed towards evil. In Freud's model, these might be seen as interpersonally supported Ego-Ideals that drive us towards death and destruction. For Allport and our social-cognitive thinkers, these are cultural traits and schemas such as prejudice that lead us and our communities in the direction of disintegration and violence. Such distorted social-cultural influences must therefore be intentionally engaged so that not only are their influences on individuals and communities mitigated, but ideally eliminated or transformed altogether.

Our spiritual formation programs must therefore work to foster God's Trinitarian Life within, to, and beyond the interpersonal factors that work to shape who we are as individuals. Our psyche, our behaviors,

17. Matt 18:20.

our relationships, and our communities are asserted to be mutually influential. Similar to the environmental organism views articulated above, who we are as well as our social-cultural contexts change in response to one another. Interpersonal contexts provide models and reinforcements for our behavior and values, for instance, while these in turn support or modify these widely seen and accepted molds of personality. Paralleling the psychological level, these social-cultural interpersonal influences are considered to be a central part of human nature.

## AWE & WONDER: EXPERIENCES OF ONENESS

As briefly mentioned above, intimate couples might come to experience a sense of oneness with each other. Similarly, most people have had experiences of awe while visiting vast landscapes, such as the Grand Canyon or a mountain range, or while looking at the immensity of the night sky. In these moments, there is a sense of oneness about creation, a sense of connection between us and the whole of it all.[18] Such experiences can be deeply formative for our lives and therefore are considered to be yet another central part of this theological anthropology.

Discussions of such experiences may be found among some of our transpersonal authors. Similar kinds of discussion may also be found in experiences of oneness with God among such writers as Augustine, Maximus, Aquinas, and Rahner. In these moments, it is as if the whole of our integrated being becomes one with that which we are seeing or experiencing. Paralleling the integrative-transcendent intrapersonal aspect, these encounters of oneness essentially seem to be moments wherein we experience an integration of what we are seeing (e.g., a scenery, another person, or an image of God) with who we fundamentally are as a person.

Looking back to the neurophysiological work of Siegel, such experiences might make sense in light of middle prefrontal cortex development. This part of the brain, Siegel points out, is connected to all three meta-regions of the brain.[19] In other words, this region of the brain has the capacity to integrate and harmonize potentially the whole of our being according to Siegel: our emotions, our sensed external experiences, our intuitions, our views of who we are, et cetera.[20] What this potentially

18. For examples of such "unitive" experiences, see May, *Will & Spirit.*

19. Siegel, *Mindful Brain,* 38–39, 127.

20. Ibid., 42–44, 191, 338, 354–55.

means is that as the integrative-transcendent capacities develop within us, we should have greater propensities for such experiences of oneness, experiences where it feels like who we are internally, as a unified person, becomes integrated with that which we are seeing and experiencing around us.

While we know that children have some capacities for experiencing awe and wonder, there have been many such as Siegel and Maximus who assert that these capacities increase as we grow older (following common developmental trajectories) and as we contemplatively develop our integrative-transcendent aspect. In other words, the theory of change that accompanies this interpersonal aspect is similar to the one asserted for our intrapersonal integrative and transcendent capacities. Indeed, as we shall see again for the Attunement aspect of the transpersonal influences below, there seems to be a sort of apex that is emerging for the human species at this level of development. It is one in which the self becomes whole, not just within itself and on its own, but also with the creation of which it is a part and even beyond.

Just as integration was considered by most of our authors to be an important ideal to pursue, and therefore taken to be a fundamental part of God's work in creation as Maximus articulated most clearly, so too are these experiences of oneness viewed as being central to the Divine Trinitarian Life. One of the most important things to note about such experiences is that feelings of love, goodness, rightness, et cetera often accompany them. In other words, there is a deep sense of intimate and compassionate connection that can fill us in these moments. Is not such uniting love considered to be a part of the very core of God's essence and desires for creation? Such oneness might therefore be viewed as experiences of God's Transcendent Life emerging within and among our interpersonal relationships. Immanently, God would no doubt be working towards the fostering of such love-filled intimacy. As Deity, grace might again be asserted to further support and augment such work as the beauty and wonder of these experiences fill the whole of our being. In short, God as Trinity is asserted within the Christian tradition to be working to move humanity, and even all of creation, towards these more unitive ends.

Given these, are there potential distortions related to such experiences of oneness? As the compiled Western Christian model claims, there are distortions in just about everything and, I assert, this includes these experiences as well. As we heard with Augustine and Luther, the "flesh" is something to be cautioned against. This is partly because its passions and desires can become such a distraction and focus that we lose sight of the greater works of God that are going on within and all around us. In Christian terms, such an overly and unhealthy focus is known as "idolatry," and it can lead us in directions that ultimately prove to be damaging to ourselves and those around us.

One of the potential distortions that is related to experiences of awe and wonder, then, might be idolatry. If the experience is so moving and captivating for the individual, they may become overly focused on the object that helped to give rise to the experience at the expense of other parts of their lives. An example of this might be someone who peers into the night sky experiences the kind of oneness that we have been discussing here. As a result, this individual is so moved that they pledged their life to the professional field of astronomy. From a Christian standpoint, such a commitment is totally fine as long as it is in accordance with the movements of God in this person's life.[21] The distortion can therefore arise if the individual ignores such considerations. For instance, if he or she has no training or education in the field and therefore is unable to obtain a job that would support her or his family. Experiences of oneness can therefore potentially be disruptive to one's growing spiritual life if it distracts them away from a fuller life in God.

Nevertheless, these experiences are considered to be a central part of the interpersonal components of this theological anthropology. They comprise our intimate experiences of oneness with the people, communities, and contexts within which we are situated. Appearing to emerge more fully with the development of our intrapersonal integrative-transcendent capacities, growth in this aspect occurs over time and with sustained contemplative and mindful efforts. With compassion and loving connection being central to them, God's Trinitarian Life is asserted to be at the very heart of nurturing these unitive experiences in our lives and our world. While they can potentially become idolatrous distractions, such oneness should be a central part of our spiritual formation programs.

---

21. How do we know what God's will is? Via a practice known as spiritual discernment. For more detailed discussions on discernment, see such texts as Ackerman, *Listening to God*; Au and Au, *Discerning Heart*; Dougherty, *Group Spiritual Direction*; Hauser, *Moving in the Spirit*; Isenhower and Todd, *Living into the Answers*; Parker, *Led by the Spirit*; Wolpert, *Leading a Life with God*.

## *Transpersonal: Beyond Our Immediate Vicinity*

We now move into the final and most controversial arena of this model of human nature. As we heard when discussing both the transpersonal-parapsychological aspect and the super-conscious component of the compiled modern science models, these considerations are challenging for both conventional Western scientists as well as some Western Christian communities. As discussed in the sections above, conventional scientists reject these views based on the myth that they are not repeatable, empirically observable, or that there is fraud or other psychological distortions involved in the reporting of these phenomena. On the Christian side, as we likewise saw, such views were asserted to be challenging to doctrinal views related to healings, miracles, and other supernatural phenomena.

Nevertheless, I am including these aspects in my own model while you, as the reader, might choose to reject these altogether. My decision is based on both my own reading of some of the literature related to these aspects as well as on my own personal experiences with charismatic Christian communities as well as with Eastern religious traditions, particularly Buddhism and Taoism. The views that I put forth below is a framework that best fits with what I have learned and experienced. These views, I assert, do affirm the conservative concerns of both conventional scientists and charismatic Christians, but also challenges both of these communities to think about the cosmos and God in more expansive ways. As with the interpersonal arena, there are three sub-components that closely parallel the core intrapersonal sub-components as we shall see below.

## ENERGY & NON-LOCAL PHYSICAL CONNECTIONS

For our transpersonal authors, there was an asserted unity with creation that we can foster. It is one that is related to the experiences of oneness discussed above but also to actual attunement, which will be addressed below. However, such unity can and also does, according to transpersonal views, happen at the physical levels. While none of the authors we have visited held such views, Eastern religions do assert trans-physical connections with their concepts of energy. Known as "chi" in Chinese versions of Taoism, "ki" in Japanese martial arts, and "prana" in some Hindu sects, such energies are asserted to underlie and more intimately connect the whole of creation at the physical levels.[22] In the West, there are some theorists who have likewise purposed similar worldviews and theologies, wherein energy becomes the basis for thinking about and describing God's nature and actions in the physical world.[23]

Similarly, it has been proposed that physical matter has the capacity to influence other parts of the material world beyond the local, immediate, and direct cause-and-effect relationships identified by Western scientists.[24] In essence, such views assert that the material realm is somehow more expansively interconnected than the mainstream Western secular view currently holds. However, these views may be changing as there are more recent developments in the field of physics that assert such non-local interactions may be possible and in line with contemporary physics, particularly quantum mechanics.[25] For instance, physicists have not only theoretically conceived of such non-local connections but also experimentally verified them with their concepts of "quantum entanglement."[26] There are also recent theologies, such as Process Theology, that incorporate such inherent and infinite potentials for the interconnectedness of creation as a whole as will be discussed later in this book. If the physical realm really is unified beyond local and immediate connections, then creation may be much more dynamic and mutually influential than is conventionally claimed by many Western scientists.

The implications of this for our explorations of human nature are significant. We have already heard just how important the physical environment is to the growth and development of our physiological aspects. As it was conceived above, however, such physical influences were confined to the direct and immediate connections that we have with our local environment. In other words, the primary concern above was to better understand how our immediate physical surroundings might influence who we are and how we develop.

However, with the transpersonal assertions that the material world might also have energies and the capacity for non-local connections, we have just now immensely widened the range of what might influence us. We have also just deepened the intimacy with which we are connected to

---

22. For further readings in this, see such texts as Reid, *Complete Guide to Chi-Gung.*

23. For examples, see May, *Will & Spirit*; Smith, *God, Energy and the Field.*

24. Radin, *Conscious Universe*, 277.

25. Ibid., chap. 16; see also "Introduction to Quantum Mechanics."

26. Pickover, *Physics Book*, 374.

our physical world. This is because, based on these claims, the whole of the universe might theoretically be acting on our physical being at any given moment. It might also therefore mean that the extent to which we are affected by another part of creation is much more extensive as the whole of our physical being is potentially being affected by the whole of any other object.

So, for example, maybe it is that the physiological effects of aggressive physical energy in one community are felt all around the world even if we never see nor hear about this community. Distortions such as these might therefore affect our world in wider ways than we currently think they do. Some writers on energy cultivation also talk about people being able to use energy for both positive or negative aims beyond their immediate surroundings.[27] These kinds of transpersonal influences can, it is asserted, be used to help foster wholeness and vitality or pain and suffering. As a result, distortions in this aspect are potentially as prevalent as they have been for each of the other components of human nature that we have considered.

If one does accept the possibility that such non-local and energy-based views are possible, the question still remains as to what extent these influences have throughout creation. At least one of our parapsychological researchers, Dean Radin, asserts that while such non-local influences (as they relate to the psychological level) are significant enough to warrant continued scientific investigation, they also seem to be minor in terms of the impact that they actually have. Repeatedly referring to thousands of experiments that have been conducted for mind-related non-local experiments (such as telepathy, mind-matter interactions, and perception at a distance), the results of success rates were only slightly above the odds that such outcomes could have happened merely by chance.[28] In other words, the results have consistently shown that there is something significant occurring in these experiments because the results cannot be explained merely by asserting that they were the result of lucky guesswork by the thousands of participants in these experiments. However, these results also show that they are consistently only slightly better than the odds given by chance, with an estimated average of being only less than 5 percent better than chance.

27. Reid, *Complete Guide to Chi-Gung*, 88.

28. Radin, *Conscious Universe*, 84, 87, 106, 135, 141, 154.

Questions can therefore be raised as to what extent such non-local influences may actually have in creation and what are the factors that contribute to their potency. For instance, are there certain conditions that a source object, such as an atom, needs to have in order for its influences to have a stronger effect on other non-local parts of creation? Similarly, does the receiving object likewise need to meet certain conditions in order for the influences of other non-local objects to have a stronger effect on itself? As Radin's results show, despite the consistently slightly better than chance outcomes, there do seem to be wide variations in the success of these experiments. In other words, while the results for many people were better than the odds of chance, for others they were much less. Hence, questions such as these need to be raised and pursued. Nevertheless, non-local effects (at least based upon these parapsychological experiments) do seem to have a significant, though slight, influence on our world.

For the conventional physical scientist conducting controlled lab experiments, this may come with some relief because to try and account for such non-local influences could be well near impossible. However, if such influences do indeed have an effect on such experiments, then scientists will have to account for them somehow. For the conservative Christian, on the other hand, Radin's results may provide further clarity into why some attempts at prayer-based physical healing (known as "faith healing") do work and why some do not. If we are able to energetically and non-locally influence the inner physiological dynamics of one another, then according to Radin such influences may only be small, though still significant. Likewise, if there are factors that do alter the extent to which such influences affect other parts of creation, then this might explain why some healing prayers seem to help while others do not.

Such non-local physical views also provide us with a cosmological avenue for asserting energetic, as well as psychic, connections with beings from other realms (e.g., angels, demons, saints, ghosts, et cetera). This is possible if: 1) there are other non-material realms or universes that exist, and 2) these non-local influences transcend and connect these multiple realms. Certainly within the Christian tradition, with our concepts of Heaven and Hell, angels and demons, et cetera, the existence of these other non-material realms is generally and doctrinally accepted. Even among philosophers and physicists, is the possibility of other such multiple universes considered to be a possibility.[29] Furthermore, within Christianity there is a long history recorded in the Bible as well as across its history of people reporting encounters with non-material beings such as angels, demons, Mother Mary, and other saints.[30] Contemporarily, people continue to report encounters with ghosts and other apparitions. Such histories and reports therefore seem to support both of the two conditions above as being a possibility.

If this is accurate, then non-local connections provide us with one more way of understanding these encounters in our world. As it relates to human nature at the physical level here, as well at the psychological level as discussed below, this means that our physiological processes may be influenced not only by non-local factors within the material universe that we are currently a part of but also by non-material realms as well. As we can see, the implications of these transpersonal views are quite extensive, particularly as they relate to our growing lives.

We might also be inclined to extend this line of theorizing to include our intimate connections with the Deity aspect of God. Such personified Life might be conceived of as influencing the physical world through these energetic and non-local channels in similar ways as other non-material beings. This essentially provides a possible cosmological theory for how God, as an "external" Deity, acts in the physical world. In other words, maybe God as Deity "supernaturally" acts in the world through these non-local avenues, adding God's energies and non-local influences to physical creation. Such a "cosmos-theology" might also help us to better understand how God, again as Deity, influences our body's physiology and contributes to its health and vitality.

However, there is also the possibility that God's immanence might be conceived of as operating within and through these non-local channels as well. For instance, as one part of creation non-locally and energetically influences another part, we can assert that God's immanent life is continually working within and through such transpersonal interactions to the extent that the free will of the entities allow. Furthermore, just as we have for each of previous aspects of human nature that we have covered above, such energetic and non-local dynamics are asserted by this Trinitarian model to be undergirded and sustained by the Transcendent, non-Being aspect of God. Theologically, then, we can conceive of God's

29. McGrath, *A Fine-Tuned Universe*, 123–24.

30. For an overview of Christianity's history where some of these experiences are discussed, see Mursell, *Story of Christian Spirituality*.

Trinitarian Life to again be fully operative and present to these energetic and non-local dynamics in creation as well as our physiological lives.

Thinking about the physical world in these energy-based and non-local terms, while quite complex and expansive, can therefore provide us with an additional way to better understand just how closely connected we potentially are with the whole of the universe (or universes) that surrounds us. Such transpersonal connections potentially penetrate not only the whole of our being but also theoretically connect our physical selves with entirety of creation—material and beyond. These transpersonal views also provide us with an alternative way of understanding how healing prayers might work as one person's energies are non-locally shared with another's. Similarly, these views offer yet another way to think about the non-material realms (such as Heaven and Hell) and our possible interconnections to them. Finally, they also theologically have the potential for helping us to understand how God, particularly as Deity, might act in creation. As a result, these transpersonal views and their possible energetic and non-local physical effects are taken to be a central part of this theological anthropology.

## PARAPSYCHOLOGICAL/SUPER-CONSCIOUS

With this transpersonal foundation for the physical world in place, extending it to the psychological seems like a natural progression. As a result, and since much exploration has already been given to this aspect above in the modern science part of this book, the reflections here will be brief. The reader is referred to these sections for more detailed discussions.

For both the transpersonal-parapsychological views and the super-conscious aspects of the compiled modern science model, humans are asserted to have the ability to psychologically "see" the world in ways that are beyond our immediate vicinity. In other words, our transpersonal psychological abilities are alleged to enable us to be able to spatially experience creation beyond the physical senses and even through time. They also assert that we can connect with one another on a feeling level in much deeper ways because of our non-local connections. Some transpersonal researchers, for instance, use meditation techniques to attempt to more deeply enter into the experiences of the people they are studying in the hopes of gaining further insights for their research.[31] If such non-local connections do permeate our physical being, then it stands to reason that our connections to one another will therefore be heightened.

However, such non-local connections are claimed to not just be at the physiological level, as we have heard. Telepathy and clairvoyance, for instance, were asserted to be a central part of what parapsychologists study. It appears that humans likewise possess the ability, though slight as it may be according to Radin's research, to see into one another's thoughts and experience each other's feelings. Again do we hear that creation, in the transpersonal scheme, is much more closely interconnected than the mainstream Western secular worldview currently asserts.

As has already been asserted above, transpersonal views at the psychological level provide an additional or alternative way of explaining our trans-psychic interactions with non-material beings and even with God as Deity. The claim here is that such beings can influence our lives through these channels by: sending thoughts, images, and words; making suggestions; endowing us with visions; influencing our psychological passions and desires; et cetera. While the extent to which such influences are possible and what the physical and psychological factors are that affect these trans-psychic connections still needs to be clarified, the possibility of their existence still remains. As stated above, such non-material psychological influences, in their cognitive-affective forms, are considered to be a long and accepted part of Christian history. These super-conscious influences are also a part of other worldviews and what "spiritual development" entails as we saw with Assagioli's framework. What these transpersonal views offer, then, are possible explanations for how such encounters transpire.

Theologically, the same line of philosophizing follows the one given above. Each aspect of God's Trinitarian Life may be conceived of in relation to these parapsychological influences for human nature at this psychological level. The distortions for this aspect are also similar to the ones discussed above with the possibility of our receiving and sending to one another the negative and more destructive thoughts and feelings that we harbor. Overall, then, we find these non-local transpersonal influences of human nature to be extended to the psychological level. In our spiritual formation programs, we can therefore work to help our communities to partner with the more God-manifesting movements of these influences

31. Anderson, "Intuitive Inquiry," 75, 81, 83.

while guarding against and working to transform the more distorted ones.

## TOTAL ATTUNEMENT WITH CREATION

Finally, we come to the last aspect of this proposed unified model of human nature. Given the non-local claims of these transpersonal views (the idea that we can connect more deeply and tangibly with other parts of creation near or far), this is perhaps the most profound of all that we have considered. Paralleling the integrative-transcendent aspect and "experiences of oneness" discussions above, this possible ability of human nature is one that asserts that we have the capacity to attune with ourselves and creation in ways that transcend what we commonly think about time and space.

Let us step back and think for a moment about all that we have been considering in this proposed unified model. We are physiological and psychological beings and we are inherently related to our physical environments and social contexts. But we also possess the ability to integrate and transcend these aspects and relationships and thereby foster a sense of oneness, awe, harmony, and wonder. Now, add the transpersonal views to this metaphysical pot that is stewing before us and suddenly such integrative and transcendent experiences are no longer mere psycho-physiological constructs. Instead, they become a lived reality in which the human being becomes concretely and more directly connected to creation in ways that are genuinely expansive through time and space. In other words, our oneness within ourselves and with the universe(s) that surrounds us may be as real as our relationship with the person sitting right next to us, according to these transpersonal views.

Such claims find support not only among transpersonal writers, but also among Christian mystics and theologians. These views assert that such integrative connections with creation are in fact real and not just perceived. Some of these also claim that they should be one of the chief aims of formative efforts and comprise the very pinnacle of human development as we heard with Maximus. Such transpersonal development does seem to closely parallel, if not directly coincide with, the growth of our integrative-transcendent capacities as well as our propensities to experience oneness. Indeed, the boundaries between these three aspects seem to collapse as our inner and outer experiences become more fully integrated into one.

However, we can again raise questions as to what extent such expansive attunement really occurs. Just because we feel connected to all of creation does not necessarily mean that we are actually non-locally connected to the whole of it. Much more research and deliberation is needed before such claims can become supportable. Nevertheless, the notion that such attunement happens to some degree is what is being asserted and it is therefore included as a central aspect of this theological anthropology.

Finally, of the three aspects of Trinitarian Life, God as Transcendence seems to be most apparent here. Many of the Christian mystics who discuss these kinds of experiences, such as Maximus, often do so in relation to talking about God as an unknowable Mystery. While we may again assert that the other two aspects play a supportive role towards the development and flourishing of such transpersonal attunement, it is God's Transcendent Life that seems to be more prevalent.

Or, we might alternatively assert, these three aspects of God become as one in the experience of the individual such that the Oneness of God, the unity of the Trinity, is realized in its' greater fullness. If integration really is happening within a person on a larger scale, then it stands to reason that one's knowledge and experiences of God's transcendent, immanent, and Deity aspects are unified into a more holistic conception and experience of God. This might help to further explain the paradoxical theologies found in such mystics as Julian of Norwich, Richard of St. Victor, and Pseudo-Dionysius.[32]

From a formative perspective, this would make sense if we assert that one of God's primary aims is to help us to grow ever more fully in God's Trinitarian Life, which is indeed a primary goal for Christian spiritual formation. If these integrative and transpersonal capacities foster such growth, then we can expect them to be one of the very pinnacles of human development. As a result, the transpersonal development of attunement is therefore a significant influence in the individual lives of human beings.

## Brief Reflections on this Unified Model

Shown below are the various aspects of this proposed synthesized model of human nature. As we can see, the three primary areas—intrapersonal, interpersonal, and transpersonal (along with their respective sub-com-

32. Kyle, "'Paradoxical-Transcendent' Mind."

ponents)—are depicted. This figure therefore provides us with an over-arching picture of these aspects and how they are related to one another.

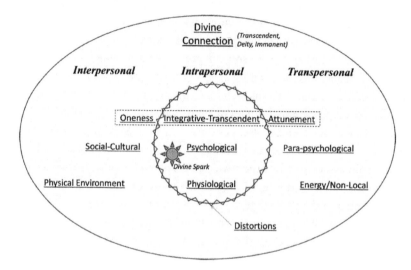

**Figure 17. A Synthesized Model of Human Nature.**

Looking at this figure, there is sort of a grid that may be seen where the three primary areas (intrapersonal, interpersonal, and transpersonal) make up the columns and the physiological, psychological, and integrative-transcendent aspects make up the rows. As we noted throughout the reflections on these various aspects, these rows essentially constitute three levels of human experience. While these three levels are closely connected with one another, they are also distinct as each one has its own associated dynamics, patterns, influences, et cetera.

For instance, as we saw, the biological brain is has own sets of neurophysiological structures, meta-regions, and dynamics. Similarly, the psychological mind is comprised of many different cognitive and affective phenomena such as schemas, traits, drives, memories, et cetera. So different are these two aspects of our personhood that some, such as seventeenth century philosopher René Descartes, have conceived of the rational mind as being completely and totally separate from the body and even the functions of the brain.[33] Yet, we know that damage to the brain does affect the mind as seen in the widely cited case of Phineas

33. Descartes, "Discourse on Method," 87–89.

Gage whose personality was altered as a result of severe brain trauma.[34] Such instances raise questions as to how these various levels of human existence are related to one another.

We might also note that the attunement, integrative-transcendence, and oneness aspects form a sort of an apex of the human person. As mentioned above, at these levels it becomes more difficult to distinguish between them. It seems that the human person has the capability to really and truly be more at one within her or his self as well as with creation, both locally and non-locally. Such integration, it was noted, was highlighted by several of our Western Christian and modern science authors. As with the mind-body example above, we might likewise wonder how such integration emerges. It is in the next part of the book that we will explore a synthesized model, or a "unified organism theory," that addresses such questions.

Finally, we can also see that distortions are an integral part of this model in accordance with our Western Christian authors. These distortions potentially permeate the entire model, affecting our core intrapersonal parts as well as all of our relationships locally and non-locally. However, all is not lost for we are also fully immersed in the Trinitarian Life of God. Following Aquinas, this model claims that the goal of all our spiritual formation efforts is to grow in this Trinity in every part of our life; in all of these sub-components. The theological anthropology shown above is therefore the general model that we will be working with as we come to see how such models might be used to help guide our spiritual formation program development efforts in the final part of this book. Before we proceed to these applications, however, we will first develop an even more generalized model that will provide deeper insights into the nature and essence of spiritual formation.

## Soulful Side Reflections: Organism Wholeness and Life-After-Death

As we saw with most of our Western Christian writers, the concept of the soul was a central part of their theological anthropologies. However, as was discussed above, this concept was excluded from the unified theological anthropology because these views of the soul varied widely and it was asserted that each one of these views was covered by the synthesized model that I put forth. Noting the importance of this concept in Western

34. Bear et al., *Neuroscience*, 570.

Christian literature, however, we might again return this notion and ask what the "soul" might be for this particular model. In concert with this, we can also raise questions related to life-after-death and what survives the transition into non-material realms, assuming that is the next phase beyond the cessation of physical life on this planet. This was not only raised by Green as an important topic but it is also a concern that is of central importance to the Christian tradition.

The concept of the soul, as we saw, was found in Green, Augustine, Maximus, Aquinas, Luther, and Barth. Contrary to Green, most of these thinkers conceived of the soul as being a separate entity from the body, one that survives physical death. Green alternatively argued, following what he asserts is more in accordance the biblical views, that the soul is inextricably bound to our embodied physical nature and our relationships as human beings. Both of these, he asserts, fundamentally shape who we are and must therefore be taken to be a central part of what one's soul is comprised of. Green is essentially arguing against the Greek-based notion that the soul is a separate metaphysical substance that is, at least to some degree, not affected by our life on this planet.[35]

In classical Christian thought, as we saw most fully with Augustine, the soul was thought of as being what makes us distinctively human and is what is made in the image of God. This soul was considered to be sent by God to raise our fallen human natures to greater spiritual, or non-material, heights. This view of the soul as a separate metaphysical substance that is potentially unaffected by our lived experiences is what Green is taking a stand against.

Based upon the synthesized model above, there is certainly a place for Green's concept of the soul. As a unified whole, one's soul could be conceived as being their totality, that which has emerged and been historically shaped by both nature and nurture. Whether or not there is indeed a metaphysical substance that is given by God cannot be ascertained based solely on these explorations. It is completely lacking from our modern authors and is a matter of faith for our Western Christian ones. What is likely, if such a metaphysical soul does indeed exist, is that it is inextricably shaped by human being and becoming as an emergent organism in this material realm, as we will discuss in more detail below. This appears to be the position that Aquinas has taken in arguing that the body and soul both take the form of one another. Such assertions are

35. Green, *Body, Soul, and Human Life*, 70, 144.

important for spiritual formation because it seems to suggest that any deformations that are not addressed in this life will affect our existence in the next. This is contrary to the more popular view that once we die, we will awake in Heaven and all will somehow be miraculously well.

The synthesized model could also assert that the Divine Spark is the soul of a person. Such a view is more reflective of our authors who assert that the soul is given "from above." Yet, there must be something more that is retained after death, something taken from the life that was lived otherwise what would be the point of this life. A third possibility might therefore be a combination of these two and that is perhaps the soul is the accumulation of those parts of ourselves that have come to identify with and attach themselves to the Divine Spark within. This would be a middle way between the two positions, one in which the pure Presence of God within us mixes with the emerging nature of our being to form a more eternal and impenetrable essence that can survive in non-material realms. Nevertheless, however we understand and define the "soul" for ourselves, my argument here is that the synthesized model above is versatile enough to cover the broader range of classical understandings of this concept.

Regarding life-after-death, Green goes on to argue that "the capacity for life-after-death is not intrinsic to humanity but is a divine gift, and resurrection signifies not rescue from the cosmos but transformation with it"[36] He is essentially making the claim that since we are so shaped by our embodied nature and the relationships that we have with our physical and social contexts, that something of our personal identity would seem to be lost when we experience physical death on this planet and proceed to non-material realms. All organisms on this planet are fundamentally influenced by both internal and external influences. Change any of these influences, something which physical death fundamentally and radically does, and the organism will likewise be altered.

Such considerations of life-after-death are central to Christian doctrine. Based on my synthesized theological anthropology, there are at least five possibilities for conceiving of a soul and what survives after death. The first obvious view is that nothing of us survives death. A second is the position of Augustine and classical Christian views wherein the soul is asserted to be an additional metaphysical substance. As noted, if such an additional metaphysical soul does exist then it is likely fundamentally

36. Ibid., 144.

shaped by the lives that we live. However, for those holding this position, one challenge would be to address the role that this substantive soul has in the human person. Between our Trinitarian theology and the unified model of human nature, all of the influences classically ascribed to such a God-given metaphysical soul have already been covered. It does not therefore seem necessary to assert the presence of such a substantive soul for this theological anthropology unless it were regarded as being the union between the Divine Spark and our emerging nature.

A third position is the one that Green has chosen and is the claim that there is no metaphysical soul and that any life-after-death existence is only made possible by God's granted gift. This view is certainly in line with the synthesized model and its' similar emphasis on the embodied and relational nature of human beings. However, one challenge that Green still needs to address is the question of who God grants such a gift to. Is it everyone? Or only those who have achieved a certain level of "spiritual development"? Only Christians? Only human organisms? On these questions, Green does not seem to offer insights.

He does, however, assert that humans stand in a precarious position between animals and God. On this, he claims, "Humans are unlike other creatures in that only humanity is created after God's own likeness, in God's own image (imago Dei). Only to humanity does God speak directly."[37] In his human-centered framework (technically referred to as "anthropocentric"), Green acknowledges that humans stand along the same embodied and relational existence as other organisms. However, humans also possess the ability to receive God's communication. This is an unusual claim for Green's scheme because he expends so much effort essentially arguing for an organism view of the human species only to insert this claim as a part of it. Why remove a metaphysical substantive soul only to replace it with Divine metaphysical communication that is only available to humans? Also, Green still needs to clarify how this communication happens and whether it is a developmental milestone or not. For instance, do new born babies possess this communicative ability? As Wilson pointed out, there are apes (genetically considered to be cousins of ours) who seem to possess similar reasoning and intelligence capacities as humans do, so why does Green believe that God does not also communicate with them? It appears that Green, while embracing something of a more universal organism theory, which will be described

37. Ibid., 62.

below, still stands in line with human-centered views of spirituality and life-after-death.

For this synthesized model, Green's claims are problematic but might still be argued for by stating that the Divine Spark is the basis for divine communication. As a result, similar questions relating to who has this Divine Spark within them can and should be raised. These are important questions to consider for the framework given in this book because God's Trinitarian life is asserted to be fully operative within, to, and beyond every part of creation, including each and every organism, to the extent that they choose in accordance with their limited capacities. Nevertheless, Green's claim that there is no substantive soul represents a second philosophical position that one can take.

A fourth position is the one that we heard from Aquinas. In essence, it lies as a middle position between these previous two positions. For this view, following Aquinas, there is still a substantive metaphysical soul, but this soul is intimately shaped by the body and human experience more generally. Being deeply impressed upon by such a life, this soul would then continue on into the next phase of existence beyond the material realm.

A fifth and final position is one that extends a theory of organisms. Christianity has long sought, as we have already heard, to create clear distinctions between humans and other species on this planet. Seeking to support the "Imago Dei" view that humans are made in the image of God and other animals are not, as we just heard with Green, Christian theorists have sought to clearly define what the distinct differences are. Whether it is a metaphysical and substantive soul that has been given to humans and not to other organisms or it is our alleged abilities to communicate with the Divine in ways different from other species, as we heard with Green, Christians have offered a number of reasons throughout the centuries for what makes us distinct as a species.

However, there may not be as much that is really all that different. It must also be remembered that not all species are necessarily on the same developmental path as humans are. Sharks, for instance, have remained relatively unchanged for millions of years. To claim that we are somehow more "advanced" than they are, I believe, is an erroneous assertion. God may be asserted to work differently with different species of organisms just as God is asserted to have a different will and developmental path for angels versus humans.

In addition, the quest to separate humans from other species and to further claim that we are somehow more loved and endowed by God is also theologically problematic. If God's ever unfolding Life really is part and parcel of the material realm and God's love is truly infinite, then it stands to reason that God cares and work intimately for the life and vitality of every part of the physical universe. If this is true, then why do we in the Western Christian tradition go to such lengths to distinguish human uniqueness from other similarly emergent species?

Based upon this, and rather than seeking to articulate what makes humans unique and therefore survives death, this final position instead seeks to clarify what some of the factors are that might contribute to an organism's survival beyond physical death. Once these potential factors have been articulated, then we can revisit the question of whether humans and/or other species might look forward to life-after-death. While some may not think such soulful and life-after-death considerations are relevant for human transformation on Earth, but there may be significant implications for them.

Soul could be conceived, in accordance with Green as we heard, as the unity of the organism in its totality as it emergently unfolds. In other words, as an organism grows so too does its "soul," or the totality of its being. If we then chose to follow Aquinas, we might argue that such a growing soul indeed has a metaphysical substance to it that survives death. Such a position is equally defensible according to these models. However, such a substantive soul would really only seem to be a philosophical add on that exists only in the background to help explain what survives death. It could still theoretically apply to all organisms and not just the human species.

However, if we chose to follow Green's position and argue that no such substantive soul exists, then we must likewise respond to Green's concerns regarding what will happen to an organism's identity once its' physical and social relationships are disrupted via death. In our unified human nature model, we have such a basis for addressing these concerns via the transpersonal aspects. Green's position that people are too physically embodied and socially relational to survive death without God's gracious intervention because these connections would be lost no longer holds in this model. Organisms could still maintain these physical and relational connections, it might be argued, through the non-local transpersonal links that transcend the material realm. In might also be argued that our transition to the non-material realms is dependent upon the strength of the transpersonal connections that we have to these realms before we die. This would seem to make sense according to this model because if we already have strong transpersonal connections to the next realm, then our transition should happen more naturally. Hence, contrary to Green's claims, the integrity of one's being can still theoretically be maintained in the non-material realms for this unified model because of the transpersonal aspects.

Philosophically, then, there are two implications for both of these views. First, it initially seems supportable that potentially all organisms can survive a transition to the non-material realms. While this is counter to some of Christianity's classical doctrines, it is fully in line with the infinite love and Trinitarian care that God has for all of creation. However, we might also ask whether such non-material survival would really be welcomed by every organism. If the non-material realm into which we transition is significantly different from physical life on this planet, then would organisms that have been living solely at the physiological emergent levels really welcome non-physical existence? Maybe it is fully in-line with God's infinite love to allow such organismic "souls" to disintegrate thereby allowing their unified, and even substantive essence to dissolve back into the material origins from which they emerged.

One of the capabilities that has been noted of the human species is our ability to at least conceive of non-material realms, if not actually connect with them via transpersonal channels. This can happen at both the psychological and integrative-transcendent emergent levels. This, it could be argued, might therefore make us better candidates and more able to deal with such radical transitions to the non-material realms. Whether other psychologically emergent species would likewise be able to withstand such a drastic transition is a question still to be wrestled with, but the possibility seems to exist. These organism-based views therefore challenge the more human-centered views of classical Christianity's concept of the soul and what survives death. We again challenge these human-centered views in the next part of the book when we offer a more "entity-centered" view of spirituality.

The other part of these discussions relate to the asserted presence of the Divine Spark in the synthesized model. If life-after-death is dependent on the extent to which one identifies and attaches themselves to this Spark, then who can be asserted to have this Presence within them and how does one come to attach one's self to it? These are questions yet to be taken up in relation to other organisms as well as for humans.

The second implication is one that has already been raised. Since the soul (in either its substantive or non-substantive versions) here might be conceived of as the totality of the organism, and this organism is partly the product of its inherited and cultivated enduring patterns, then it stands to reason that these patterns and influences may continue to some extent after death. In other words, the life that we live on this planet, the histories of which we are a part, and the choices we make may very well continue to shape and influence us into the next realm. This is not necessarily to say that they will influence us in exactly the same way or to the same extent since the next non-material phase of our existence will be very different as we leave our physical bodies behind.

Nevertheless, and contrary to common hopes of going to Heaven where all will be taken care of, the formative implication is that our spiritual progress, or lack of it, may very well continue into the next realm. Such a claim seems to actually argue against the view that we will awake in Heaven, especially if Heaven is conceived of as those parts of creation where God's Trinitarian Life is fully manifest without distortion. If we live a life that embraces such distortions, and we take at least some of these distorted patterns with us, then the next realm cannot be "Heaven" by definition because of the distortions that we bring along with us. There must be, as classical Christian views of Purgatory allude to, some intermediate realm where we will continue, with the on-going help of God directly and via non-material beings, to work towards the perfect spiritual life to which all organisms and all of creation is invited. It therefore behooves us to make as much progress as we can in this life.

It also seems plausible that a case may be made for arguing that if one has cultivated a life that is too full of distortions, they will be unable to transition to the next non-material realm. We already know that it is possible to live such a distorted existence on earth that one's physical life cannot be maintained. Drug addictions, poor nutrition and lack of exercise, negative and stress-filled habits of thoughts/feelings, et cetera can all lead to an increasingly disintegrated life and even to death. Based on this, we might therefore expect that the next realm might also only be able to sustain a certain amount of distortions. Hence, it might be argued that not all organisms will be able to survive a transition to the next realm of our existence because of the extensiveness of distortions that are present in this one. Regardless of where one stands in relation to all of these claims, however, these are some of the soulful reflections that

So the people who have their lives together the best
go on and those who don't, don't?.
    This is utter bullshit.

the synthesized theological anthropology presented herein might offer to classical Christian views of the soul and life-after-death.

## CLOSING REFLECTIONS

In this third part of the book, we have embarked upon quite an extensive quest to see how we might synthesize our own theological anthropology in light of our Western Christian and modern science authors. After reviewing some of the considerations for how such model construction might proceed, a proposed unified model was presented as one possible outcome for such synthesizing work. While this synthesized model is very different from many of the ones found in classical Western Christianity, it does offer one way to merge the findings of modern science with many of these classical views.

Nevertheless, depending on one's own cultural locations and which models that one takes as their primary basis, the view of human nature that they synthesize may be quite different from the one constructed here. Another central part of such synthesizing work, it was noted, are the dynamics of one's local ministerial context. The people and communities that we are directly working with must influence the models that we choose to use or create. If these models do not accurately represent our community, if they do not help us to better understand them, then they are not worth having.

A challenge therefore lies in having more generalized models to turn to for all of spiritual formation efforts. Spiritual formation is not just involved in the transformation of individuals, but also relationships and whole communities as well. While we could and should perform a similar synthesizing activity for each of these other levels of spiritual formation, we might also be able to develop a more generalized model of formation based on the work that we have already done, with some inductive extensions. In the next chapter of this book, we will be doing just this. We will be seeking to develop a more generalized model from which we hope to extract some of the more central insights and guidelines for our spiritual formation craft.

# CHAPTER 4

# Spiritual Being and Becoming

*A General Model for Spiritual Formation*

THE UNIFIED OR SYNTHESIZED model of human nature given above achieves the second of the three primary goals for this book as we now have a general model based on both Western Christian and modern science views that we may work with for our spiritual formation programs. At this point, we might therefore proceed on to the final part where we will explore how such theological anthropologies might be used to help guide the development of specific spiritual formation programs. However, as we just heard, there are still some unanswered questions for this model in terms of how the three levels (Physiological, Psychological, and Integrative-Transcendent) are related to one another. One could, therefore, seek to create a more generalized model.

Why might developing a generalized theory be helpful? There are at least three reasons: 1) such a theory might provide basic insights into some of the fundamental dynamics of the people and communities that we will be working with; 2) a systematic model can help to ensure that we are not missing any major elements to consider in our work; and 3) an inductively generalized model may provide us with basic guidelines and insights into the more fundamental nature of our formative work.

To pursue these benefits, it may be helpful to take a philosophical step back and to propose a much more generalized model. Perhaps being considered a "universal organism theory," it is a model that seeks to move towards capturing some of the evolutionary and lifespan developments of, ideally, any organism or entity on our planet, but the human species in particular. This theory, as it is developed here, will not really be this comprehensive but merely an attempt to move in these inductive directions and answer the questions raised above whilst simultaneously providing further insights into the nature and work of the transformation of people and communities. As such, it is more of an intellectual work of philosophy than a work of rigorous science, offering possibilities rather than actualities that have been empirically verified.

Since our work as spiritual formators is primarily concerned with change, it behooves us to learn and reflect on all that we can about such transformation dynamics. However, it is also recognized that the discussions that follow are much more abstract and theoretical in nature. For those pragmatists who are seeking more practical insights into the relationship between theological anthropologies explored in the previous chapters and spiritual formation program development, this part of the book may be passed over. At any rate, I will be as brief as possible merely providing a cursory sketch of the more philosophically generalized model presented below.

## A BRIEF REVIEW OF FORMATION DYNAMICS AT VARIOUS LEVELS

To begin, it will be helpful to have a general architecture that undergirds the fundamental nature of human beings, organisms, organizations, and the material realm more generally. For this underlying philosophical foundation, I turn to separate communities for insights into how various aspects of our being might be made up. As we shall currently see, each of these communities articulates some similar components therefore allowing for a more generalized philosophical architecture of entities to emerge. As we move quickly through these sections, what we are looking for are the more basic and fundamental elements that might come to form a more generalizable model. We will therefore briefly touch upon these basic elements in each of the sections below and then summarize our explorations at the end.

### Neurophysiological Structures

The first community to which we turn is neuroscience. As we have already covered the basics of this field, we can be much briefer than we were in the previous chapter. What is important to recall from our reflections above are neurons, the meta-regions, and the actions of the limbic system specifically. Neurons, it was asserted, comprise one of the foundational components for the central nervous system. Neurophysiological dynamics occur largely because of these fundamental nodes of the biological brain.

These neural nodes alone, however, are not all that there is to this system. Equally important, if not more so, are the vast and diverse networks that these neurons form with one another as they make connections via their axons and dendrites. Such neural networks, on a global neurophysiological scale, comprise the foundation for the three meta-regions that we learned about. By firing individually and in harmony with one another, these meta-region networks have been observed to be associated with many of our behaviors and actions as human beings.

An additional consideration is the neurophysiological operation of such regions as the limbic system. As we may recall, this network is partly responsible for our feelings and it does so by releasing hormones and other chemicals that can have system-wide field effects on the brain. It is therefore not only the neurons (and other cells, such as glial cells) and the networks that they form, but also these system-wide field effects that at least partially influence who we are and how we act in the world.

Finally, we also note that neurophysiological change only occurs when, as the now often repeated Hebbian mantra claims, "neurons that fire together, wire together." This means that neurons are able to form temporary connections together that may not endure with time. A common phrase in our culture is, "use it or lose it," and this principle seems to apply here as well. Those connections that are repeatedly (but also heatedly)[1] made will be the ones that are more likely to endure across time and form sustained networks.

---

1. Sustained connections can also be made if neuro-chemical conditions are ripe. An example of this is traumatic experiences and the enduring memories that we have of them. Due to the hormones emitted during these experiences, the underlying neurophysiological structures that support their continued existence within us endure even though such connections may only have been stimulated once. For more discussions on these kinds of neural connections, see Metcalf and Mischel, "A Hot/Cool System Analysis of Delay Gratification"; Mischel, "Personality Coherence and Dispositions"; Mischel and Shoda, "Toward a Unified Theory of Personality"; Mischel et al., Introduction to Personality, 415–16.

## The CAPS Model: A Social-Cognitive Model

Next, we turn to the psychological level, particularly to one group of social-cognitive theorists. In order to help draw out the basic elements that will be developed more fully below, we will spend more time on this model than the others. Walter Mischel and Yuichi Shoda are personality psychological researchers. Mischel and Shoda have sought to create a model of personality that addresses what is known as the personality paradox in this discipline, which may be captured via the following question: "Which is correct, our intuitive belief in the existence of stable personality differences, or the repeated research findings of behavioral inconsistency across situations?"[2] The result of their work was the Cognitive-Affective Processing System, or CAPS model. The following is a brief description of this model and its basic architectural elements.

The most fundamental elements in the CAPS model are referred to as "Cognitive-Affective Units" (CAUs).[3] In essence, CAUs are cognitive and affective mental representations that come to influence such factors as one's perceptions, expectations, values & goals, affective dynamics, and external behaviors.[4] Their origins and development can be found in one's genetic predispositions, their neurophysiological make-up, and also in their life experiences.[5] Examples of these CAUs include the schemas, constructs, representations, and subjective maps of traditional social cognitive research, all of which give meaning and guidance to one's life.[6] "In the proposed theory," they assert, "individuals differ in how they selectively focus on different features of situations, how they categorize and encode them cognitively and emotionally, and how those encodings activate and interact with other cognitions and affects in the personality system."[7] These CAUs are therefore viewed as the fundamental node-like

2. Mischel et al., *Introduction to Personality*.

3. Mischel, "Personality Coherence and Dispositions"; Mischel and Shoda, "A Cognitive-Affective System Theory of Personality."

4. Mischel and Shoda, "A Cognitive-Affective System Theory of Personality"; Mischel and Shoda, "Toward a Unified Theory of Personality"; Mischel et al., *Introduction to Personality*, 423–25.

5. Mischel and Shoda, "A Cognitive-Affective System Theory of Personality."

6. Ibid.; Mischel and Shoda, "Toward a Unified Theory of Personality"; Mischel et al., *Introduction to Personality*, 423.

7. Mischel and Shoda, "A Cognitive-Affective System Theory of Personality"; see also Mischel, "Personality Coherence and Dispositions"; Mischel and Shoda, "Toward a Unified Theory of Personality."

elements that influence all of these processes as they are organized into a complex and highly dynamic inner network of interacting variables.[8]

While all of this may seem complicated, the basic idea that they are trying to convey is that our internal and external dynamics are largely influenced by enduring mental representations, or "schemas," that have both cognitive and affective components to them.[9] These CAUs are therefore understood by Mischel and Shoda to be influential and guiding nodes in the overall personality network and are therefore the most fundamental elements of their CAPS model.

As briefly mentioned above, these CAUs are developed, initiated, and then influence one's behavior in various ways. In particular, CAUs interact in the personality network via external situational factors as well as by internal organization and interactions. Externally, Mischel and Shoda highlight four important aspects relevant to these CAUs and the personality system. First, as we have already noted, environmental encounters across the lifespan help to shape and give rise to the CAUs that one has.[10] One's culture, for example, influences the cognitive and affective schemas that one has and how they are related to one another. Secondly, external stimuli at least partially determine which CAUs will be activated in any given moment.[11] For instance, the CAUs that are activated for a child with their peers at a summer camp will sometimes be different than the ones activated when they are with an adult camp supervisor.[12] Third, the CAUs that are currently active influence what one will notice and perceive in their current situation.[13] If we are in a "bad mood," for example, we are more likely to see the glass as half-empty rather than half-full.

Finally, because of these CAU-situational dynamics, they assert that individuals will generate distinctive "if . . . then . . ." situation-behavior patterns.[14] In other words, they write, "[The proposed theory] predicts that the person's behavior in a domain will change from one situation to

---

8. Mischel, "Personality Coherence and Dispositions."

9. Mischel and Shoda, "A Cognitive-Affective System Theory of Personality."

10. Ibid.

11. Ibid.

12. Mischel and Shoda, "Toward a Unified Theory of Personality."

13. Mischel and Shoda, "A Cognitive-Affective System Theory of Personality"; Mischel and Shoda, "Toward a Unified Theory of Personality."

14. Mischel, "Personality Coherence and Dispositions"; Mischel and Shoda, "A Cognitive-Affective System Theory of Personality"; Mischel and Shoda, "Toward a Unified Theory of Personality"; Mischel et al., *Introduction to Personality*, 417.

another—when the if changes, so will the then—even if the personality system were to remain entirely unchanged."[15] These "if . . . then . . . " patterns, they hypothesize, may then be the basis of a stable "personality signature" that characterizes the individual.[16] What makes a personality network enduring, in other words, is the repeated activation of these if-then responses. These CAUs are therefore highly influenced by and interactive with the external environments that one finds themselves or chooses to be in and therefore form the basis of their approaches to personality studies.

Internally, on the other hand, these CAUs are additionally influenced by at least the following primary factors: their organization and how they are encoded. Organizationally, Mischel and Shoda conceive of these CAUs as being arranged into a complex mediating network of interrelationships.[17] This highly interconnected network is not viewed as "separate, independent discrete variables, forces, factors, or tendencies," but rather as a dynamic organization that acts as a whole.[18] This complex network is therefore viewed as guiding and constraining the activation of its various parts; i.e., "the specific cognitions, affects, and potential behaviors" that a person has available to them in a given situation.[19] Such "relationships and interactions," they claim, "may operate at many levels of awareness, automaticity, and control" and they therefore act more like a parallel-distributed processing system rather than a serial one.[20] Mischel and Shoda further view this organization as being stable unless, they assert, "new learning, development, or biochemical changes occur."[21] The internal organization of these CAU networks is therefore a central aspect of the CAPS model and is central to how the personality system is viewed.

15. Mischel and Shoda, "A Cognitive-Affective System Theory of Personality"; see also Mischel and Shoda, "Toward a Unified Theory of Personality"; Mischel et al., *Introduction to Personality*, 417.

16. Ibid.

17. Mischel and Shoda, "A Cognitive-Affective System Theory of Personality"; Mischel and Shoda, "Toward a Unified Theory of Personality."

18. Mischel and Shoda, "A Cognitive-Affective System Theory of Personality."

19. Mischel, "Personality Coherence and Dispositions"; Mischel and Shoda, "A Cognitive-Affective System Theory of Personality."

20. Mischel, "Personality Coherence and Dispositions"; Mischel and Shoda, "A Cognitive-Affective System Theory of Personality"; Mischel and Shoda, "Toward a Unified Theory of Personality."

21. Ibid.

A final internal factor that influences these CAUs is related to how they are encoded. In the CAPS model, CAUs can become organized into subsystems that are either "hot" or "cool."[22] The "hot" system is related to emotions, impulsiveness, passions, et cetera and is therefore viewed as an affective "go system" that is intended to move us to action in certain situations.[23] The "cool" system, on the other hand, is posited as being specialized for rational, emotionally neutral, flexible, strategic, and reflective processing and is often referred to as a "know system."[24] Not only do the hot and cool systems work together to "produce experiences that are both cognitive and emotional," but they also "underlie the individual's distinctive, characteristic internal states and external behavioral expressions."[25] The CAPS model therefore asserts that these encoded hot and cool CAU networks, and their appropriate balance and harmony, to likewise be a central aspect of their model. As with neurophysiology, we can see that nodes, networks, field effects, and the transient nature of dynamics and structures are some of the basic elements that might make up the architecture of a more generalized model as we shall see below.

## An Organizational & Community Development Architecture

Continuing to move quickly and briefly, we turn to another couple of fields to consider, this time at a sociological level. Here, we are only seeking to verify the presence of these basic architectural elements and will therefore not spend too much time on the models at this level. In his book, *Strategic Organizational Change*, Michael Beitler identifies six target groups that organizational developers must direct their transformational efforts: individuals, dyads, intergroups, groups/teams, large subsystems, and the entire organization.[26] By monitoring, diagnosing, and developing interventions for each of these levels, organizational change may be facilitated in healthy ways. Such interventions, however, must not only engage with these individually, but also structurally, culturally, and stra-

22. Metcalf and Mischel, "A Hot/Cool System Analysis of Delay Gratification"; Mischel, "Personality Coherence and Dispositions"; Mischel and Shoda, "Toward a Unified Theory of Personality"; Mischel et al., *Introduction to Personality*, 415–16.

23. Metcalf and Mischel, "A Hot/Cool System Analysis of Delay Gratification"; Mischel and Shoda, "Toward a Unified Theory of Personality."

24. Ibid.

25. Ibid.

26. Beitler, *Strategic Organizational Change*, 57–58.

tegically.[27] In other words, organizational developers must not only work with the specific individuals and groups that make up the organization, but also the more system-wide dynamics that guide and make up their sociological dynamics.

In a similar way, community builders are sometimes encouraged to consider the assets that each aspect of a community has.[28] These include the basic units of a neighborhood such as its citizens, but also the associations and institutions of which these individuals are a part of. The steps towards building stronger and healthier communities include such activities as: mapping a community's assets as well as needs; building relationships among people and institutions; mobilizing members to build economic development; collectively working to develop community vision; and drawing from necessary and helpful resources beyond the neighborhood.[29] Again, do we see an emphasis at these sociological levels on the need to engage with the basic units of the community (i.e., the citizens) in the social, political, and economic networks of which they are a part. We also see the need to engage the broader field dynamics that affect them as these organizations and communities continually across time.

## Process Philosophies

Finally, we turn to a community that we have referred to repeatedly above: Process theology/philosophy. This final exploration will provide us with a model that seeks to universally describe some of the basic elements of any part of creation and will therefore comprise a stronger foundation for the development of the generalized model below. This philosophy primarily originated with the works of Alfred North Whitehead who sought to articulate a "philosophy of organism."[30] Basing this philosophy and theology on his background in physics and mathematics,[31] Whitehead provides a distinctive view into the cosmos. In this philosophy, there are four essential elements to the Process model of creation that are relevant for our purposes here.

---

27. Ibid., 86.

28. See: Kretzmann and McKnight, *Building Communities from the Inside Out*, 7.

29. Ibid., 345.

30. Cobb and Griffin, *Process Theology*, 7.

31. Suchocki, *God, Christ, Church*, 4.

The first element of this model is the "actual occasion." According to Process theologians John Cobb and David Ray Griffin, these occasions "are momentary events which perish immediately upon coming into being."[32] The core assertion of Process philosophies is that all of life is ever in a process of becoming; never being fixed, substantial, or enduring.[33] Instead, there are only instances of these actual occasions that come into being, become concrete for a fleeting moment, and finally perish. In this way, they thereby exert an influence, as will be discussed more below, on the next set of actual occasions that come into existence. All of creation is asserted by Process philosophers and theologians to be made up of these abstracted fundamental instances of reality known as actual occasions.

The second essential element of this model is the idea that these actual occasions form themselves into collective "societies" that we give such labels as organs, humans, plants, galaxies, et cetera.[34] In other words, actual occasions, being discrete nodes of existence, form enduring networks with one another that endure across time and throughout space. Each set of momentary actual occasion existence is therefore asserted to exert an influence on the next set of actual occasions that come into being such that these societies or network survive across time. As a result, substance-like properties appear to be enduring realities when, according to Process philosophies, they are actually the result of momentary network existences that are repeated across time. An analogy would be a film reel where the enduring image that is projected onto a screen is the result of a series of individual frames that contain the image. This view of reality is very similar to what we heard with the CAPS model as it sought to explain how personality might endure across varying situations with "if-then" dynamics.

The third important element in this model is what is known as the "cumulative penetration." In its essence, the cumulative penetration is the field of influences from all prior existing actual occasions that act on any given and newly becoming actual occasion.[35] There is, therefore, an "extensive continuum" of connections and relationships between all actual occasions in creation through which they act upon and mutually

---

32. Cobb and Griffin, *Process Theology*, 14.

33. Ibid.; Suchocki, *God, Christ, Church*, 11.

34. Bracken, *Divine Matrix*, 61; Cobb and Griffin, *Process Theology*.

35. Odin, *Process Metaphysics and Hua-yen Buddhism*, 137; Whitehead, *Adventures of Ideas*, 191.

influence one another in field-like ways.[36] Actual occasions exert not only directionality on the newly becoming actual occasions, it is further asserted, but also an "emotional intensity."[37] It is the presence and affective influences of this cumulative penetration field that impacts the becoming of each new actual occasion.[38] This cumulative penetration is what partly explains the phenomenon of enduring substances that we observe in our lives, since the previous moment's existence inclines the next moment's actual occasions to become and behave in certain and specific ways.[39]

The final foundational element of this Process model is the "initial aim." The initial aim, according to Marjorie Suchocki, is conceived of as God's creative influence acting on each actual occasion in creation.[40] This aim has the purpose of directing the occasion to optimally unify the cumulative penetration that is acting on its becoming thereby opening it up to the best possibility that the actual occasion can realize during its momentary existence.[41] Conceived of as "Creative-Responsive Love," this optimal initial aim from God is to be distinguished from the subjective aim that the actual occasion finally chooses for itself during its own becoming.[42] In other words, each actual occasion is free to choose between the initial aim of God and another more subjective aim that it creates for itself in light of all of the influences that are acting upon it via the cumulative penetration. God's goal for all actual occasions is for each one to actualize the initial aim of God thereby conforming them to the truer realities of peace and harmony in creation rather than to the more illusory appearances that actual occasions might subjectively try to create for themselves.[43]

---

36. Bracken, *Divine Matrix*, 66; Odin, *Process Metaphysics and Hua-yen Buddhism*, 70; Whitehead, *Adventures of Ideas*, 134.

37. Odin, *Process Metaphysics and Hua-yen Buddhism*, 84.

38. Cobb and Griffin, *Process Theology*, 19; Faber, "De-Ontologizing God," 217; Odin, *Process Metaphysics and Hua-yen Buddhism*, 87; Suchocki, *God, Christ, Church*, 9.

39. Whitehead, *Adventures of Ideas*, 186.

40. Suchocki, *God, Christ, Church*, 39, 258.

41. Cobb and Griffin, *Process Theology*, 53; Suchocki, *God, Christ, Church*, 258.

42. Cobb and Griffin, *Process Theology*, 56; Faber, "De-Ontologizing God," 213; Suchocki, *God, Christ, Church*, 39.

43. Cobb and Griffin, *Process Theology*, 53, 65; Suchocki, *God, Christ, Church*, 45; Whitehead, *Adventures of Ideas*, 293.

## Common Elements Among These

Whew, so that's a lot of abstract theorizing! But, we might ask, towards what ends? We began this section by saying that what we are looking for are some of the more fundamental elements that might comprise a basic architecture for a more generalized model of entities or organisms. These entities might be an organ of the body, an individual person, an organization that one is a part of, or a community that one lives in. By extracting these common elements, the hopes are that we will be able to derive some of the more fundamental principles that can guide our spiritual formation endeavors, particularly at the individual level.

Looking at these physiological, psychological, sociological, and philosophical models, we can identify at least four common elements. First, each of these models asserts the presence of basic nodes for the systems that they are focused on. At the neurophysiological level, these were the neurons. For the CAPS model, these were the CAUs while the sociological models held these to be the individuals of the organizations and neighborhoods. Finally, in the Process model, these were the very abstracted actual occasions that we just learned about.

Second, each set of theories had networks that these nodes were organized into. Neurons form regions and meta-regions of the brain. CAUs coalesce to create schemas in the personality system. Individuals make up dyads, teams, institutions, and the like in organizations and communities. Actual occasions orient themselves to comprise societies in the Process model. Organized networks therefore seem to be another essential component to a generalized model of formation.

Next, we also heard throughout about the necessity of being aware of field effects in each system. Chemicals that wash entire systems of the brain are one example. Hot and cool influences can act more generally to influence one's psychological encoding states. Cultural norms more broadly affect communities and institutions. In the Process model, the cumulative penetration element is another example of such wider field effects, effects that influence wider parts of the system beyond the nodal level. As a result, I assert that field effects are another basic component that we must consider in the construction of a more generalized model.

Finally, we also heard of the transient or continually changing nature of systems to varying degrees. Most clearly seen with the Process model, parts of a system—the nodes and networks themselves as well as the connections between and among them—can come and go across time. In the

CAPS model, we heard of "if-then" dynamics wherein different CAUs were only activated under certain situations. In the biological brain, enduring connections are sustained only after repeated firing but even then may be lost or fade away. At the sociological levels, we can imagine the transitional nature of communities and institutions as people, businesses, departments, et cetera come and go. In line with this, we have already heard one principle of formation—it is the repeated engagement of a system's components that leads to their enduring across time—and we shall discuss this in more detail below. As a result, our general model must also capture the enduring and non-enduring dynamics of any system, entity, organism, et cetera that we are seeking to formatively work with.

With these basic elements in place, it might seem like we are in a good position to now move forward with proposing a generalized model; a more "universal organism theory" if you will. However, there is still one more major issue to consider that was raised in the previous part of the book. In discussing my own synthesized theological anthropology, the question arose as to what the nature of the relationship might be between the physical, psychological, and integrative-transcendent levels. As briefly mentioned, there are some such as Descartes who have considered these various levels to be independent and distinct from one another. Yet, our own experiences as well as neuro-psychological research suggest that they are somehow inseparably connected. So, how might we conceive of these interrelationships? Emergence theories, which will be discussed next, provide one possible way to understand and respond to such complexities. These discussions will become relevant for our generalized model here because they will help us to better capture the emergent properties that can arise in the systems that we find ourselves working with whether these are individuals, relationships, organizations, or whole communities.

## EMERGENCE THEORIES

Our goal in exploring emergence theories is to better understand the nature of how we develop as living organisms, communities, and societies—collectively termed "entities" in this scheme—in response to our evolutionary histories and our daily lived experiences. In the process, however, we shall come to see how the physiological, psychological, and integrative-transcendent aspects are related to one another and how social dynamics emerge out of the interactions of individuals and groups. In the end, we will find that these theories can be incorporated as another basic component of our more inductively generalized model.

## Philosophy, Physics, and "Monistic Stuff"

In the secular scientific worldview, the universe is considered to be a closed system that is made up of one general kind of "monistic stuff." Theologian Philip Clayton, in his book *Mind and Emergence*, describes this scientific worldview noting that "reality is ultimately composed of one basic kind of stuff" and that all of the phenomena that we observe and study, such as physical and mental properties, emerge out of this monistic stuff of creation.[44] It is then the responsibility of the sciences, Clayton goes on to explain, to examine and uncover the "law like" properties of this monistic stuff.[45] This monistic stuff comprises the atoms, molecules, et cetera that make up matter. Following the basic philosophy above, and in particular the Process perspective, the series of actual occasions of existence are asserted to endure across time and form the networks of connections (or "societies" in the Process view) that give rise the atomistic elements of this monistic stuff. Process philosophers might go so far to assert that actual occasions are the fundamental philosophical building blocks of this monistic material "stuff."

To put this more simply, think about the elements of matter (e.g., electrons, protons, and their more basic quantum make up). At this level, these essentially are the nodes of the material realm that sometimes join together in enduring ways to form more complex networks such as atoms, molecules, and the substances (solids, liquids, and gases) that are then made up of these. The basic idea here is that material creation is comprised of nodes that form networks (enduring and non-enduring) of increasing complexity. In other words, this view asserts that the material realm arises out of more basic nodes that join together in increasingly complex structures and networks as we heard above.

In the secular science view, however, creation is also considered to be a "causally closed system" with there being no need to assert the presence of any sort of external influence or guidance such as a Deity; i.e.,

---

44. Clayton, *Mind & Emergence*, 4, 158.

45. Ibid., 188.

creation is fully able to "run on its own" as it were.[46] For the synthesized model of human nature put I forth above, however, such a non-theistic worldview is not held. Not only does our model of human nature and its Trinitarian theology assert the presence and actions of God's Life in creation, it also holds a place for other non-material realms of reality as well as non-local interactions within and among them. Nevertheless, this theological anthropology and its associated philosophy of organism, still affirms this science-based view of monistic stuff and the claim that all matter and life in this material realm arises out of the increasing complexity of this basic "monistic stuff."

## Emerging Life

Central to these views of increasing complexity are theories of emergence.[47] Generally, these theories "recognize nature's tendency to produce more and more complex forms of organization,"[48] as just noted. Spanning "the entire spectrum of cosmic history,"[49] these theories of emergence assert that new forms and levels of life and complexity arise as evolution progresses from the same basic monistic stuff of which material creation is comprised.[50] Such theories of emergence and complexity are important, because they are becoming a central part of contemporary scientific worldviews and science's abilities to help explain some of the enduring phenomena of our monistic-material world and how life is arising and developing across evolutionary history.

One of the challenges that scientists in different disciplines face is the seeming duality between different levels of existence. As a specific example, we have already heard of one of these in relation to the brain and the mind. It is clear that these two are closely related but that they are also somehow distinctly different. Given this, there have been at least three primary philosophical approaches used to describe such independence and interrelationships between brain and mind.

46. Clayton, *Adventures in the Spirit*, 77, 186; Peacocke, *Paths from Science towards God*, 34, 70, 75, 83, 93, 146.

47. McGrath, *A Fine-Tuned Universe*, 210.

48. Clayton, *Adventures in the Spirit*, 64–65, 90; McGrath, *A Fine-Tuned Universe*, 215.

49. Clayton, *Adventures in the Spirit*, 66, 191.

50. Ibid., 74, 87; McGrath, *A Fine-Tuned Universe*, 205–6.

As we have already heard, Cartesian dualists such as René Descartes assert that the nature of the relationship between the mind and the body/brain is one that is completely distinct and separate from one another.[51] However, dualism is problematic because it fundamentally does not address the causal connections that have been observed between the mind and brain as seen, for instance, in the widely cited case of Phineas Gage's altered personality that resulted from severe brain trauma.[52] These dualistic views therefore do not seem to provide a satisfactory explanation for how the mind and brain are distinct but interrelated.

An alternative philosophical view is provided by biological reductionists, such as Richard Dawkins, Stephen Jay Gould, Edward Wilson, and others. The reductionist view asserts that all higher levels of organism functioning, such as the mind, can be fully explained solely in terms of the lower level dynamics of the biological brain or even gene expression.[53] The basic claim is that there really is no higher level of ontology and existence and that all seemingly "higher" properties are really the result of causal influences that have their origins in lower levels such as the biological level. In other words, biological reductionists might assert, as our understanding of biology, or in this specific case neurophysiology, continues to grow so too will our understanding of the mind and that all mental functioning will eventually be able to be described fully by biological sciences. It might therefore be argued, then, that as this happens there will no longer be a need for the field of psychology for all causal explanations and understandings of the mind will be derived solely from biological laws and principles. Of course, the physical sciences (such as physicists and chemists) could reductionistically make the same claims towards the biological sciences.

However, some neuro-psychiatrists, such as Dan Siegel, challenge this view. On this, Siegel writes, "It is too simplistic to say merely that the "brain creates the mind" as we now know that the mind can activate the brain."[54] The core of the problem that these researchers are attempting to address is that both mind and brain appear to have their own distinct

51. Descartes, "Discourse on Method," 86. For other dualistic relationships, specifically between our animal self and our symbolic self, see Becker, *The Denial of Death*, 26.

52. Bear et al., *Neuroscience*, 570.

53. Dawkins, *The Selfish Gene*, 264; Gould, "Challenges to Neo-Darwinism," 224. For further discussions on such views, see Clayton, *Mind & Emergence*, 114.

54. Siegel, *Mindful Brain*, 24, 48–50.

properties, laws, dynamics, et cetera, which is the claim of the dualists, but that they also seem to be interrelated if not indistinguishable from one another, which is the claim of the reductionists.

In between these two positions, is the increasingly accepted third philosophical position known as the theory of emergence. A theory of strong emergence mediates both of these polarized positions (i.e., dualism and reductionism) by asserting "ontologically distinct levels" that emerge out of the dynamics of previous and "lower" levels. Strong emergence recognizes that complex and qualitatively different wholes are created out of the interactions of its more simple parts. Each new emergent level, asserts theologian Ian Barbour, is "relatively integrated, stable, and self-regulating, even though it interacts with other units at the same level and at higher and lower levels."[55]

So, for example, the mind is asserted to emerge as a result of the biological functions of the brain. However, this newly emergent psychological level of reality has its own set of dynamics, principles, et cetera that cannot be reduced to or completely explained or predicted by neural network operations alone. Another example of emergent levels would be individuals who join together as a group. While each person in the group has their own unique personality, the work that they do together will be something more than a mere sum of the parts. Each new level of complexity, these emergence theories therefore claim, have their own integrity and cannot be fully reduced to the level that they are emergent from. Nor, however, are the newly emergent higher levels completely independent from the lower levels from which they emerged, as dualists claim. Damage the brain and the mind will be altered, which is what we see in the case of Phineas Gage. Remove or alter an individual's behavior and the dynamics of the overall group will be changed.

Emergence theories therefore offer one way of understanding how evolution and increasing complexity unfolds from the monistic stuff of the material realm. Atoms coalesce to emergently form molecules whose properties cannot be fully predicted or described based solely on the observations of individual atoms. Molecules structure themselves in relation to one another to form more complex substances such as water. From this matter, living organisms emerge and the long history of evolution's increasing complexity progresses. As these emergence theories assert, each of the progressions in complexity essentially represent a new level of

55. Barbour, "Neuroscience, Artificial Intelligence, and Human Nature," 383.

emergent reality complete with their own nodes, networks, field effects, et cetera that are interrelated but not completely reducible to the lower levels from which they emerged. Whether these are the brain's neurons and their associated meta-regions or the CAUs and their corresponding personality networks, emergent monistic life is wonderfully dynamic and complex.

## Human Emergence: Body, Mind, & Integration

With this monistic, emergent philosophy in place, we are finally in a better position to understand the three levels of the synthesized theological anthropology asserted in the previous chapter. Emergence theories can provide us with a greater understanding of how these emergence theories might help us to better understand the dynamics of the people and communities that we are formatively working with. As it relates specifically to the human species, generally following Clayton's framework in his book, *Mind and Emergence*, there are three primary levels of emergence that are significant for the study of human nature: physiological, psychological, and integrative-transcendence.[56] These three levels, and their corresponding interpersonal and transpersonal relationships, can help us to better understand the human person in ways that not only provide us with further insights into the synthesized theological anthropology set forth above, but also in how we can better work with our communities. In order to see how emergence theories help us to reinterpret this theological anthropology, let us briefly revisit each emergent level.

The physiological level of emergence, as we have heard, includes all of the biological and pre-biological levels of emergence that are operative within humans—such as quantum, atomic, molecular, chemical, physical, and physiological levels and their corresponding networks and field effects of cells, organs, hormones, and the like. This level of emergence, as we have already heard, also includes genetic influences, "appetites and aversions," our "animality" and physical drives, as well as the full range of biological factors that have worked to shape us throughout our long

---

56. These three levels roughly follow the chapters that Clayton uses in his book, though he asserts that "the human person is a physical, biological, psychological, and (I believe also) spiritual reality." See Clayton, *Mind & Emergence*, 148.

evolutionary history.[57] As amazing as it sounds, we possess within our bodies millions of years of increasing monistic emergent complexity.

At this level, as we can see, we are able to interact with and are deeply shaped by our physical environments. As we heard, the foods we eat, the ecosystems we are a part of, et cetera impact how our physical body grows and functions. Furthermore, if transpersonal views are accurate, then this emergent level will also possess the capacity to interact with other non-local parts of creation in energy-based and other non-local ways. Since we are not the only species to have achieved this physiological level of emergence, other organisms and species are asserted to share these interpersonal and transpersonal relationships.[58]

Next, at some point in this evolutionary history, the psychological level came into emergent being. To distinguish it from the physiological level, some have asserted that it uniquely includes such mental capacities and dynamics such as "the capacity for reason," human innovativeness, and our abilities for symbolic functioning as we saw above. Yet, we also seem to share some version of these, as well as many other psychological capacities, with other species of animals.[59] In other words, the psychological level of emergence does not appear to be relegated solely to the human species alone.

With this level also comes the social-cultural interpersonal influences that help to shape who we are. The words we hear, the images we see, et cetera all help, as we have heard, to form our own being and becoming. Prior to this emergent level, and for the many non-psychological organisms, such mental impressions did not have an effect. It is also at this emergent level that parapsychological and super-conscious abilities come into existence, according to the synthesized theological anthropology set forth in this book at least. Seeing through time, using our mind to influence one another and other objects, communicating with beings from other realms, et cetera are all transpersonal phenomena that can theoretically emerge at this level. Since humans are not the only psychologically emergent species, then we would expect that other similarly emergent animals to possess such capacities and there are those who do

---

57. For a more lengthy discussion of such factors, see: Gould, "Challenges to Neo-Darwinism," 224; Roughgarden, *Evolution's Rainbow*, 6.

58. Irwin and Watt, "An Introduction to Parapsychology," Kindle Locations 130–31.

59. Wilson, *On Human Nature*, 283.

indeed claim that there is some evidence to support such claims.[60] We are now beginning to see more clearly here how emergence theories enable us to better understand how human evolution and development unfolds intrapersonally, interpersonally, and transpersonally.

Finally, the integrative-transcendence level of emergence is one that appears to lie somewhere beyond the previous levels and may be a newly unfolding epoch in human evolution. As we have heard, this emergent level is the integrated state of being that was described above. Clayton most concisely describes the integrative-transcendent nature of this emergent level when he writes, "We might define it as that level that emerges when an integrated state is established between a person and her body, her environment, other persons, and her overall mental state, including her interpretation of her social, cultural, historical, and religious context."[61] Such integrative-transcendence, according to Clayton's emergence position, is therefore a level that lies distinctively beyond the previous two levels, yet is still causally related to them.

Siegel's neuroscientific research also offers data for why this may be and how this level emerges. Siegel's research asserts that it is in a mindful state of awareness, as is induced by many meditative and contemplative practices, in which many diverse parts of our brains are integrated together into a more unified whole and this then gives rise to the integrative-transcendent experience.[62] Associating such experiences with the middle prefrontal regions of the brain's cortex, Siegel argues that mindfulness practices can nurture this new and characteristically different state of mind.[63] Overall, then, the integrative-transcendent experience is considered to be a new level of emergence that is recently dawning upon the pages of human history.[64] Whether or not this level of emergence is shared with other species of animals remains to be seen, but it is one that can fundamentally reshape who we are as human beings.

With this level, as with the other two, come new ways of relating to the world around us interpersonally and transpersonally. As we heard,

60. Irwin and Watt, "An Introduction to Parapsychology," Kindle Locations 129–31.

61. Clayton, *Mind & Emergence*, 195.

62. Siegel, *Mindful Brain*, 41, 119.

63. Ibid., 339.

64. At least in the past 4,000 years as recorded by human history, particularly by many of the world's religious traditions, a timespan that is relatively "recent" in relation to evolution's multi-million year history.

we come to possess the ability to experience oneness with creation. While no doubt are such experiences partly the product of physiological and psychological dynamics as we heard from Clayton and Siegel, they also seem to entail more holistic non-local connections according to the transpersonal views of attunement. To realize that we are possibly seeing this newly emergent level of influences in human evolution is exciting as we realize the potential implications that it has for us personally as well as for our relationships with the universe that is all around us.

These emergence theories therefore help us to better understand the nature of individual and social evolution and development. They can provide us with a framework for better understanding the relationship between emergent levels in non-dualistic and non-reductionistic ways, thereby retaining both the integrity and interrelationships for each of these levels. They can also help us to realize how human development has and continues to unfold both across evolution's history but also across the lifespan as the three levels of human emergence discussed herein gradually arise as we develop from a biological egg, to a psychological endowed organism, to a more integrated and transcendent being.

To reiterate, none of these emergent levels can be reduced to and explained solely in terms of previous levels. Neuroscience will not replace psychology nor will psychology replace sociology for each of these fields of study focuses on a different level of human emergence. Nor, however, can any of these fields ignore the findings of the other, for each emergent level as we heard is causally interconnected; though in less direct ways than may be seen within each emergent level. In other words, neuroscientists, psychologists, and sociologists still need to study and understand at least the basics of one another's disciplines because each new level of emergence affects the others to some degree. These emergence theories are therefore considered to be another central part of the generalized model that will now be discussed.

## THE NFNE MODEL: A GENERALIZED THEORY FOR FORMATION

With these theories, we have just covered the diverse physiological, psychological, sociological, and philosophical aspects of our world. Yet, in spite of this diversity, I assert that there is a common structure that emerges from among them. As we saw, it is one that has at least the following common elements to consider for formation work: nodes, fields, networks, their transitional nature, and emergence. These collectively seem to capture some the essential basics for an architecture of people and communities. For lack of a more creative name, we might therefore refer to this generalized model as a Node-Field-Network-Emergent (NFNE) Model, or one might refer to it as a "universal organism theory." As we moved through the sections above, we could have also highlighted additional models from other disciplines (such as molecular science and other physiological fields of study) many of which seem to share these same common elements in one way or another. This basic architecture, I am asserting, therefore comprises a fundamental structure with which we might better understand human life and growth. As such, it may therefore be used to help provide insights into some of the basic principles and guidelines for formation work.

## Basic Components

Before reflecting on some of the insights that such a model might provide, we will first briefly revisit this model's basic components to see more clearly how they are interrelated. The goal here is twofold: 1) to pull the discussions above together into a more cohesive presentation of this model; and 2) to outline steps that one might use to apply this model to their own formative endeavors. Our discussions here will be more summative and brief in nature because we have already discussed each of these in greater detail above. The reader is therefore invited to recall our physiological, psychological, sociological, and philosophical discussions above to help think more concretely about this more inductively abstracted model. Once in place, this NFNE model will provide us with a better understanding of the nature and work of spiritual formation.

### Defining the System's Boundary

The first step in developing any model is to decide what the system will be that we are formatively focusing on. This might be a congregation's youth group, a close relationship in counseling, or a specific part of the body that we are working to bring more health and vitality to. By stating this focus, we are essentially establishing the borders that make up the boundaries of the system that we will be working with. Such clarity can not only help us to stay focused on only those parts that we are called to work with but it can also help to simplify our work. This is because defining the boundaries of our work from the beginning can help us to realize just how complex the formative work might be and, if it is too complicated, to narrow our focus. Defining our system is therefore a first necessary step to developing and applying this generalized model.

Once we have defined these boundaries, then we have also automatically defined intra-system, inter-system, and trans-system relationships. Any direct influences that exist within the system's boundaries would be "intra-system" dynamics. Direct connections that exist outside of the system's boundaries are "inter-system" influences. Influences that occur non-locally and that act on one or more parts of the system would be considered to be "trans-system" connections. So, for instance, if the system is defined as being the physical body, then any physiological dynamics are intra-body. If we lived in a toxic health environment with polluted water and air, these would be inter-body influences. Finally, if our worldview included the presence of physical energies on the body, these might be labelled as trans-body influences. The first basic component and step to using this more generalized model is therefore to define the system's boundaries and begin to note some of the intra-, inter-, and trans-system influences as shown in the figure below. As we continue to develop this model below, of course, these various influences will emerge with much greater detail.

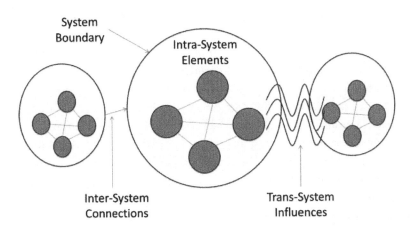

Figure 18. Intra-, Inter-, and Trans-System Influences.

*Nodes, Connections, and Fields*

The next set of elements to consider for this model are the most basic ones: nodes, direct connections between nodes, and fields that exist across these. As we heard above, nodes are essentially the core components of the system that we are working with. If we are focusing on working towards the health and vitality of the brain, they might be the neurons. If we are working for organizational change, these might be the individuals or teams of the corporation. At their core, the "nodes" of our defined system are those more fundamental elements and basic units that we will be formatively working with.

Of course, as we've heard above, each node can be seen as a system within itself (e.g., neurons have inner workings just as do people). Our challenge as formators therefore lies in discerning just how deep to go; deciding at what level to stop at. For instance, do we really need to know and identify all of the inner workings of each individual in order to effectively reshape an organization's dynamics? We will likely need to know general internal thought and attitude patterns among our community, but possibly not each person's detailed inner psychic life. If this is the case, then our basic node might be the person as a whole and not all of the complex inner dynamics of each individual.

Of course, the nodes of any system are connected to other parts of the system in varying ways. Some nodes might be influenced by other nodes, networks, and dynamics within the system. These connections are therefore intended to capture the more direct and specific cause-and-effect influences that are present within a system. These connections do not only need to capture these influences for specific nodes, but also for networks and meta-networks, which will be discussed below. Such connection tracing is essential for our formative work because it helps us to not only identify the more direct and causal influences within the system but also the means by which we might be able to enact change within the system. For instance, if we know that a person's identity is more directly shaped by their perceived performance on tests, then we might focus some of our identity formation efforts on helping this individual to reflect on their performance and the potential implications for their self-perceptions. Knowing how one part of a system is more directly connected to another can therefore be very beneficial for guiding our formative efforts.

Finally, we can also note the presence of what I term "field effects." Seen in Process philosophy's concept of cumulative penetration, which is the total sum of influences from the previous generation of actual occasions that creates a field-like effect that greatly influences the next generation. The limbic system was presented as a neurophysiological example of field effects in the brain that are caused by hormones and other chemicals that affect the system on a wider scale. Overall, the idea here is that entire sets of nodes, networks, and other parts of a system can be influenced by these more generalized field effects. These differ from the influences that a part of the system experiences via the more direct connections discussed above. Rather than acting locally and on a specific part of a system, which would be a direct connection, field effects are asserted to act more globally and systemically. As a result, they therefore comprise another central aspect of this generalized NFNE model. Below is shown a basic figure that is intended to represent these three basic components.

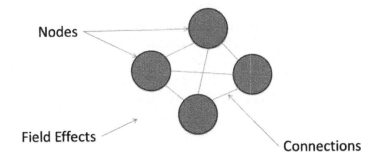

Figure 19. Nodes, Connections, & Fields.

## Networks and Meta-Networks

As noted repeatedly above, these nodes do not exist in a vacuum. On the contrary, they often form vast networks of complex connections with one another. In the Process model, these were the "societies" that actual occasions form and propagate from moment-to-moment. In the brain, these are the widely interconnected neural networks that contributed to the structures of the three meta-regions. In essence, a "network" might be understood as any well-defined collection of interconnected nodes.

Identifying these networks would therefore be a necessary next step in developing and applying this generalized model. These networks might also have their own field effects, be they locally or non-locally within or beyond the system.[65] Another example of these defined networks might be the organs in the body. Each one has their own physiology that is separate and distinct from the other organs. Within a system, these networks might also have direct connections with other nodes or networks. Knowing these should provide us with greater insights into the nature and dynamics of the system that we are working with just as it did at the nodal level.

Of course, just as any identified node of a system is likely composed of its own inner dynamics, so too is each network likely to be a part of larger network. These "meta-networks," or networks of networks, might be helpful for us in terms of better understanding the organization and hierarchical structure of the system that we are working with. Returning to the body example given above, the central nervous system, digestive system, et cetera are all meta-networks that are comprised of numerous organs, which are themselves networks within the body. Extending this, we might also find it helpful to identify "meta-meta-networks," or networks of meta-networks. For simplicity's sake, I include these larger networks in the term meta-networks. Again, the goal of identifying these complex interrelationships is to help us to more clearly understand how a system is organized and what the relative relationships and influences among its components might be. The figure below is intended to conceptually depict this increasing complexity.

---

65. Remember, transpersonal influences are defined to be ones that occur non-locally only. Such non-local influences can occur both within a system's boundaries as well as from beyond. For instance, it might be possible that the operations of the heart non-locally influence the functioning of other organs in ways that are not directly mediated via the bloodstream, magnetic fields generated by the heart, etc. Such influences might be considered to be "transpersonal" influences. We must also note that non-local influences might act only on specific parts of a system or in a broader and more network or systemic-wide way. As a result, such trans-system influences might be modelled as either single line connections or as field effects.

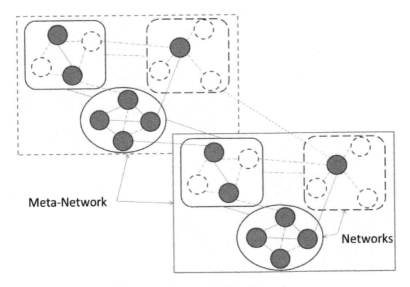

**Figure 20. Networks & Meta-Networks.**

## Transient Dynamics

As we heard above, any part of the system that we are working with is enduring to a limited degree—nothing lasts forever. The question, then, is to what degree are the system's elements enduring and what is the impact of these nodes, networks, fields, et cetera on the rest of the system. As we heard with the Process model, societies only endure across time if the influences of the previous generation are strong enough to ensure that the society will be replicated in the next generation of actual occasions. In a very similar way, the CAPS model claimed that aspects of the personality network only endure with "if-then" responses that are activated over many different situations. Such assertions are not unlike the Hebbian principle wherein neural networks are sustained at least partly, if not largely, by their repeated firing. In general, then, the networks that are formed only endure across time and space if they are continuously engaged to some degree, which is one of the basic principles of formation. Otherwise, they will likely fade away and dis-integrate; i.e., lose the nodal connections and influences that give shape to them. In detailing the nodes, connections, fields, networks, et cetera, some consideration must therefore be given to the transient nature of each element and whether we would consider them to be enduring, non-enduring, repeated but at sporadic moments, et cetera as shown below. How one defines what is "enduring," "non-enduring," or somewhere in between, is dependent upon the specifics of the spiritual formation program that one is developing.

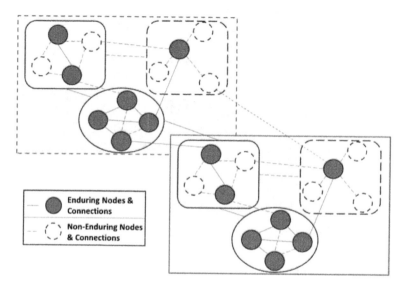

Figure 21. NFNE Transient Dynamics.

*Emergent Relationships*

As we have already discussed these kinds of relationships in detail above, we will not do so again here. What is instead relevant for our purposes is the uniqueness of influence that emergent relationships have. The fundamental characteristic of these relationships is that they are not really direct connections or field effects, but rather constraining relationships that exist between one emergent level and another. Recall that each level may be studied separately to some degree and general patterns, laws, et cetera identified for each level. For instance, psychologists study the enduring patterns of the mind while neuroscientists similarly explore the physiology of the brain. However, each level is connected to and influences one another though it is not always exactly clear as to how. Such emergent relationships between levels go both ways (e.g., the brain dynamics affect the mind and vice versa, as we heard above from Siegel).

We must also remember that emergence can happen between any part of a system and another: such as between nodes and networks, networks and meta-networks, meta-networks and systems, and/or systems and their surroundings. For formation work, then, what is therefore important is to identify where these kinds of non-direct and non-field relationships exist and what the effects of them might be on our system. We must also consider the emergent levels that are directly above and below the system that we are working with because these will help us to identify further influences on the system itself.

For instance, if one is working with some part of the psychological level, then one should also be familiar with the neurophysiological and integrative-transcendent dynamics that are likely to influence one's focus area. As a more specific example, if we are focusing on identity formation of a group of adolescents, then such an identity might be understood as an emergent relationship with the many CAUs, complexes, personas, et cetera that make up the inner life of each youth. Also, because identity is understood as a psychological phenomenon, we might also want to consider the "lower" physiological influences of each youth as well as the "higher" sociological ones of which they are a part of because both of these are emergently related to our identity focus. As just noted, we should consider what effects each youth's growing integrative-transcendent capacities might have on their own identity. While such influences may not be as clearly defined or well understood as direct connections and fields, identifying their presence and constraining effects may be helpful for us in our formation efforts. The figure below depicts how we might begin to visualize such emergent relationships.

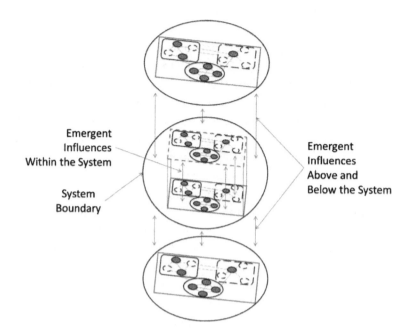

Emergent Influences Within the System

System Boundary

Emergent Influences Above and Below the System

Figure 22. Emergent Relationships.

## Trinitarian Life

The final step in developing this more generalized model is related more specifically to the theology of it. Up until this point, each of the discussions above may be embraced by theists, non-theists, and atheists. For our purposes in theistic spiritual formation, however, we need to additionally assert how God might be conceived of in relation to these various components. Such added reflections will result in a "theistic NFNE model" that can help to further guide our spiritually formative efforts.

In the Process model, which is very similar to this one, God's presence and action is primarily conceived of as an initial aim that acts on each actual occasion in creation. Following the Trinitarian theology outlined throughout this book, such action would essentially capture the influences of the Deity aspect of God's Life. While each community's theology will vary, my own version dictates that God acts much more expansively and non-dualistically within, to, and beyond the NFNE model than even the Process theory asserts. As Deity, God's grace might be understood as externally acting on each part and whole of the system and its surroundings. Every node, connection, field, emergent influence, et cetera, it may be asserted, is continually acted upon by this Deity aspect of God. Immanently, God's incarnational Life seeks to manifest Itself with ever increasing purity throughout the entire system and beyond. Emerging out of God's utterly transcending Non-Being (both within and beyond each component), God continually invites the system to root itself ever more deeply in God's non-existence, or so this Trinitarian theology asserts.

But towards what ends, we might wonder. This is where religion sometimes differs with its secular counterparts. As a theist, I claim that the direction of God's aims and invitations within, to, and beyond creation are always towards attuning to and becoming one with God's Life. According to my own western Christian background, it is a Life of peace, justice, love, truth, goodness, beauty, et cetera (i.e., all positive attributes that have been ascribed to God in this and other religious traditions). In such a theistic spiritual formation framework, then, our work with our system is to seek to partner with these movements towards these aims. Every node, connections, field, et cetera is therefore discerningly worked with via this theistic lens. It is a worldview that asserts that God is not only present within, to, and beyond each component of our system, but that God actively works to spiritually form it in part and as a whole. Our goal as spiritual formators, the very essence and nature of our work, is therefore to discerningly partner with this Trinitarian Life of the system and its formative developments.

## Spiritual Entities: Applications of This Model

These are the basic components of this proposed theistic NFNE model are therefore intended to comprise the core of our craft to better understand and work with the systems to which we are called. This model can help us to identify the essential components and dynamics of any system that we are working with: What are the basic nodes/units of the system? What are the connections among these? What networks, meta-networks, et cetera make up the system and is the system a part of? Are there any emergent relationships (below, at level and/or within the system, and above) that we need to be aware of in order to better understand the dynamics of the system? What are the enduring and non-enduring dynamics that are major influences on and/or within the system? It is from this basic model that we will be deriving some of the core characteristics and principles of deep spiritual formation. However, this model may also seem to be somewhat abstract. As a result, we briefly consider how it may be used in more concrete and practical ways. The following are two examples of such applications. We will also return to this model in the final part of the book as we seek to build a specific program.

### Spiritual Human Beings: Towards an NFNE Model of Human Nature

Shown in the figure below is the application of the theistic NFNE model to the synthesized theological anthropology from the previous part of this book. As we can see, this model begins to capture just how complex human nature is in reality.

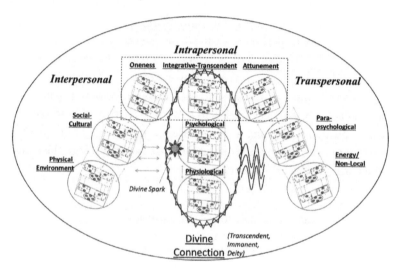

**Figure 23. An NFNE Theological Anthropology.**

While the synthesized theological anthropology can help us to iden-tify some of the major components of human nature, the NFNE model can help us to begin to better understand the complexity of each of these areas as well as how they might be interconnected. Each area, such as the physical environment or the psychological aspect, can be considered to have its own set of nodes, networks, fields, and meta-networks. This model philosophically asserts that these will be enduring to varying degrees. There may also be emergent relationships within each area as well. For instance, one might assert that the relationship between the CAUs of the CAPS model and a person's identity is an emergent one, with each of these levels having their own sets of dynamics, "laws," et cetera and yet being closely interrelated. We can also see that this model asserts that the three core intrapersonal levels (physiological, psychological, and integrative-transcendent) are related to one another in an emergent fashion as are their corresponding interpersonal and transpersonal levels. Overall, this model helps us to more clearly see the immense complexity that is an inherent part of human nature.

The practical implications of this model are significant. Any program wishing to address the "whole person" has quite a task set before them if they are to do this thoroughly. Not only is the current number of identifiable areas rather large, as we have seen, but the dynamics as well as the direct and non-local relationships of each area is quite complex. In order to address the whole person effectively, a formator would need to be well versed in each area, from neuroscience to psychology to integrative-transcendent resources and beyond. In the final part of this book, a case example will be presented to show how one might begin to develop a program that addresses specific areas in light of such complexities. In order to address the whole person, systems of programs, even entire ways of life, are needed across one's lifetime. This complexity in and of itself, it can be argued, is enough to support the need for comprehensive and holistic approaches to spiritual formation as are found in some religious communities.

### Spiritual Organisms: Towards an Entity-Centered View of Creation

As was noted above, without the Trinitarian reflections, the NFNE model could be affirmed by proponents of non-theistic and atheistic worldviews. Such views might include mainstream secular science as well as other religious traditions that do not have a God-concept as a central part of their belief system. However, as this text is written from a western Christian theistic position, some more still needs to be said about a theistic spirituality in relation to organisms more generally.

As we heard with Assagioli, "spiritual development" was conceived as being associated primarily with the growth of super-consciousness. This represents a very limited view of spirituality that confines it to certain developmentally emergent psychological and integrative-transcendent capacities in only one aspect of a person's life, namely the transpersonal capacities. Similarly narrow views of how one can relate to God were found among some of our Christian authors. Augustine, for instance, asserts that the more spiritual aspects of our self are the rational, knowing, and psychological parts while the more physical, sensing aspects are viewed as being the primary source of distortions in our life. Again, we hear a narrow view of what spirituality is and limitations being placed on how we can relate to God. More broadly, such narrow views of spirituality abound. In addition to psychological kinds of knowing or transpersonal abilities it is also often associated with the achieving of self-transcendence.[66]

If we were attempting to apply a theistic NFNE model to organisms more generally, these narrow views of spirituality are challenging because they limit the range of possibilities for how an organism is asserted to relate to God. However, we can note that such limited views come from a more human-centered perspective and do not seek to intentionally reflect on how non-human organisms might relate to God. Nevertheless, we could try to extend these common views to other organisms, but we would only be able to do so to a limited extent due to their already narrow conceptions. For instance, we might take Augustine's and/or Assagioli's views and argue that they equally apply to other species, such as apes, who have achieved psychological emergence. Yet, this still excludes the many more organisms that inhabit our planet and the wider universe(s). The primary theological challenge to such exclusions is the classical Christian doctrine of omnipresence, which asserts that God is actively present within and through all of creation (i.e., the immanent aspect of God). If this is true, then each part of creation is already relating to God, we just now need to find ways of articulating the nature of this relationship.

What is needed, then, is a different and less human-centered (or "anthropomorphic") foundation from which to conceive of all entities as spiritual organisms. In the Process framework, we already have such a foundation with its concept of the initial aim. The basic idea here is that every actual occasion, of which the monistic stuff of the material realm and therefore all organisms are made of, receives direct communication from God. We also have a similar foundation with the Trinitarian theology articulated throughout this book. Here, God's life is asserted to act

66. Conn, "Toward Spiritual Maturity," 356–57; Schneiders, "Theology and Spirituality."

within, to, and beyond every part of this monistic material creation via God's immanent, Deity, and transcendent aspects, respectively.

Building upon the Trinitarian Life foundation and this NFNE model, we now have a way of considering each organism to potentially be "spiritual." In my own framework, this term is used to refer to the extent to which any part of creation is a direct part of God's manifesting Life (immanently, transcendentally, and/or as Deity). Such a relationship or manifestation, as we saw with the NFNE model, can happen for any one of the aspects that were outlined. This theologically means that any organism, regardless of its current node, field, network, emergent capacities, et cetera, can be an intimate part of God's Life as God is continually seeking to manifest within, to, and beyond all of creation. Every organism, then, can be "spiritual" in any moment to the extent that it is directly participating in this manifesting Life. Whether it is a tree, a bee, a human being, an organization, a culture, an ecosystem, a government, a galaxy, an electron, et cetera an entity-centered spirituality asserts that God's infinitely loving Life ever seeks to manifest Itself within, to, and beyond all that is in existence (and even non-existence) in a myriad of diverse ways. Contrary to what some might claim, I assert, no part of this material realm is excluded from the abundant, all-loving, and everywhere present Life of God. Every single entity can therefore be "spiritual" by participating fully in the very Source of its own existence.

Does this mean, however, that each entity relates to God in the same way? Are single-celled organisms, for instance, conscious of God in the same ways that humans are? Of course not. Based upon emergence theories, we can assert that God's infinitely diverse and complex Life relates to each entity fully in accordance with the capacities that it currently has. For physiologically emergent organisms, God will be present with them via their inner biological dynamics, through the relationships that they have with their physical environments, and by the energetic and non-local connections that are acting upon them. For psycho-socially emergent entities, God will additionally relate to them via their social-cultural contexts, the inner psychic dynamics that they have, and the parapsychological phenomena that they are privy to. At the integrative-transcendent levels, these entities will additionally have the capacities to relate to God via the experiences of oneness, transcendence, inner integration, and attunement with larger parts of creation. As an entity or organism emerges and develops, in other words, God's Life continues to be fully present and available to them in accordance with their current capacities; i.e., to the extent that they are currently able to relate to God's infinitely complex Life.

One of the wonderful experiences of being human is that many of us are afforded the opportunity to experience God's abundant life through each one of these three emergent levels across our lifetime. As an in-vitro egg, our psychological life has yet to emerge so our relationship with God is one that is purely at the physiological levels. At this stage, our spirituality is one that is therefore more purely related to our biological processes as we develop, our relationship with the womb, and possibly the energies and non-local influences to which we are subjected. Here, our relationship with God might be asserted to primarily happen with the immanent aspect of God.

Continuing to grow, however, consciousness dawns upon the pages of our life and suddenly we can relate to God in new and psychologically profound ways. From the inner dreams, thoughts, and motivations that we experience internally and non-locally to the interpersonal relationships that are a part of shaping our lives, spirituality takes on a new shape and form for our life. Many people find that their relationship to God as Deity flourishes with this emergent level. Finally, as our nature allows and as we work intentionally towards it, sparks of integrative and transcendent experiences begin to impact us. Here, our spirituality again transforms as we connect more deeply in oneness and attunement with the world that is around and beyond us and we come to relate more intimately to God's transcendent aspect with awe and wonder.

Throughout it all, this spiritual entity theory asserts, can we be fully present to God's ever manifesting Trinitarian Life. Such Presence, following the theistic NFNE model, does not happen solely at the level of the organism as a whole, but also each of its respective parts. Our organs, for example, can be asserted to each have their own spirituality as God works to foster their life and vitality individually as well as the health and functioning of the body as a whole. These entity-centered views of spirituality also claim that such a holistically growing spirituality is not narrowly confined to the human species, as the human-centered views above assert. Rather spirituality is available to every entity—and every part of each entity—with which we co-inhabit the material and non-material realms.

However, this does not automatically guarantee that all is well on our planet as we know so very well. A true Heaven on Earth would be one where God's Life is fully manifesting always and everywhere and, I believe, this is God's desire for this monistic material realm. Nevertheless, as noted repeatedly in the synthesized model, distortions abound for us humans as well as for our world. Parasitic organisms that destroy themselves by killing their hosts, for me, are one example of such distortions to God's Life. They are not only destructive towards the flourishing of the lives to which they are related but also to themselves and their own species. Are such ends in harmony with the Life and will of an all loving God? I do not personally think so.

As a part of the Trinitarian theology laid out at the beginning of the section for the synthesized model, I asserted that free will extends to the whole of this material realm. For this more universal spiritual entity theory, this would mean that such free will is an integral part of the monistic material stuff out of which all life in this material realm is asserted to emerge from. Such is integral to the Process model as each actual occasion is free to choose between God's initial aim and the subjective aims to which it is subjected. At every level and in every part, then, distortions may enter in as each part of the material universe is free to choose in each moment the extent to which it will be a part of God's Life that is seeking to manifest within, to, and beyond it. Distortions therefore are asserted to have the potential to enter into our lives and our world at anytime and anywhere, at least in relation to monistic material sources.

Overall, then, a more fully entity-centered view of spirituality is one which asserts that each entity and its various parts possess the ability for a direct relationship with and manifestation of the Trinitarian Life of God. These are an expanded view of the more human-centered views described at the beginning of this section which located such a spiritual relationship largely in the psychological, transpersonal, and integrative-transcendent aspects of human personhood. Instead, each entity truly can be spiritual at every step of its developmental journey to the extent that it is truly a part of God's manifesting Life. Nonetheless, distortions abound as free will is asserted to be yet another inherent attribute of the monistic stuff out of which all material entities emerge. By combining the NFNE model with our Trinitarian theology, we therefore see possibilities for re-envisioning how spirituality might be conceived of more broadly.

## Limits and Adaptations

Before continuing on to some of the general characteristics and guidelines that the theistic NFNE model might be able to provide us with, we must first note a few of the limitations and adaptations of using this model. First, this is only intended to be an inductively abstracted model that may be used to initially guide a practitioner in their own theory building processes. It may be used to help ensure that one does not overlook any of the major components or dynamics (i.e., nodes, fields, emergent relationships, et cetera). However, once a formator has chosen a specific area to focus on, a process which will be discussed in the next chapter, they still have the task of learning about the details of that area. A first limitation of this model, then, is that it is only intended as a general guide and an initial starting point.

Another major limitation and necessary adaptation is that it can be cumbersome to apply in practice because of its complexity and abstractness. When developing an actual program, practitioners may not find it necessary or helpful to identify each of the major components of the NFNE model. If one were to teach the concept of the Trinity to a youth group, for instance, it might be helpful to identify each concept as a node and note the various connections between the three persons or aspects of the Trinity. However, the religious educator might not find it helpful to try and identify fields, emergent relationships, et cetera. As a result, this model should only be used to the extent that it provides useful insight and guidance.

Overall, then, like any other model or theory that one draws from, the NFNE model should be used with caution. Every theory has within them the inherent limitations and biases of their creators and we therefore need to be very discerning when we apply them to our own applications.[67] Any theory should only be used to the extent that it helps us to better partner with God's formative Life in our midst and therefore improve the quality and effectiveness of our programs.

---

67. For a more detailed discussion on theory building and their limitations, see Kyle, *Living Spiritual Praxis*, Appendix B.

## DEEP SPIRITUAL FORMATION (DSF)

Based on the theistic NFNE model, we are now in a position to reflect on the human organism and transformation in more general ways. Our goal here will be to highlight some of the basic characteristics and core principles that can help to guide our formative efforts. Again, we have embarked on these more abstracted reflections in an attempt to generalize the synthesized theological anthropology proposed above. By having a more universal model, we hope to outline some of the core principles that we may follow when working with any one or more of the nine different aspects of the synthesized theological anthropology and/or with other aspects of our world.

## Basic Characteristics and Guidelines for Working with Entities

As a part of the compiled model for our modern science authors, we listed some of the basic characteristics of human nature as being well-ordered, malleable, and having enduring parts. We similarly find these characteristics to be illustrated clearly by the basic components of the NFNE model. However, there are also other basic characteristics that have emerged as we have progressed through the development of this model. According to these reflections, there are at least seven such basic characteristics of entities that will be helpful for us to remember in our formative work with our communities.

First, *entities are well-organized.* Nodes, connections, fields, networks, and meta-networks create definite order and structure to an entity. Such systems may be highly organized in a hierarchical fashion thereby creating processes within the organism that contribute to its functioning and well-being. For humans, at the physiological level, examples might include homeostatic processes while at the psychological level these may be constructs of self that one creates and lives by.[68] In Maslow's framework, we learned of the basic needs of the human person being arranged in a distinctive hierarchy that unfolds across one's life.[69]

Regardless of what aspect of human nature we are working with, then, one of our tasks is to identify what some the existing hierarchies and structures that are present. Some of this organization may serve the

68. Rogers, *Client-Centered Therapy*, 191.
69. Maslow, *Motivation and personality*, 97–98.

organism well, while others may be hindering or even damaging its over-all health and well-being. When deciding what formative actions to take, then, we must consider what these enduring structures in the system are and how to modify them if necessary.

Second, and in contrast with the first, *entities are also malleable and in a constant state of change.* Whereas the first characteristic asserts that entities do have "being" (i.e., enduring qualities), we are also continually "becoming." Nodes themselves may come and go as might the connec-tions that they form with other parts of the system. As we saw with the CAPS model, the CAUs and their corresponding "if-then" dynamics may change from one situation to another. Similarly, neurons might also form temporary connections with one another but if these are not repeatedly stimulated they can fade away from the system as we heard with the Heb-bian rule.

In our formative work, then, we must seek to understand at least two sets of change dynamics. First, we must be aware of the kinds of nodes, connections, networks, field effects, et cetera that come and go for the anthropological aspect(s) that we are working with as well as what the effects are of their temporary presence. Second, we can also seek to understand how to help or hinder their appearance and influence on our communities. By working more intentionally with these non-enduring and ever-changing dynamics, we should be able to help our constituents to progress in their growing spiritual life with the Triune God.

Third, *entities are asserted to seek their own unity, integration, well-being, growth, self-actualization, et cetera.* As a unified whole, such as a dis-tinct society in the Process framework, organisms (and even each of their parts) possess their own directionality and drives. Evolutionary history, and the continually increasing complexity that has emerged throughout, is a clear example of such self-care. As we heard with our geneticists, species are asserted to seek the health and well-being of their own gene pool. The ego, in the psychoanalytic scheme, works for the safety and preservation of the psychological system.[70] Similarly, self-actualization was claimed to be a central psychological need by humanistic theorists such as Maslow and Rogers.[71] Overall, then, entities are asserted to in-trinsically work towards their own health, vitality, and well-being.[72]

---

70. Mischel et al., *Introduction to Personality*, 161.

71. Maslow, *Motivation and personality*, 68; Mischel et al., *Introduction to Person-ality*, 307; Rogers, *Client-Centered Therapy*, 193, 195, 487, 491, 507.

72. Ryan and Deci, "Self-Determination Theory," 656.

In the work of human transformation, then, we must be attentive to the goals and directions that the people, or the aspects that we are focused on, are headed towards. Again, some of these directions may be distorted but many of them will also likely be connected to some to degree in God's will for their lives. As a result, much of the formative work that we do with people must come from a continual stance of discerned listening. We must also discerningly trust in these movements as they work, as this characteristic asserts, for their greater good. So much of the work of human transformation lies beyond our abilities to control or even guide. We must therefore trust in these integrating and self-actualizing movements as they do seem to be an integral part of an entity's make up.

Fourth, and again in contrast with the previous one, *entities are permeable, being fundamentally shaped by both internal and external influences.* While an entity and its many parts consist of their own holistic integrity, their boundaries are also highly permeable. This characteristic, then, is most focused on the connections that are made between nodes and networks, as well as with the field effects within which entities find themselves to be in. Perhaps the most obvious and often noted of all the characteristics, who we are and how we become moment-by-moment is directly influenced intrapersonally, interpersonally, and transpersonally according to our synthesized model of human nature. These interactions provide feedback and help to guide the paths that we progress along.[73] From innate drives and processes to social learning and conditioning, the inner and external boundaries of organisms allow for it to continually adapt to changing influences.[74] As Maslow writes, "Certainly there are almost no closed systems within the organism. Within the organism everything does actually relate with everything else, if only sometimes in the most tenuous and distant fashion."[75] It is when an entity attempts to deny such influences, Rogers asserts, that it eventually does so to its own detriment.[76] In a permeable fashion, then, organisms and their various aspects are greatly influenced by the connections that they have with those around them, locally and non-locally.

---

73. Wilson, *On Human Nature,* 76.

74. Dollard and Miller, *Personality and Psychotherapy,* 88; Maslow, *Motivation and personality,* 28, 323; Mischel et al., *Introduction to Personality,* 259; Rogers, *Client-Centered Therapy,* 483; Ryan and Deci, "Self-Determination Theory," 659.

75. Maslow, *Motivation and personality,* 319.

76. Rogers, *Client-Centered Therapy,* 510.

As it relates to the work of human transformation, knowing and working with these connections becomes key. Three important guidelines are important here. First, we must be aware of the range of influences that affect the person or aspect that we are working with. We must also be aware of how these connections shape this person or aspect. Finally, it will be very helpful to know whether and to what extent we can alter these connections and the influences that they are having. For enduring connections, pursuing these will be much easier than it will be for non-enduring ones that have a temporary but significant impact because enduring connections are generally more predictable. Nevertheless, such intrapersonal, interpersonal, and transpersonal connections must be a central part of our formative work.

Similarly, *the historical location of entities* is a fifth important characteristic. As we saw above, for the Process, Neurophysiological, and CAPS models, nodes and networks only endure because they have been repeatedly reinforced across time and situations. Such enduring dynamics are therefore given shape by the history of recurrences that they have been a part of. Biologically, these are the evolutionary adaptations that have been selected and adaptively passed on and reaffirmed by each successive generation.[77] Behaviorally, these are the enduring schemas, CAU networks, and stimulus-response mechanisms that have worked well across the history of our lifespan.[78] Physiological, psychological, and integrative-transcendent capacities emerge, as we saw, in historical dialogue with the previous levels upon which they are causally founded. These histories are therefore important because they are what largely determine the enduring nodes and networks that shape our spiritual being and becoming.

Knowing these histories is therefore essential for the work of human transformation. Such knowledge can provide us with insights into the kinds of enduring nodes and networks that we are likely to encounter. They may also help us to anticipate how a person, and their various aspects, might develop across time and respond to different situations. In essence, then, such historical entity insights can provide us with useful predictive knowledge, though we must caution against taking such histories too literally. In other words, as was just pointed out, phenomena are only enduring because they are repeated across time and space and this has the potential to change from one moment or generation to the next.

77. Mischel et al., *Introduction to Personality*, 140; Westen et al., "Psychoanalytic Approaches to Personality," 74.

78. Dollard and Miller, *Personality and Psychotherapy*, 181.

Sixth, *entities are developmental by nature and nurture.* The emergence theories we reviewed most strongly supported this attribute as one level is only able to take shape based upon the previous level. Evolutionary history, it was asserted, has had increasing complexity that has dawned upon our planet. Similarly, we can note the developmental phases that humans traverse through from cradle to grave. Such developmental unfolding, as we have heard, is supported by predispositions, such as genetic expression, but also by the contexts in which we grow in. Working together, nature and nurture therefore play a significant role in an entity's developing life.

For formators, such a developmental unfolding is important to remember because it can help to determine what we do and how we go about it. For instance, we would not expect a new born infant to comprehend the more intricate details of Shakespeare. Nor should we expect every person to possess integrative-transcendent capacities if these are indeed developmental as has been asserted in accordance with emergence theories. Each aspect outlined in our synthesized model of human nature might therefore be viewed through such developmental lenses. For our work, then, we should be cognizant of the developmental stages that each aspect has been observed to progress through. Doing so will help us to further refine and hone our approaches that are more appropriate to the aspects we are working with.

Finally, and directly related to the previous one, a seventh characteristic of entities is that *they only possess certain limited capacities.* For instance, write Dollard and Miller, "A parrot can learn to imitate words but not to become a great thinker."[79] While this is an obvious point, it is one that is crucial to remember. For the transpersonal aspects, it was theorized that there potentially exist an infinite number of connections that any given organism might make with both material and non-material realms. Similarly, the Process concept of cumulative penetration asserted the potential for each actual occasion to be influenced by all occasions of the previous generation. With views such as this, it can be tempting to think that an organism possesses an unlimited number of capacities through these infinite connections. However, the possibility for such unlimited capacities does not match with our lived experiences as Dollard and Miller rightly point out in my own view. Even though it could be argued that the parrot has the potential to access the thoughts of great

79. Ibid., 101.

thinkers via transpersonal mediums, it does not seem to match with our experiences with parrots in general—at least they do not seem to share these with us if they do transpersonally access such thoughts. Additionally, even if the parrot can access such thoughts, as far as we might be able to tell from its neurophysiology, it only has the cognitive capacities to process them to a limited extent. Overall, the point is for us to affirm that each organism, as well as each of its aspects, only possesses certain and limited capacities that have historically developed and emerged. For our work, this is again important because we can only formatively engage with the capacities that a person or community currently has rather than the ones that we might wish that they had.

## The Nature of DSF

With these characteristics and guidelines in place, it will also be helpful to briefly reflect on the nature of deep spiritual formation in light of the NFNE model. To help us with these reflections, we turn to the field of education and their notions of deep learning. By bringing these insights into dialogue with our discussions here, we hope to develop a greater understanding of the nature of DSF and how we might begin to foster it more generally.

In learning science and instructional design literature, there are at least five characteristics of deep learning that are given, as shown in the figure below. First, students should be able to articulate the details and nuances of the concepts or skills that they are learning about in scaffolded, critically reflective, and metacognitive ways.[80] These concepts or skills should also be able to be engaged from multiple perspectives both within the discipline and among classmates.[81] Thirdly, students should have the ability to adapt and apply course material to multiple and diverse contexts.[82] Research into cognition has also shown that deeper learning is more likely to occur when the concepts or skills are more directly related to a student's own life, experiences, and already existing knowledge.[83] Finally, such learning transpires when it is engaged repeat-

---

80. Sawyer, "Introduction," Kindle Locations 595–600, 776–84, 909–15.

81. Ibid., Kindle Locations 793–804; Slavin, *Educational Psychology*, 12.

82. Linn, "The Knowledge Integration Perspective on Learning and Instruction," Kindle Locations 9300–303, 9309–12, 9316–19.

83. Sawyer, "Introduction," Kindle Locations 595–600.

edly across time in spiral learning ways.[84] With each of these characteristics present in educational systems, it is asserted, deeper learning is more likely to unfold.

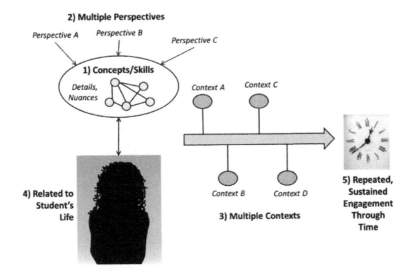

**Figure 24. Characteristics of Deep Learning.**

These five characteristics of deep learning can become the basis for helping us to better understand the nature of DSF in light of the NFNE model. The inductive assertion being made here is that since education deals more primarily with cognitive capacities and development, which were a part of the fundamental basis for the NFNE model, then theories of learning should have the capacity to be inductively generalized. While more general research is needed to verify that this is indeed the case, we will be moving forward based upon this assumption in order to see what insights it may provide us. Let us therefore take each one in turn.

First, *deep spiritual formation results in some significant change to the system.* This may seem like an obvious point, but the question that we really need to ask ourselves is whether our interventions really will have a tangible impact on the people and communities that we are working with. In education, this means helping students to better understand the concepts and skills that they are learning with greater detail. In close

---

84. Bransford et al., "Foundations and Opportunities for an Interdisciplinary Science of Learning," Kindle Locations 1398–1405; Collins, "Cognitive Apprenticeship," Kindle Locations 2469–80; Richey et al., *Instructional Design Knowledge Base*, 78.

relationships, this might mean helping couples to simultaneously move in the direction of greater self-differentiation as well as attunement. In organizational development, this might mean working with teams to better understand their roles in the developing organization and to carry them out with greater efficiency.

As viewed through the NFNE model, this essentially means increasing the complexity of the various components in the system. This might entail increasing or decreasing the number of nodes or connections. It might mean adding to or detracting from the fields that are active within the system. Or it could result in the creation or elimination of new networks, meta-networks, or even emergent levels. Overall, deep spiritual formation should result in some kind of significant change to the system, particularly in terms of its complexity, dynamics, and structure. The kinds of change sought should therefore be clearly articulated by the formator when designing their spiritual formation program.

Second, *deep spiritual formation should engage the system in multiple ways.* For education, this means exploring a topic from multiple perspectives. More generally, it means approaching the formative work from a multitude of ways. Studies of western Christian spiritual formation literature reveal a "praxis" approach to this field that entails at least the following elements: knowledge, reflection, action, and stillness.[85] Each of these is essentially a different avenue through which we can engage with human systems at the individual level. We can provide knowledge and insights that help our constituents to better understand the change that we are working with them to make. We can help them to reflect on their lived experiences in transformative ways. We can walk side-by-side with them as they engage in experiential activities and projects. Finally, we can use spiritual practices and recreational activities that help them to find the rest and silence that is needed for deeper change to unfold in our lives and our communities.

As it relates to the NFNE model, this would mean working with each of the main system components in a myriad of ways. Here, we can analyze the range of influences and connections that are available to us to impact the system through. By knowing these avenues, we can and should utilize the full range of possibilities that we have available to us given our limits such as time, resources, et cetera. Such diverse approaches can therefore help to foster lasting transformation because it is through them

85. Kyle, *Living Spiritual Praxis*, 144.

that we can have a greater impact on the system. These multiple channels can thereby increase the number of influences that can affect change. Deep spiritual formation should therefore seek to use multiple ways of fostering change in a system.

Third, *deep spiritual formation should be engaged in multiple contexts, particularly those in which our constituents are most likely and often to find themselves in.* In education, as we heard, this meant that students should have the ability to apply course material to multiple contexts. For a couple, this might mean having them practice communication skills and conflict mediation activities at home and not just while on a couple's retreat. The idea here is that if we really want the people and communities that we are working with to be able to integrate the desired changes into their own lives, then they will need to engage them in contexts that are similar to the ones that we are hoping to have an impact in. More ideally, of course, is that they would engage in the transforming activities as a part of their normal life outside of the spiritual formation program. In addition, the more contexts that people engage in the transforming activities, the more likely they will be to adapt them to changing circumstances.

From the perspective of the NFNE model, this essentially is a work that is similar to the previous point. By having people and communities engage in transforming activities in diverse contexts, particularly those most related to their daily lives, we are helping them to sustain and adapt to those changes. Such diverse engagements will likely, but not necessarily, utilize multiple avenues of influences. But, more importantly, it will also provide the support and empowerment that they will need in order to adapt the program's intended changes to their daily lives thereby increasing the depth of transformation. The more that a system intentionally works to adapt these transformations for diverse contexts, the more likely will the depth of change be for that system. As a result, these theories assert, nurturing deep spiritual formation necessarily entails engagement in multiple and diverse contexts thereby fostering one's adaptive abilities.

Fourth, *deep spiritual formation must be directly connected to a system's already existing structures, dynamics, et cetera.* For education, this meant that students were to relate the concepts or skills to their own lives, experiences, and prior knowledge. In essence, this means that we must take the time to learn extensively and deeply about the people and communities that we are working with. Following this, our spiritual formation programs must then be designed to work with our constituents from where they are currently at. While this might sound like an obvious point, one time-saving temptation in formation work is to simply engage with our communities with little to no pre-analyses or reflections on who they are or what they might actually need. We might also fall into the trap, particularly in working with youth, of assuming that they are very similar to ourselves and we therefore design a program that is appealing to and appropriate for us personally with little relevance and connection to each youth's background and current capacities.

Reflecting on this through the lens of the NFNE model and its applications, we must remember that each entity and system has its own set of capacities, dynamics, structures, et cetera. Not only will these be different from our own capacities, they will also change over time. As a result, great care must continually be given to where the system is currently at in terms of its internal and external influences and dynamics. As we do this, we will find that our formative work is far more influential because it will be designed to work with the actual state of the system as best as we can understand and conceive of it. Deep spiritual formation therefore requires a primary focus on the system's current and ever-changing structures, dynamics, et cetera.

Finally, *deep spiritual formation must be engaged repeatedly with increasing depth.* As we heard, deeper learning transpires when it is engaged frequently across time in spiral learning ways. Any new skills or change that we work with must be engaged regularly or we are likely to lose them. This point is inherent in some of the others above. As we engage with our groups in multiple ways and in multiple contexts, there is the opportunity for sustained engagement. Such engagement, however, is not a repetition of the exact same activities, material, et cetera over and over again. Contrary to behaviorist-like claims, rote memorization activities have actually been found to decrease retention of material.[86] We can think about our own experiences of doing monotonous tasks and the boredom, mindlessness, and day-dreaming that they can foster. The ineffective dynamic here is not a greater or deeper engagement with the task but rather a dulling of it. Deep transformation, on the other hand, should foster an ever increasing engagement with the changes.

Set prayers, such as the Lord's Prayer for instance, should not be mindlessly recited with little commitment of one's being to it. Rather, each recitation should foster a greater connection between one and God as well as between themselves and the world around them. Such depth can come about in a spiral way, where we think more deeply each time

86. Matlin, *Cognition*, 174.

about the words and their connection to our own lives. Such is the nature of deep spiritual formation when it is engaged repeatedly.

From the NFNE model's perspective, this essentially entails engaging the system over and over again. It is one of working with the inherent malleability of the system over time to foster the changes that one is seeking. A review of western Christian personal transformation literature shows that human change takes time and continual engagement.[87] As a result, deep spiritual formation requires that we expend the repeated time and energy needed to foster the changes that we are working towards.

Taken collectively, these five characteristics of deep spiritual formation can help to guide our formative efforts. Adapted from educational literature on deep learning, they can provide signposts for us as we seek to design and implement our programs. They can also help us to better understand the kinds of transformation that we should be working towards. For in the end, this author asserts, deep spiritual formation is what God is proactively working to manifest in our midst.

## CLOSING REFLECTIONS

In this chapter, we have pursued more abstracted and generalized reflections. The goal was to develop models, characteristics, and guidelines that we might use to help us in our spiritually forming endeavors. While the resulting theistic NFNE model and its accompanying insights may have limited applications to our more detailed and localized work, it can nevertheless be used as both a starting point and touchstone for us. However, it did result in a much more complex view of human nature than was seen in the previous chapter with the synthesized theological anthropology. The challenge that now lies before us is to explore how we might actually begin to use both these synthesized and generalized theories for concrete program development. In the next and final chapter, we will be doing just this. We will be looking at how to adapt such models for our own spiritual formation systems and ensure that they are indeed an insightful and centrally guiding part of our craft.

---

87. Kyle, *Sacred Systems*, 280–84.

# CHAPTER 5

# Spiritual Groundedness

## Moving from Theory to Practice

THESE SYNTHESIZED AND MORE generalized models can provide us with a helpful overview of some of the different areas and dynamics related to the human person and our transformation. In essence, they are a broad map of the landscape for working with individuals and their own growth and development in God. As such, these models may be used to think about the kinds of programs that a community should have in place if they are seeking to develop a holistic approach to personal spiritual formation.[1]

For instance, looking at the proposed synthesized theological anthropology, we can use this as a guide to ensure that our ministries are addressing all aspects. At the physiological level, we can develop programs that help to teach about and foster healthy eating habits, body care, and exercise. Psychologically, we should work with our communities to help them develop positive self-esteem, strong emotional intelligence, and other factors that contribute to the flourishing of God's Life in the psyche. To the extent possible, our spiritual formation programs can help to foster great integration and self-transcendence. We can also look to our models for insights into what interpersonal and transpersonal capacities need to be addressed. We might also use them to help us to generally reflect on the distortions that are present within our communities and where we might begin to focus our efforts around these. In short,

---

1. For relational and communal spiritual formation programs, additional and/or alternative models will be needed.

our theological anthropologies can serve as general guides for evaluating personal transformation in our congregations and classrooms.

However, as was noted in the section on the challenges and limits of constructing a theological anthropology, such generalized models can only go so far in helping to guide our program design and development. If we are to create specific programs that are spiritually formative for one or more of the nine components of the synthesized model presented herein, then much more information and detail will be needed if we are to base our programs on this model. While the generalized model from the previous chapter can provide us with some greater insights and detail, more is still needed. Such is the aim of this final chapter, to explore how we might further expand upon our models so that we can develop our formation programs in light of them.

Of course, using such models as a central guide is not the only way to create a program or design a class. In fact, we need not use models at all for our program development work. There are at least four other methods by which we may develop our spiritual formation programs. We will therefore briefly review these alternative methods that we have available in this part so that we may turn to these if the need arises. However, one the core aims of this book is to explore methods for intentionally and directly using our theological anthropologies in program development. As we shall see, such methods are termed "Strong Model-Based Methods," and we will be following these in the sections that follow. In order to help us to see how such methods may be used, a detailed case example will be presented. By the end of this final chapter, we should have a clearer idea of how we might begin to develop our own strong model-based programs using the theological anthropologies that we have synthesized.

## FOUNDATIONS FOR DEVELOPING A STRONG MODEL-BASED SYSTEM

In order to better understand how we might begin to use our theological anthropologies as a more centrally guiding construct in our formation programs, it will be helpful to better understand the nature of this work. In the brief sections that follow, we will be laying a foundation so that we might work towards developing strong model-based methods. After introducing the formation framework, which is a theoretical construct that is insightful for better understanding the nature of our work, we will then review five different program development methods that are commonly used. With one of these being model-based methods, we will explore this in more detail. These sections will therefore lay the foundational groundwork for the case example that is presented below.

## The Formation Framework

At its heart, the work of spiritual formation is essentially a feedback system.[2] Feedback Theory has had wide ranging applications in such fields as engineering, theater and acting, and neuroscience-based approaches to formation.[3] In its most fundamental and simplified essence, "feedback processes," write professors of psychology Charles Carver and Michael Scheier, "involve the control and regulation of certain values within a system."[4] It is referred to as "Feedback Theory" because it is based on the assumption and/or observations that in order for a system to maintain or achieve these "certain values" it must have some way of monitoring its current values in relation to these desired ones. A very simple feedback loop may be pictured as follows:

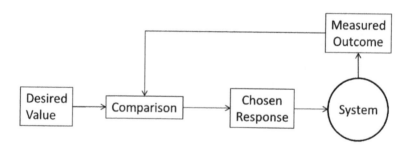

Figure 25. A Simplified Feedback Loop.

In education, for instance, there may be certain objectives that a teacher discerns are appropriate for her or his students. Based in part

---

2. For discussions on the nature of feedback and its application to human systems, see such texts as Carver and Scheier, chap. 2. For similar discussions on this section, see: Kyle, *Living Spiritual Praxis*, 237–40; Kyle, *Sacred Systems*, 6–8.

3. For examples of texts in these fields, see Bilgrave and Deluty, "Stanislavski's Acting Method and Control Theory"; Dispenza, *Evolve Your Brain*, 292, 303, 326, 439–42; Franklin et al., *Feedback Control of Dynamic Systems*.

4. Carver and Scheier, *On the Self-Regulation of Behavior*, 10.

upon understandings of cognitive development, or other theories of human learning, she or he may then develop lesson plans of activities that are intended to help students to move towards these objectives. As most of us know (sometimes regretfully) educational classes do not stop here because the teacher is also expected to assess each student's progress. Tests, quizzes, group projects, research papers, reflection assignments, et cetera may all be utilized towards these ends. Diagrammatically, this educational feedback process might be envisioned to be something similar to the following:

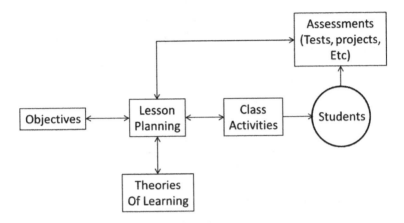

**Figure 26. Feedback Processes in Education.**

In ministerial spiritual formation, we can likewise find there to be a basic feedback architecture that may be used in our field. Indeed, education may also be viewed as a spiritually formative activity.[5] Whether we're working with individuals, relationships, or communities, there is some set of ideals that we discern an invitation to partner with the Spirit to work towards. Given these goals, we then need to discern a set of approaches that we believe will help our constituents to grow towards/in them. As we engage in this formative work, we then need to continually monitor and evaluate the progress that is being made in relation to these ideals. This is the essence of all feedback loops. We can therefore see that the field of spiritual formation may be fundamentally approached as a feedback-oriented discipline.

Given this, we can propose a more systematic "Formation Framework" for spiritual formation that is primarily based upon

5. For an example of such views, see Downs, *Teaching for Spiritual Growth.*

feedback theory and its basic architecture. The figure below captures this formation framework. In the sections that follow, we will briefly explore each of these aspects of this framework in relation to our work in spiritual formation.

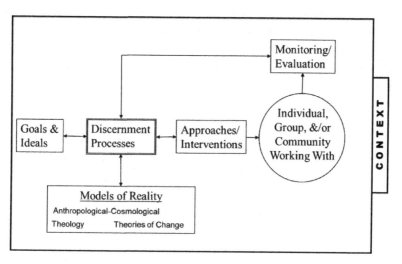

Figure 27. The Formation Framework.

## Context

Context is, as we saw with the various models of human nature, one of the most important aspects of any spiritual formation program. As we have heard repeatedly throughout this book, when we are working with people and communities, it is very important to note the many diverse contextual influences that have and continue to shape them both historically as well as locally (i.e., in both time and space). Such influences might involve the close relationships that one has or the socio-economic influences that surround them. It is therefore essential in developing spiritual formation programs that we understand these contextual factors in the development and implementation of our programs.

## Models of Reality

As we have also seen through this book, models of reality are the theories that have been developed to provide greater insight and understanding into some of the dynamics that we will be formatively working with. In particular, there are at least three specific set of such models that are important for spiritual formation work: anthropological-cosmological, theological, and theories of change. Each of these models of reality essentially strives to explain the nature of life, the cosmos, the Divine, and human transformation. These models form, as we shall see, a foundation of knowledge out of which spiritual formation systems might emerge in dialogue with. Let us briefly consider each of these in turn as a way of recapping what we have already seen so intimately with the models of human nature that we have explored and worked with.

## ANTHROPOLOGICAL-COSMOLOGICAL ASPECTS

These aspects are fundamentally concerned with describing, explaining, modeling, et cetera the dynamics and complex interrelationships within creation. I term these aspects "anthropological-cosmological" because these models of reality often seek to detail both what happens within and among humans (anthropology), the happenings of creation as a whole (cosmology), and the intimate interconnections between the two. At the level of the individual, these would include the views of human nature that one has. For relationships, these models might describe what intimate relationships are and the complex interpersonal dynamics that accompany them. These models will also often include discussions of other non-material realms of the cosmos, angels and demons, et cetera as we have seen. Anthro-cosmological models therefore seek to explain the nature of life as it is being lived here on earth in relation to the wider cosmos of which we are all a part of.

## THEOLOGICAL ASPECTS

While the anthro-cosmological aspects might detail the dynamics of individuals, relationships, communities, and creation as a whole, they do not necessarily or directly address God's relationship to them. We saw this with our more secularly-oriented modern science models of human nature. We may therefore consider theological aspects to be quite distinct from anthro-cosmological models. Theological models are taken to address the essence and nature of the Divine and intentionally seek to describe how God is present to creation and how creation relates to God.

Even though not all spiritual formation systems might explicitly address these theological aspects, such as with "non-theistic" systems which do not have a God-concept as a central part of them, I assert that all of them inherently have a theology contained within them for the beliefs that there is no God or that God is not a central part of formation work are still theological claims. We must therefore be as explicit as possible in identifying the implicit theologies that undergird our spiritual formation systems.

## Theories of Change

Finally, we come to what is one of the most important parts of any spiritual formation program. Spiritual formation is fundamentally concerned with fostering some kind of intentional change in creation. In order to do this, however, it helps to have an understanding of how such changes occur and the processes by which they come about. Any models that address this are what I call "Theories of Change." Often, they flow directly from the anthro-cosmological models that one has. However, since spiritual formation is fundamentally a field that is focused on nurturing change, I assert that it should be given a specific and separate focus. These models are, therefore, a central part of what informs the discernment of what practices, actions, and guidance to offer to the persons, relationships, and communities that we are working with. These theories of change are therefore a necessary and integral part of any effective spiritual formation program.

### Ideals & Goals

Most every spiritual formation program has a set of ideals and goals that it is actively seeking to work towards. Most, if not all, spiritual formation programs that I have both learned about and worked with over the years have some set of ideals, transformations, et cetera that its practices, theologies, worldviews, and communities are intentionally striving after. Some of these goals may be anthro-cosmologically based, such as emotional well-being, relational vitality, or transpersonal development. Others may be more theologically and religiously centered, such as seeking after a more Christ-centered life. One of the keys to this category is therefore that each community is able to articulate the goals that they are explicitly working towards and to then tangibly move in those directions. It is therefore important to identify, as clearly as possible, what these horizons include.

## Approaches

This is perhaps the most obvious of all of the categories. Every spiritual formation system seeks to bring about intentional, positive change through the use of specific approaches. Some of these approaches may be practices that nurture the general transformation of the individual, relationship, or community or they may be very focused, such as meditative techniques that are intended to bring about specific states of consciousness. These approaches, when utilized effectively, are chosen as a result of one's discernment processes and are intended to move one's constituency towards the intended goals. It therefore behooves us to know the full range of approaches to transformation that are available to us for the specific kinds of spiritual formation that we are seeking to foster.

## Monitoring & Assessment Techniques

As we have heard, the whole field of spiritual formation is one that inherently sets out to bring about some sort of intentional transformation. In order to do this, ministers must therefore have some ways of monitoring and evaluating the progress (or lack of), that their individuals, relationships, and communities are making. Doing so enables spiritual formators to provide better direction to their constituents and to continually modify their approaches in well informed and clearly discerned ways. In addition, since discernment is inherently rooted in knowledge (from this realm or beyond), this further establishes the need for effective techniques for observing and evaluating the Life of the Spirit within and to the moment-by-moment dynamics of the people that we are working with. We must therefore have ways of monitoring the progress that our communities are making.

## Discernment & Ongoing Implementation

Just as lesson planning is for an educator, spiritual discernment should be the centerpiece for all formative endeavors in theistic ministry. For instance, once a community lays out a set of goals to work towards, they must then develop ways of discerning how to go about moving towards them. Spiritual discernment is absolutely essential in this, I assert, because each community's journey towards the ideals is as unique as they are. How does one know, for instance, which practices to use for each person, relationship, et cetera at different stages of their journey? How does one know if the program they have designed is indeed what God's formative Trinitarian Life is seeking to do at this time, in this place, with one's community? I assert that spiritual formators must therefore develop methods and approaches to discern and answer such questions. They must therefore do so as they seek to guide their flock along the spiritual path ever moving in harmony with the unending and all-pervasive movements of God.

## The Framework & Systematic Program Development

This formation framework seems to capture many of the essential aspects of any spiritual formation system. It is intended to provide a more systematic way of exploring program development at any of the levels that we formatively work with (personal, relational, communal, et cetera.). From a systematic perspective, a well-designed program is one where each of these framework elements is directly related to one another. In other words, there is a clear and direct alignment between the ideals that the program is working towards, the approaches that one chooses to pursue these aims, the models of reality that inform the design, the assessments that one uses, and significant and relevant contextual factors. Likewise, any discernment processes that one uses should draw from each of these elements in both the design and implementation phases. Diagrammatically, we might think of these systematic connections as shown in the figure below.

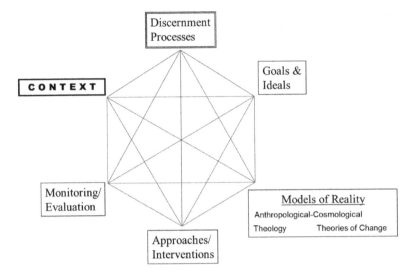

**Figure 28. A Systematic View of Spiritual Formation.**

Here, we can see how each part of the framework should be inter-connected with each of the other parts. In other words, as we work to develop each element, we can do so with each of the other elements in mind. In short, this formation framework is therefore intended to provide a more systematic way of thinking about program development and some of the different methods that are commonly used to develop them. As a result, this framework will be the foundational lens through which we think about how we might begin to develop strong model-based programs using the theological anthropologies that we have synthesized. Before considering this, however, we must first realize that there are many different program design methods that we may draw from for our work.

## Five Methods for Program Development

Based on the formation framework, we may begin to think about how to develop specific programs for our community. As mentioned above, there are a number of ways of approaching such design and implementation. Looking at the framework, we might see that there are at least five characteristically different sets of methods that we can use. They follow the major components of the framework: ideals, models, approaches, assessments, and discernment. Each one of these methods has its own basis and processes for program development. Furthermore, there are examples from different fields of human transformation, secular and religious, that seem to favor one of these methods more than the others.

We will now briefly explore each of these in turn. What follows is a description of each set of methods as they might be embodied in their pure forms. Specifically, we will be exploring what they more primarily base their program development on, examples of formative fields that seem to use each one, and discussions of some of their strengths and limits. However, it must be noted that most programs are usually developed using a combination of one or more of these methods. As we shall currently see, using one of these sets of methods exclusively without drawing from the others can lead to distortions in one's programming. Healthy program development therefore requires a discerned and more holistic use of these methods together. Nevertheless, in order to help us to better understand what is distinctive about each of these methods, they will be presented in their purer forms. Overall, the goal of this section is to paint the broader landscape of program development methodologies so that we understand where strong model-based methods stand in relation to them.

### Objective-Oriented Methods

This first set of methods primarily bases it program development on a set of clear objectives that have been defined for the community to work towards. The achievement of these objectives is the central aim and all efforts in the program are geared towards these ends. As a result, each of the formation framework's elements are, in a purer version of these methods, centered on these objectives. Hence, the assessments are articulated in relation to the objectives as they measure the community's progress towards these aims. Similarly, the approaches are chosen solely based on how effective they are anticipated to be in moving the community towards the objectives. Furthermore, discernment in these methods centers on the objectives and how the community is moving towards them or not. Finally, the models of reality are chosen based on the insights that they provide to the formator in understanding how they can better help the community to achieve the given aims. This first of the methods are therefore objective-oriented because program development is largely based on the achievement of some set of given ideals.

Examples of this method include standards based public education and twelve-step programs such as Alcoholics Anonymous (AA). In these fields of human transformation, a heavier emphasis is often given to meeting a given set of objectives that have been defined for these programs. In public education, these would be the learning objectives or standardized tests that schools are working to prepare their students for. In twelve-step programs, such as AA, a primary aim is helping members to fully abstain from drinking. With these sets of objectives in mind, teachers and AA mentors then work to build and continually adapt their approaches such that their communities continually move towards these ends. Again, in reality lesson planning and AA meetings also draw from the other methods below, but they still are illustrative examples of these more objective-oriented approaches.

If embodied in its purer form, this method has a number of strengths and limits. One of the primary strengths is that there are clear aims to journey towards. Formators can therefore more easily know where they are at any given time in relation to them. They can also evaluate the "success" of their programs based upon how well these clearly defined objectives have been met by each member of their community. Conversely, one of the possible limits to these methods is that rigidly defined and pursued objectives can become damaging to the community. If the objectives chosen are not developmentally or culturally appropriate, for instance, formators can be tempted to try and force their constituents into molds that just don't fit. Such approaches to program development must therefore be integrated at least with the data-driven methods discussed below so that the objectives that are chosen are indeed relevant and appropriate for one's community. In other words, we must have the community that we will be specifically working with in mind when we develop such objectives.

## Model-Based Methods

Model-based methods primarily base program development on the models of reality that have been chosen and/or developed. In their purer forms, or "strong model-based" versions as will be discussed in greater detail below, the entire human transformation system is designed based solely on these models. The ideals are defined in direct relation to components of the model. For instance, for our synthesized theological anthropology we might want to design a program that addresses the intrapersonal psychological aspects. To do this, following these model-based methods, we would first define which parts of the psyche we wanted to specifically work with and then outline what our goals are for those parts. If nurturing a more positive self-esteem was one of the aims, for example, then we would work to more clearly define what this looks like in terms of our models, such as the number of reported self-constructs or narratives that depicted the individual in a positive way. Hence, these methods also strive to define what is monitored and how this data is evaluated in relation to the models.

Furthermore, we would choose approaches that seem to provide a means to move our community towards the objectives according to our models. Following our self-esteem example, we might use a personal reflection activity where people write out all of the positive qualities and gifts that they have and encourage them to appreciate and celebrate these about themselves and one another. Such activities would be chosen based primarily on the theories of change that we have. Finally, our discernment for these methods would center on our models, seeking to further refine both them and the program itself (based on the changing models) as things unfold.

An example of this method might include applications of behaviorism-conditioning views, such as Dollard and Miller's learning theories. In Dollard and Miller's scheme, we can recall, there were four primary components to learning in their scheme: drives, cues, responses, and reinforcements. Drives are those things that compel us to act, cues initiate the drives, responses are our resulting actions, and reinforcements ensure that this entire behavioral pattern either continues or is discouraged. We might then, based on this learning theory, develop a program that seeks to work with these components such that our community comes to behave in certain ways. A part of this work would be mapping the more common drives and responses that individuals have in response to certain cues. If we wanted to work to modify these, following this model, we would then provide positive and negative reinforcements to encourage or discourage some of these drive-response mechanisms.

From this, we can see how each element of the formation framework may be articulated in terms of the model. The set of desired drive-response reactions that we want to cultivate are the ideals, the means of positive-negative reinforcements are the approaches, and the assessments track how the community is progressing in relation to the set of the desired reactions. Discernment then focuses on continually updating the models and modifying the program accordingly as we learn more about our community's inherent drive-response mechanisms and how they are responding (or not) to the positive and negative reinforcements being given. In other words, the behavioral-conditioning model guides the development of each of the formation framework's elements.

Strengths of model-based methods include the insights that models can provide into the dynamics of our community and how they change. In a purer objectives-oriented method, there might be no such models at all and the primary way of choosing approaches could be merely trial-and-error. For stronger model-based systems, then, the advantage is that these theoretical constructs ideally yield insights into the interconnections and influences that continually shape the people and communities that we are working with. They can therefore empower us to better work with them in partnership with God's formative Trinitarian Life in our midst.

However, and particularly with human transformation fields, such models may also have serious limits. First, they might not accurately capture the dynamics of our local community and can therefore be very misleading. Just as it is possible to have objectives that are not developmentally or culturally appropriate for our community, so too is it possible to have models that are misrepresentative. Secondly, as discussed and seen in the previous parts of this book, these models can become so complex that their use becomes too cumbersome for practical applications. Finally, and closely related to these first two limits, our models can be too narrowly defined. In the behaviorism example above, for instance, we can note that there is much more going on both within a person's psyche in relation to the drive-response mechanisms as well as around them socially than the proposed model alludes to (such as motivations, cognitive reflection, peer pressures, social norms, et cetera). If we used this overly simplified model to develop a strong model-based program to the neglect of these other dynamics, much damage could be done by trying to force people to conform to the behavior-response mechanisms that we have set out as ideals. This is, in fact, one of the primary criticisms of behaviorism and its applications to therapy.[6] While model-based

---

6. Mischel et al., *Introduction to Personality*, 288.

methods seem very appealing and empowering because of the insights that they seem to give, they must be used with much caution due to such potentially misleading limits.

## Approach-Centered Methods

This third set of methods is one that primarily bases program development on a specific set of given approaches that are considered to be of particular importance. Often, these treasured approaches have been used and passed on for many years or even generations as part of the traditions of the community. Turning to the framework, many of these approaches will often have a certain set of aims that they are intended to help the community move towards and these are adapted as objectives by the formator.[7] Similarly, each approach will yield certain kinds of data and feedback that may be used as a part of the program's assessments. Typically, many of these approaches will come with models and explanations for how and why they transformatively work in the ways that they do. Discernment is then focused on better understanding, adapting, and working to implement these "tried and true" approaches in the specific community that one is currently working with. Overall, and in their purer forms then, these methods are centered on a certain set of approaches that are considered to be vital to the program that is being developed.

In many religious communities, particularly local churches, this is a method often used for community formation. Worship services, the Lord's Prayer, specific spiritual practices, regular Scripture reading, mission trips, and the like are examples of approaches that congregations use in the spiritual formation of their communities. Many of these practices have been passed on for generations. The Order of Worship, for instance, is often one that follows a structure that has been followed by the community for many years, sometimes dating back to the denomination's founding.[8] Such approaches are considered to be the bread and butter of the community's spiritual formation as each person is ideally expected to fully engage in them. The extent to which members may be participating in these is what is often monitored and discernment might center on improving not only the quantity but also the quality of their engagement.

7. For more discussions on the details of approaches, see Kyle, *Living Spiritual Praxis*.

8. Thompson, *Liturgies of the Western Church*.

While there may also be an understanding of what is being spiritually formed through these approaches, and even theories of how this happens, the more primary focus lies in deepening the community's involvement in and engagement with them. As a result, these religious practices are one example of an approach-centered method as it sometimes plays itself out in local congregations.

One of the strengths to these methods is that discernment related to which approaches to use is greatly simplified. Rather than having to try and choose from amongst a vast number of approaches, formators turn to the smaller subsets of choices found in their local community and/or the traditions of which they are a part. A strength of this approach is that by doing so, one is relying on the collective wisdom that has hopefully been cultivated across generations in relation to them. If these practices really are transformative for one's life, then why would we not draw upon and use them? Overall, then, approach-centered methods can seem to greatly simplify program development because they can seem to come as a ready-made system that just needs to be implemented (just open and add water, right?).

One of the limits that can creep in, however, is when the specific approaches are not appropriately adapted for one's current context. Such approaches, while they may have been powerfully formative for a different group of people at a different time in history, may not have the same intended effect today. Cultural, developmental, and similar considerations must therefore be taken into account when using these methods. Similarly, the accompanying models for how the approaches formatively work and why, may not accurately match the community that one is working with right now. Furthermore, the set of approaches that one has may only address specific anthropological aspects; i.e., they may not make up a more fully holistic formation system. If this is the case, then the formator still needs to discern whether or not the aspects addressed by the approaches are indeed the ones that their program should focus on.

Finally, there is also the danger of not allowing for new approaches to emerge and/or be integrated into the life of the community. As long as the current approaches are working, then there may not be a need for change. However, if the community begins to stagnate with these, then alternatives may need to be introduced. Of course, if the community is already rigidly attached to the current approaches then resistance to such changes may fervently ensue. We must all remember that the primary goal for all Christian spiritual formation endeavors is our continually growing life in Christ. Anything that hinders such growth is a distortion that needs to be addressed. Approach-centered methods can therefore become a source of idolatry that no longer supports these God-given aims.

## Data-Driven Methods

Data-driven methods are those that are more rooted in the moment-by-moment unfolding of the community. Practitioners that use these methods expend a great deal of time and energy deeply listening to and continually reflecting on what participants in their programs say and do. Deeply immersed in this observed and self-reported data, these methods often build upon and modify programs in response to the patterns, trends, and themes that emerge. In their purer forms, the program's ideals are considered more like general horizons towards which we float than concrete objectives that must be achieved. Similarly, approaches are chosen and honed based upon the community's engagement with them and the extent to which such engagement is vital or not. If a particular exercise does not seem to resonate with participants, practitioners of this method have no qualms about dropping them immediately and moving on to something else. Models, theories, and insights into the community are likewise held loosely and are considered to be in an unending state of change and adaptation as one comes to know the community more intimately. In short, discernment for these methods of program design and implementation is primarily driven by the data that the formator continually collects and reflects on as the things unfold.

One popular well-known example of these methods is community organizing and building.[9] Practitioners in this field seek to work very closely and continually with neighborhood residents to address problems and foster healthier physical and social environments in their community. Rather than coming into the community with their own agenda, organizers will meet with diverse segments of the neighborhood—from residents to businesses to government agencies—to formulate goals for the region. Creating models by mapping the needs as well as the assets that are in the community, they will then work to identify interventions

9. For an overview of these methods, see such texts as Kretzmann and McKnight, *Building Communities from the Inside Out.*

and solutions to difficult problems. With the social, political, and economic vitality of the neighborhood being the standards against which all activities are evaluated, community builders diligently work to stay attuned and responsive to the stake-holders for no progress can be sustained without their willing investment. Such work in our midst is therefore one example of these data-driven methods in action.

As with each of the others, these methods have a number of strengths and limits. In its purer forms, one of the potential limits is that substantive, long-range work might not be achieved. As we heard repeatedly throughout this book, lasting change requires a sustained and focused effort. However, since these methods primarily seek to stay closely connected to the moment-by-moment movements of the community, there is the danger of initially heading in one direction only to drop this and veer off in another thereby not giving the sustained focus that is needed for substantive transformation in a specific area. This method might therefore be tempered with the discipline found in either the objective-oriented or approach-centered methods.

Nevertheless, one of its great strengths is that practitioners can be much more attuned to the community and therefore better able to adapt the program based not only on local cultural considerations but also on significant incidents and situations that arise. For instance, imagine that a major news event just occurred, such as a school shooting in one's own neighborhood. Rather than continuing on with the planned program as if nothing happened, these methods would encourage us to listen more deeply with our constituents as to the impact that this unexpected event is having on our lives. Overall, then, these methods primarily focus on staying attuned and responsive to the moment-by-moment data that we collect from our community.

### Authoritative Source(s) Methods

Finally, we turn a set of methods that is quite unlike many of those found in mainstream, secular society but are more common among religious institutions. Each of the methods that we have considered thus far has had a clear basis and foundation for program development. Whether these were the concrete objectives that we work for, the models that we have synthesized, a given set of tried-and-true approaches that we rely on, or the in-vivo data that we continually collect, these first four methods were very intentional about what they were basing their programs on. Furthermore, these epistemological foundations can be clearly articulated, discussed, and even debated among formators and their communities.

For this fifth set, such foundations are no different. Here, practitioners look to some specific and clear set of sources that they deem as being "authoritative" for their work and their communities. Development of the formation framework elements therefore largely depends upon turning to these authoritative sources for guidance in what to do. Examples might include the sacred texts that a community has, gurus that are recognized in one's field or community, or specific ways of knowing that are used as the primary basis for discernment. Overall, the formator would continually turn to one or more of these authoritative sources for insight and direction in developing their programs.

As a specific example, consider formators who primarily relies on alternative ways of knowing as the basis for their discernment, such as in charismatic traditions.[10] Here practitioners seek to primarily base their program development on the "movements of the Spirit" which is understood as being rooted in either one's own intuitive-affective movements or in the transpersonal (particularly parapsychological) capacities that one has. By attuning to these intrapersonal and transpersonal dynamics, in purer applications of this method, practitioners would listen attentively to the "Spirit's movements" to and through these alternative ways of knowing as they decided upon which ideals to pursue and which approaches to use. They might also use such ways of knowing as the basis for their data collection as they strive to allow "God" to reveal to them, through these intra- and transpersonal channels, what it is that they need to know in order to develop and implement the program.

Examples of these alternative ways of knowing sources include charismatic and Ignatian approaches to spiritual discernment.[11] Each of these approaches has a central emphasis on listening to the affective movements of one's life, while some charismatics might place an alternative or additional weight to "revelational seeing" (something that is considered to be a parapsychological phenomenon in the synthesized model). In Ignatian discernment, for instance, a central part of decision-making is listening to the inner, affective movements of consolation or desolation that one has. The goal here is to discern whether or not any given decision is in

10. Parker, *Led by the Spirit*.

11. For further discussions on these, see such texts as Au and Au, *Discerning Heart*; Hauser, *Moving in the Spirit*; Parker, *Led by the Spirit*.

tune with the will of God by noting the impressions that it makes on one's heart. Of course, Ignatian discernment is not a pure form of these methods because practitioners are likewise encouraged to utilize their rational faculties as well as their communities in decision-making. Nevertheless, the affective listening that is central to Ignatian approaches is illustrative because at every step of program development, from the models that one chooses to the assessments that they develop, such inner affective listening is supposed to be occurring. These alternative methods may also be used with the community that one is working with by encouraging them to listen for the "movements of the Spirit" as well.

In Christianity, the Bible is another obvious example of such authoritative sources. As Christian religious educators, we can look to the scripture for guidance on how to develop each part of the framework. From the ideals that we choose, to the approaches that we draw from, to the assessment techniques and discernment processes that we engage in, the Bible can form the primary basis for developing each element of the framework. Throughout Christian history, such has been the case for many systems of personal transformation.[12] Overall, then, these are examples of methods that look to specific authoritative sources as the primary basis for program development.

In their purer forms, these methods can be very misleading, though they also have their strengths. The primary strength that these methods have is that they take seriously the authoritative sources to which the community is committed. These become the foundational basis for the programs that are developed thereby allowing the fruits of cultivated wisdom in the source to be extracted and applied within the community. These are methods that are committed to sources in the community that are considered to be central pillars and can therefore help to foster closely connections to these sources.

In its pure forms, the primary limit or potential for distortion lies in only relying on such authoritative sources. If the use of these sources are not verified and checked against common sense, critical reflection, other sources, the experiences and culture of our community and our field, then they can lead us down distorted paths. Similar to model-based and approach-centered methods, these authoritative sources might not accurately capture what God is actually doing in our midst right here, right now. In other words, turning solely to these sources can lead us to

12. For descriptions of some of these, see Kyle, *Sacred Systems*.

overlook or ignore the work that God has already done and continues to do in our midst. Indeed, as we shall see next, each of these methods has something valuable to offer to holistic program development.

### Holistic Program Development: Factors to Consider

As was stated at the beginning and has been reiterated throughout, we will only rarely use one of these methods in their pure forms. Instead, it is often better to blend these together in more holistic ways to ensure the on-going strength and vitality of our programs. One possible approach to such merging of methods is to engage each one of these equally and as fully as possible. This might perhaps entail the following processes. First, one could collect as much data as they could about their community that would be relevant for the program. If one were to create a program to address self-esteem among teenage girls, for instance, one might send out a survey or set of questions to potential participants ahead of time in order to gauge where they were in relation to such development. Secondly, one might then research some of the models on self-esteem and identity development among this population. Based on this, one might then synthesize such research with the results of the survey in order to generate a set of models that will help to further inform and guide the program's design and implementation. Using these models, the formator could then discern, based partly on the authoritative sources one has as well as in consultation with their community, the objectives to pursue. Finally, such discernment might then turn to the approaches that will be used in pursuit of the objectives, particularly drawing on any specific ones that the local community regularly uses. As the program begins, one would continually collect data, which might then spark the need for further research, and discerningly update the models, objectives, and approaches as one goes. Overall, this more holistic method therefore seeks to draw on the strengths of each one of the five methods whilst simultaneously mitigating their limitations. However, much more research and development is needed in this area.[13]

Nevertheless, not all situations will allow for such a holistic approach to program development. There may be certain kinds of programs that are better suited for only a smaller subset of these methods. As a result,

---

13. For further discussions on spiritual formation program development carried according to a similar process, see Kyle, *Living Spiritual Praxis*.

it will be helpful for practitioners to know what factors they should consider in choosing which methods to utilize and merge. There are at least four such factors to consider.

The first is the situation itself. How much information does one have available to them? Do you know who will be participating in your programs? Have there been similar programs developed in the past that you can look to for further insights? Are there models and research available to further support and inform the kinds of formation that you are hoping to foster? Are there approaches that are already commonly used for this kind of formation? Are there expectations that the program already has, such as its graduates needing to demonstrate certain levels of development, knowledge, skills, et cetera (e.g., knowing the parts of the Bible, being equipped for ministry, et cetera)? Situational considerations such as these can help to us to know if it is even possible to use one of the methods above or not. For instance, if there is no research available on the kind of program that you are developing and no one else seems to have attempted a similar program and you do not know who exactly will be attending, then it will be difficult to use the model-based methods because you will not have much information to base the development of your models on.

A second consideration is the personality characteristics/traits of the participants that the program is being designed for. Which of these methods might they respond to best? Some people respond very well when given clear objectives to work towards, while others respond better to more of a free-flowing and less pressured program. For the former, a more objective-oriented program might be better suited while for the latter data-driven methods might be more welcomed by them.

Third, and relatedly, also depends on the expectations and aims associated with the program. For example, if you were designing a relaxing weekend getaway for parents this would probably not be too compatible with a heavy objective-oriented approach which had a rigid schedule with set tasks to be achieved by couples in a timely fashion. Rather, a more data-driven approach would seem to match this program wherein the facilitators would be more flexible and willing to adapt to the needs and wishes of the group as they find rest in their own ways.

Finally, formators need to consider their own personality characteristics. Are you more laid back and a "go with the flow" kind of a facilitator or are you much comfortable being more routine-oriented, structured, and disciplined? Are you more by the book and like to follow a given set of authoritative sources or do you prefer to be more open to the "winds of the Spirit"? In reading through these brief descriptions, you will no doubt have noticed that some of these methods appealed and resonated with you more than the others. It is important to note these inner movements because you will probably find that you are more naturally inclined and gifted for some of these methods more than the others. This does not mean, of course, that you should only use these few methods to the neglect of the others. This is because different programs and situations, as we just heard, may require specific methods be used so we must all be well versed and comfortable with using each of them. Nevertheless, we may find that some of these appeal to us more than others and, where possible, we should not be afraid to draw on our own strengths and inclinations because: 1) if developed in healthy ways, they can be considered to be one of God's gifts to the world through us, and 2) engaging in our ministries from our gifts strengthens both the quality of and our passion for our programs. So, while there may be many others, these considerations are some of the key ones to consider when merging these five methods in the development of our spiritual formation programs in more holistic ways.

## "Strong" Versus "Weak" Model-Based Methods

In this book, we have been working towards building our own theological anthropologies. The final goal of this work that we are pursuing is exploring how we might use these models to help guide our spiritual formation program development in more intentional ways. In other words, we are interested in primarily utilizing the model-based methods discussed above. When doing this, there is a spectrum along which models might be used to guide our program development. For the purposes of simplifying things, we will consider the two ends of this spectrum, which I have named "weak" and "strong."

In weak model-based systems, models are used as more of an overall guide for the program's development. We heard something of this briefly above in the introduction to this chapter. There, it was asserted that we could use the synthesized theological anthropology as a general guide for setting up a community's personal spiritual formation system. Based upon this general use, the ministers would make sure that their congregation had programs that addressed each of the various aspects depicted by the model. Or, they might use the model to help them to know which areas a specific program was going to address. For weak model-based methods, therefore, the model is being used in a very general ways with little to none of the program's planning or implementation being directly based on the model. In other words, very few (if any) of the formation framework's elements are articulated in terms of the model in a weak model-based method.

For strong model-based methods, at the other end of the spectrum, every element of the framework is defined in terms of the models being used. The description of model-based methods above was essentially a description of strong model-based approaches. Some of the strongest model-based examples may be found in the field of engineering control systems design. Here, equations describing the physical dynamics of every part of the system are generated and used to design the control system. For example, a cruise control on a car must continually monitor the vehicle's speed in order to maintain the desired value set by the driver. If the car is traveling faster than this set speed, then the cruise control lets up on the gas. If the car is going too slow, it gives more gas. The amount that the cruise control lets up or "steps on it" is precisely determined moment-by-moment by the physics equations that model the car's dynamics.

For human transformation systems, following strong model-based methods, each part of the framework would likewise be defined by the models. For the ideals, this means that the concrete objectives are able to be determined and articulated directly in relation to the models. Similarly, one should be able to derive from the models what to monitor and how to assess progress (or lack of) towards these aims. The models should also provide clear guidance in what specific approaches to use so that progress is continually made throughout the program. Ideally, these models should provide sufficient insights into what, more specifically, fosters transformation so that these approaches may be selected and appropriately adapted to the local context. Finally, these models should directly inform one's discernment processes by aiding them in knowing how to proceed next and what to modify should the program not unfold as expected. In short, then, the models being used should be sufficiently detailed in order to provide this level of detail and guidance. If they are, then strong model-based methods may be used. Otherwise, one will need to draw from one or more of the other four program development methods outlined above, something which is advisable nonetheless.

In the case example that now follows, we will be looking at one example of a strong model-based design. We are following the strong model-based method in order to help demonstrate the extent to which our theological anthropologies may be used for program development. We will also be exploring the kinds of additional information that are needed in order to develop such strong model-based programs. This final section is therefore intended to round out our theory-to-practice journey related to models of human nature and their uses in spiritual formation program development.

## CASE EXAMPLE: A SPIRITUALITY & PEACEBUILDING WORKSHOP

As we have just heard, it is not always advisable to use only one of the methods to the exclusion of the others. Each one has its own strengths and unique perspectives to bring to the program development endeavor. As we shall see below, certain elements of the other methods will be integrated into what follows. However, for illustrative purposes, we will be closely following a strong model-based approach. Since such methods are ones that primarily use models to develop and inform the various elements of the formation framework, we will be using these elements to guide the development of this case example. As we journey through this example, we will be highlighting some of the central factors that need to be considered when developing strong model-based systems using the theological anthropologies that we have developed for use in our local communities. Let us now consider each one of the formation framework's elements to see how they might be developed using strong model-based methods for the case example that is presented.

## Context & Background: Women's Leadership Empowerment

A local faith-based nonprofit has approached a minister to develop a workshop on spirituality and peacebuilding. The mission of this organization is the leadership development and empowerment of women in the community. In particular, they seek to develop the "mind, body, and spirit" of women. In line with this mission, they have discerned that the women connected to their organization could benefit from a two-hour per week, fourteen-week program that teaches peacebuilding skills from a faith-based perspective. Such skills include conflict meditation, restorative justice, nonviolent direct action, and how to better listen to and integrate one's inner psychic life. Intended only as an educational introduction and overview of this material, the organization hopes to help these women to begin to incorporate these skills into their personal, familial, and communal lives. Their hopes are that these women will then become more empowered leaders in the community. As a result, they have asked a local minister to develop and offer such a program for their constituents.

Demographically, the women who typically participate in this organization's programs are somewhat diverse. While the organization regularly serves as many as 1,200 women across all of its programs on an annual basis, this particular program has been limited to twenty five to thirty people. Participants in similar programs typically range in age from eighteen to sixty years, with the average age being approximately twenty five years old. Many of these women have young children and a number of them are single mothers. While the majority of participants are European-American, approximately 25 percent are of other ethnic backgrounds. Finally, because this particular program will incorporate spirituality, it is also important to note that about 60 percent of this organization's constituents self-identify as Roman Catholic, though only about 20 percent are practicing (i.e., they participate/attend church on a regular basis). The remaining persons are a mix of various Protestant denominations and about 3 percent self-identify as either agnostic or atheist. It is for this organization and its diverse constituency that the minister has been asked to develop this spirituality and peacebuilding workshop.

## Models of Reality: An Increasingly Complex Cognitive Foundation

Since strong model-based systems are derived most directly from the models that they embrace, much intentionality needs to be given to their development. As these models are to become the basis for each of the other framework's elements, we will be seeking to ensure that the models we develop here are able to provide the kinds of insights that they need to fulfill this function. Let us now consider each of these models in turn.

*Anthro-Cosmology*

As we have seen, models can be used in either general or specific ways. Generally, they can provide an overall landscape in which we locate our programs. Specifically, they can help us to develop one or more of the other framework's elements. In order to develop strong model-based programs, it is helpful to use both of these. By first considering the general aspects that the program will be focusing on, we may then research and develop more specific models that can provide us with the more detailed understandings that we will need in order to fill out the rest of the formation framework. Using the synthesized model of human nature from this book, we will be following this approach by moving from generalities to specificities for this particular spirituality and peacebuilding program. Let us now consider each in turn.

## GENERAL MODELS: LOCATING THE FOCUS OF THIS PROGRAM

A first step for developing our strong model-based program can be to more clearly discern what kind of a formation program it is. In other words, before we can choose more specific models to work with, we first need to know which specific aspects it will be attempting to spiritually form. Once we have done this, we can then refine and develop the more specific models that we will base our program development on. To help us to more generally locate this particular program, we turn to our synthesized model from above. By reviewing the intrapersonal, interpersonal, and transpersonal aspects, we can more clearly identify what the primary foci of our specific programs are. For this spirituality and peacebuilding workshop, let us briefly consider each of these areas in turn.

Looking at the intrapersonal aspects, it is clear that this workshop will focus primarily at the psychological level, more specifically on the cognitive aspects because it is an educational workshop. While this program could incorporate physical health as one of the peacebuilding skills, due to time constraints diet and exercise will not be covered in the material that is presented. Similarly, integrative-transcendent development is not taken to be a central focus even though participants might be engaging in a few contemplative practices as a part of it. Since this program is really only intended to provide an introductory overview to peacebuilding skills, the more primary focus of this program is cognitive development or deep learning in relation to the material. At this stage, the hopes are that the participants will learn enough about these skills so that they are not only able to recall them beyond the life of the program but to also begin incorporating this knowledge and these practical skills into their lives and communities. While it was stated that cognitive and affective dynamics are inseparably interrelated, the affective and more unconscious dynamics were also noted to require more long-term formation approaches. As a result, this program is considered to primarily focus on the more cognitive and educational aspects in relation the material that will be covered.

Turning next to interpersonal considerations, we similarly find the primary focus to lie at social-cultural levels—though for different reasons. While care for the environment is a significant peacebuilding issue (and such topics might be covered in the session on nonviolent direct action), the relationship with the physical environment is not a core aim. Similarly, oneness with creation is also not a central formation focus, though any contemplative and mindfulness practices used in the workshop might nurture this. What is central, however, are the relationships that one has with others because many of the peacebuilding skills address this communal aspect. Furthermore, relationships have been noted to be a fundamental means through which women learn, make decisions, and develop.[14] While this program is not primarily intended to cultivate healthy, spiritual (i.e., God-manifesting) relationships, social learning theories such as Bandura's are important models for helping formators to better understand such interpersonal modes of learning. As a result, this program will need models to help us to better understand how to work through such interpersonal modes for the women who will be attending these workshops.

Finally, none of the transpersonal aspects appear to be relevant for this specific program. Neither the cultivation of physical energies nor attunement with creation are topics or levels of formation that will be directly addressed. Similarly, participants will not be explicitly introduced to parapsychological phenomena and the minister will not seek to nurture such capabilities. Hence, this program will primarily focus on cognitive development in relation to the workshop's topics and will seek to partly do so through interpersonal modes of learning because of the demographics of the participants who will be attending.

---

14. For example, see such texts as Gilligan et al., *Making Connections*.

## SPECIFIC MODELS: REFINING THE DETAILS WE NEED

As we can see, the synthesized theological anthropology developed in this book has enabled us to hone in on the more primary foci for this program. Such progress is tremendously helpful because it has greatly simplified the model-based work that we now need to do. While the synthesized model has provided us with general insights, however, it lacks the more refined details that we will need in order to develop a strong model-based system. Each one of the framework's elements, following these methods, must be defined in terms of the central models being used. So, for instance, while the synthesized model alludes to cognitive development, it does not provide the details that we will need in order to develop the workshop's objectives, know which specific activities to choose, how to implement sufficiently informative assessment techniques, or continually guide our discernment as the program unfolds. For this, we need more detailed and well developed models. Fortunately, the synthesized model has helped us to know what specific kinds of models to now look for: models of cognitive dynamics and social learning theories.

### Cognitive Dynamics: Revisiting the CAPS Model

To help us to better understand the basics of learning from a cognitive-affective perspective, we refer back to the CAPS model that was discussed as part of the generalized model in the last chapter. At this point, we might turn to the generalized model to help ensure that the more specific model(s) that we select address the elements of the generalized model (e.g., nodes, connections, fields, et cetera). However, since the CAPS model was used in the derivation of the generalized model, we already know that it embodies these general elements and we can therefore proceed with it. Nevertheless, we will be discussing the CAPS model in terms of these generalized elements.

There are three basic aspects of CAPS model that will be helpful here. Each of these captures an essential part of the inner cognitive-affective system and will therefore provide more detailed insights into the nature of learning for this particular workshop. First, as we may recall, cognitive-affective units (CAUs) make-up the basic elements of this model. As it relates to this workshop, these would be the already existing beliefs, attitudes, knowledge, assumptions, behavioral patterns, et cetera that participants already have about spirituality and peacebuilding for each of the four levels that will be covered (individual, relational, communal, and societal).

For instance, participants will most likely come with their own ideas about what conflict is, how it has impacted their own life, and what their general feelings and attitudes are in relation to conflicts. Some may view conflict as being inherently negative and therefore should be avoided at all costs, while others may view it constructively and see it as an opportunity for growth. As we heard above, these CAUs have been formed as a result of nature and nurture, as well as by the ongoing choices that one has made throughout their life. In essence, these beliefs, attitudes, behaviors, et cetera make up some of the fundamental nodes that the minister facilitating this workshop will be working with.

Secondly, these basic CAU elements, or nodes, make up networks that can form enduring structures within our personality system. In other words, our beliefs, knowledge, et cetera can be related to one another in complex, enduring, and emergent ways. In addition to having an understanding of what conflict is, for example, participants will likely know what violence is based upon past experiences and exposure. These two concepts might then be related to one another with violence being understood as one way to respond to conflicts. Participants might even have their own typology of violence, noting that there are different forms or kinds of violence in our world. Seeing these differences between conflict and violence and constructing a landscape of different kinds of violence are examples of such cognitive-affective networks that help to influence and guide our understanding and actions in relation to peacebuilding. As was noted with the CAPS model, some of these networks may be encoded as hot or cool systems, motivating us towards action and/or helping us to make better sense of the world around us. The workshop must therefore work not just with the basic concepts of spirituality and peacebuilding but also with the hot and cool relationships that participants have in relation to them.

Finally, we may recall that these already existing CAUs and their networks are triggered by both internal and external stimuli. These were understood by Mischel and Shoda to be "if-then" stimulus-response mechanisms (e.g., "if a scary monster appears, then I will run"). Each CAU node and network may be set in motion by either one's current situation or by one's inner attitudes, thoughts, daydreams, et cetera. These nodes/networks of CAUs may be triggered because they are similar in structure to the stimulus. For instance, if we were walking outside in the dark through the woods and saw an S-shaped stick, we might immediately mistake it for a snake. Sometimes, however, CAUs are triggered when we are in situations that are similar to the ones that the triggered CAUs were encoded. Soldiers experiencing PTSD (post-traumatic stress disorder) symptoms may be reminded of combat experiences by situations at home such as a backfiring car or loud and disorienting social environments.

For this workshop, knowing this is essential because a central part of what it will be seeking to do is to modify how participants respond to the inner and outer conflicts that they encounter in their lives and communities (i.e., working with their CAU nodes and networks that have to do with conflict, peacebuilding, violence, et cetera). Understanding these three basic elements of cognition are essential for helping the minister to better understand how to work with participants in this workshop and therefore develop each aspect of the formation framework. However, what is still needed is an understanding of how to work with and change this inner cognitive-affective system, which is something that will be discussed below.

## Social Learning Theory: Some Basics

In addition, as was mentioned above, because of the particular context that this workshop will be taking place in, namely a women's group, an additional social learning theory is needed. For greater insights into how we learn via the relationships that we have, we turn once again to Albert Bandura's social-cognitive model that was reviewed in the modern science chapter above. As we can recall, this model argues that we fundamentally learn from one another by observing each other's behaviors and their resulting consequences. Furthermore, Bandura argues that it is by being exposed to many different ways of engaging life, we formulate our own integrated version. On this, he writes, "When exposed to diverse models, observers rarely pattern their behavior exclusively after a single source, nor do they adopt all the attributes even of preferred models. Rather, observers combine aspects of various models into new amalgams that differ from the individual sources."[15] In other words, according to Bandura, one of the primary ways that we learn and grow is by interacting with many different people from which we then craft and construct

15. Bandura, *Social Learning Theory*, 48.

our own understanding. For this particular workshop, then, this model is a foundational one because it helps us to better understand how learning happens interpersonally. As such, it is adopted as a second key model of reality, though we will only be referring to it in limited ways for this case example for simplicity's sake.

## Theories of Change

While these specific models are helpful, however, we still do not have a more detailed understanding of what is being inwardly formed according to them. For instance, we can ask more details in relation to how these CAU/Networks change based on day-to-day experiences as well as developmentally across one's lifetime. Are they forming genuinely new neural and psychic connections or simply rearranging already existing ones? How, more precisely, are the schemas and enduring psychic patterns changing as they interpersonally learn from one another? Understanding such inner cognitive-affective dynamics can be helpful when choosing activities and particularly for when people are not progressing as expected.

With as complex as these inner psychic systems are, we might expect the resulting theories of change to likewise be quite complex and they can be. For the purposes of preparing for this workshop, however, there are a few basic models that will be helpful. The first is for us to better understand the fundamental types of transformation that are possible with these inner CAU systems. Following this, we will turn to Neo-Piagetian models of cognitive development that will help us to better understand how a person's grasp of a set of material can developmentally increase in complexity across time and with intentional engagement. While understanding this general trend will be helpful for designing this workshop, we will also need to better understand the increasingly complex processes by which such development might occur. To help with this, we turn to a model known as Bloom's Taxonomy. Finally, we will reflect on how social learning can help to foster these kinds of cognitive change. What we must remember throughout this section, especially given the complexity of these models, is that for model-based approaches to human transformation the theories of change are the most central models that we have. As we shall see in the coming sections below, most of the rest of this workshop's design flows directly from them. It therefore behooves us to ensure enough detail for these subsequent framework elements.

## BASIC TYPES OF CAU SYSTEM CHANGES

If we think about the CAPS model and how these internal nodes and networks are formed and reshaped, we might notice that philosophically speaking there are at least four fundamental ways that this internal system might be changed.[16] Each of these represents a basic type of change that can be made to a person's existing CAU system. Knowing each of these four basic types of systemic change is helpful because they capture the fundamental ways that we can work with people for transformation at these levels.

The first is that we can modify the existing CAUs and their associated networks. For this workshop, we can work with what the participants already know about and have experienced in relation to conflict, violence, peacebuilding, et cetera. More specifically, there are at least three ways that we can work with these areas. First, we can expand upon this knowledge and their experiences. This might involve broadening their definition of conflict by helping them to explore and revisit some of the different kinds of conflicts that they have encountered in their life. Secondly, we might also work to reshape or reorganize what they currently know. An example of this might include introducing a typology of violence that helps them not only to think about violence in different ways but also categorizes their own experience of violence according to the typology. Finally, we can modify these internal CAUs/Networks by adding greater complexity and nuances to them. For this, we might work to help participants to analyze and critically reflect on their own definitions and experiences of conflict, comparing and contrasting them with one another, et cetera all for the purpose of fostering a more detailed and complex understanding of conflict. Shown in the figure below, each of these is therefore a way of working with and modifying the already existing CAUs and their networks that people have and they follow some of the principles of deep spiritual formation outlined in the previous chapter of this book.

16. For similar discussion, see Richey et al., *Instructional Design Knowledge Base.*

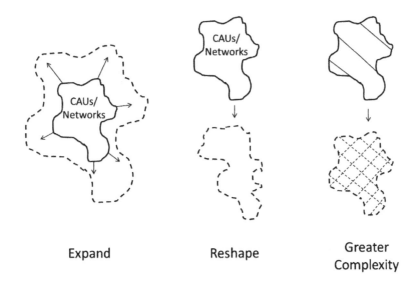

Expand                    Reshape                    Greater Complexity

**Figure 29. Modifying Existing CAU Networks.**

Secondly, we can also add completely new CAU nodes and networks to the system. For the first basic type of change above, new information might have been introduced in order to help foster one of the three modifications mentioned above. In this one, however, this new information stands as genuinely new and different nodes/networks apart from existing ones. An example of this might be discussing Walter Wink's "myth of redemptive violence" wherein participants learn of the history of myths that have portrayed violence as the best and sometimes only way of handling conflicts.[17] If they have not heard or learned of this before, then it would constitute new information that is being introduced to them. Such information might be linked to existing knowledge and experiences that they already have or it might stand alone all on its own. Studies in cognition have shown, however, that the more closely linked such new information is to existing nodes/networks of knowledge and experience the more likely a person will be to retain and integrate it into their life.[18] This second basic type of change, pictured below, is adding new CAU nodes/networks to the already existing system.

17. Wink, *Engaging the Powers*, chap. 1.
18. Matlin, *Cognition*, 188–89.

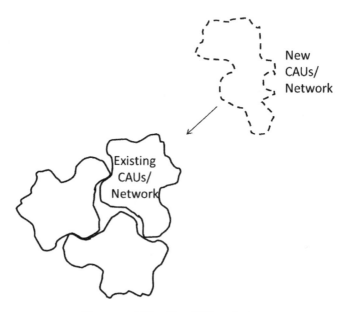

**Figure 30. Adding New CAUs to the System.**

Third, which might seem obvious based on the previous one, is that we can combine CAU nodes and networks. We can add new ones to existing ones, or we can combine existing ones together in new and/or different ways. As stated above, this might mean teaching new definitions of violence that we then relate to the ones participants are already familiar with. Or, it might mean relating their understanding of conflict more directly to their thoughts about violence. Overall, as may be seen below, this kind of change works to combine these CAU nodes/networks together in new and/or different ways.

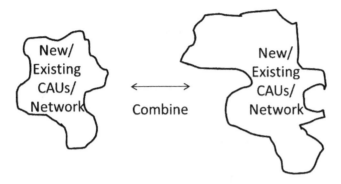

**Figure 31. Combining Existing CAU Networks.**

Finally, and this is most unusual of the four kinds of change for the system, genuinely new CAU nodes and/or networks can be created. Such manifestations represent genuine movements of creativity and novelty. Here, participants might realize things that they have never thought of before. They might have new ideas for how to create and apply the peacebuilding skills to their own lives or communities in ways they have not seen or thought of before. These epiphanies might come as a result of existing concepts, memories, et cetera and/or they might spontaneously emerge as new information and/or activities are engaged. Whatever their origins, these novel nodes/networks are new to the person and are more than the mere sum of the contributing parts. This final basic type of systemic cognitive-affective change is therefore the emergence of genuinely novel CAU nodes/networks in the system as is depicted in the figure below.

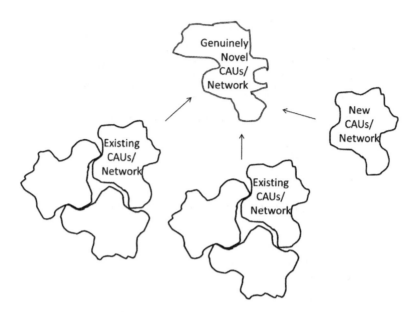

Figure 32. The Emergence of Genuinely New CAU Networks.

These four basic types of change are helpful for providing essential insights into how cognitive-affective change can come to our inner cognitive system. By understanding that these are the fundamental ways to impact and modify the existing CAU system, we are in a better position to be able work with the participants in this more educationally-centered workshop. However, it will also be helpful to better understand what happens to the overall system as one develops cognitively. In the literature, there are at least two types of cognitive development that are highlighted. The first is related to the increasingly complex cognitive structures that we form in relation to a specific set of material as we engage with that material more often. The second type is related to the increasingly complex processes that we use to engage with the material, processes that help to foster the first kind of cognitive development. By looking at these two types in more detail, our goal here is to further understand what is being transformed, as well as how, so that we are better able to work with the participants in this workshop. Again, strong model-based methods require very detailed theories so that there are sufficient insights to help develop the other aspects of the framework.

## Increasingly Complex Content: Neo-Piagetian Perspectives

Based on the original work of child cognitive psychologist Jean Piaget, neo-Piagetian researchers assert that as we develop cognitively the structures that we use to represent and understand our world become increasingly complex and more interconnected. An example of this may be found in the work of those who have studied skill development.[19] When we are initially introduced to a concept or a skill, our inner representations of them form only single and simple concepts. For example, when we are first introduced to an area of mathematics such as geometry, our understanding of the material will only be very basic.[20] However, as we continue to work with it, our understanding and insight into geometric proofs and theorems will become more nuanced and detailed. So, as it relates to this workshop, a participant may initially only have a very simple definition and understanding of what violence is. However, as they explore the different kinds of violence and its typologies, their understanding will become more nuanced, complex, and interconnected with other knowledge and experiences that they have had. Recall that such increasing complexity was one of the central characteristics of deep learning.

What has been noted by Neo-Piagetians, as well as by those studying adult learning, is that as we develop in these ways our inner representations can come to form ever more complex systems of representation and even meta-systems or networks of complex understanding.[21] In other words, we might only begin with simple concepts of geometry or violence, but as we study, explore, reflect on, apply, et cetera this material, our understandings of it become increasingly complex and interconnected. Moving from a single and simple definition of violence to a typology or mapping of all of the different kinds of violence that there are would be an example of such increasingly cognitive complexity in relation to this material. As this development relates to our CAU system, referring back to our generalized model, this development essentially captures the movement from single nodes to networks of nodes to meta-networks, as shown below.

19. Morra et al., *Cognitive development*, chap. 5.

20. Ibid., 151.

21. Kegan, "What "Form" Transforms? A Constructive-Developmental Approach to Transformative Learning," 62–63; Morra et al., *Cognitive development*, 158.

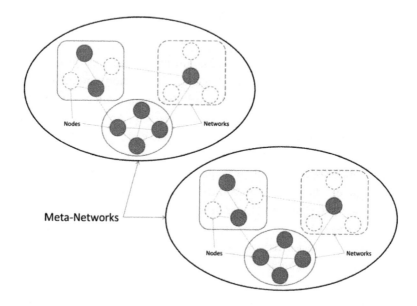

Figure 33. Meta-Networks in Cognitive Development.

One of the key assertions that can be made is that the greater cognitive complexity that we develop in a particular area, such as peacebuilding, the more able and likely we are to integrate into our daily life. Following this claim, one of the central goals of this workshop is to therefore help the participants to develop in these increasingly complex ways. While understanding the general trajectory of this development is helpful, however, we still only have a basic idea of how to help foster it. We can, of course, turn to the four basic types of change discussed above to aid us in this. Nevertheless, cognitive development researchers and practitioners also provide more detailed insights into the specific kinds of processes that seem to help support this increasingly complex cognitive development, which is what we will turn to next.

## INCREASINGLY COMPLEX PROCESSING: BLOOM'S TAXONOMY

As it relates to cognitive developmental learning theories, a common one that is widely used in the field of education is Bloom's Taxonomy.[22] While the full taxonomy addresses cognitive, emotional, and psychomo-

---

22. Krathwohl, "A Revision of Bloom's Taxonomy," 213.

tor aspects of the person, our identified interest here is primarily in the cognitive arena. Originally developed as a way to compare assessments across educational settings, the model has been used as a way to classify objectives, refine and focus assessments, and to help educators to choose and improve their activities and pedagogies.[23] It is therefore a very helpful model for guiding the development of programs that seek to nurture cognitive development in relation to a specific set of material such as our peacebuilding workshop is seeking to do.

In essence, revised versions of the Taxonomy divide learning along two dimensions. The first is related to the kinds of knowledge that a program can address. According to this revised model, there are four such kinds of models: Factual, Conceptual, Procedural, and Metacognitive Knowledge.[24] Factual knowledge essentially encompasses the basic facts, definitions, terms, et cetera that a discipline has for its foundation. For our workshop, these would of course be the definitions of violence and conflict that we explored. Conceptual knowledge, alternatively, comprises the interrelations among these basic facts. An example of this might be the typologies of violence that was presented to participants. Procedural knowledge, however, has more to do with the skills, techniques, methods, et cetera that a field uses to pursue knowledge. For this workshop, these would include the skills that were taught in relation to such topics as conflict mediation, restorative justice, and nonviolent direct action. Finally, metacognitive knowledge, differing from the others, is intended to capture strategic knowledge, knowledge about cognitive tasks, and self-knowledge. In cognitive psychology, metacognition is essentially the knowledge that we have about cognitive processes in general as well as our own ways of thinking and processing.[25] Following this, participants would be engaging in metacognitive thinking if they were asked to notice and reflect on their own inner attitudes and responses to conflict in their life. According to the Taxonomy, then, these are four fundamentally different kinds of knowledge that we can intentionally work with communities to develop and we can see how they are helpful for identifying and classifying the kinds of learning that can happen in the spirituality and peacebuilding workshop.

The more widely known and used aspect of the Taxonomy, however, are the six stages, or processes, of cognitive development that a person can

23. Ibid., 217–18.
24. Ibid.
25. Matlin, *Cognition*, 190.

progress through in relation to a set of material. In the revised version of the Taxonomy, these six cognitive processes are: Remember, Understand, Apply, Analyze, Evaluate, and Create.[26] Each essentially represents an increasingly complex interaction with the material that is being learned.[27] The action verbs commonly associated with each of these, which are used by educators to develop objectives, provide us with greater insights into their nature. Some of these are the following:[28]

- *Remember*—recognizing, recalling, identifying, retrieving, listing, describing, naming, locating, finding

- *Understand*—interpreting, exemplifying, classifying, summarizing, inferring, comparing, explaining, clarifying, paraphrasing, representing, translating, illustrating, instantiating, categorizing, subsuming, abstracting, generalizing, concluding, extrapolating, interpolating, predicting, contrasting, mapping, matching, constructing models

- *Apply*—executing, implementing, carrying out, using, change, choose, compute, demonstrate, discover, dramatize, employ, illustrate, interpret, manipulate, modify, operate, practice, prepare, produce, schedule, show, sketch, write

- *Analyze*—differentiating, organizing, attributing, discriminating, distinguishing, focusing, selecting, finding coherence, integrating, outlining, parsing, structuring, deconstructing, comparing, finding

- *Evaluate*—checking, critiquing, coordinating, detecting, monitoring, testing, judging, hypothesizing, experimenting, concluding, contrasting, defending, describing, discriminating

- *Create*—generating, planning, producing, hypothesizing, designing, constructing, inventing, devising, making, rearrange, reconstruct, relate, reorganize, revise

The purpose of these descriptors is to help us to understand the kinds of increasingly complex cognitive processes that are being used in relation to specific content and/or skills. While they are helpful, it might also be useful to reflect on these in light of the four basic types of CAU

26. Krathwohl, "A Revision of Bloom's Taxonomy."

27. Ibid., 215.

28. "Bloom's Taxonomy Action Verbs"; Churches, "Bloom's Digital Taxonomy"; Heer, "Model of Learning Objectives–based on A Taxonomy"; Krathwohl, "A Revision of Bloom's Taxonomy," 215.

system change that were covered above. Remembering is basically the ability to access one of the domains of knowledge that the Taxonomy outlines (e.g., factual, conceptual, procedural, and metacognitive). In essence, it is most related to the first type of CAU system change wherein one simply accesses an existing CAU node/network. While somewhat similar, understanding is more complex in that a person must not just be able to remember a skill or piece of information, but also be able to relate it to other material and/or represent it in different ways. Participants in the workshop might be asked to explain what conflict is in relation to their life experiences, for instance. To be able to do so might represent a form of understanding according to the Taxonomy. The basic type of change here, then, could be understood as combining CAU nodes/networks or it might be modifying existing ones.

Being able to apply the material, skill, et cetera in one way or another represents a further advancement in one's cognitive processing capacities. Here, the individual must be able to identify an appropriate place for the application to happen and be able to adapt it to fit with that unique context. Such processing might involve any of the first three kinds of CAU system change. This is because new material may need to be introduced, existing knowledge modified, or combinations of these made in order for the application to be carried out.

In a similar way, when we set about analyzing something, it might require each of these three basic types of CAU change as well. However, it is more fully an act of giving greater complexity to an existing CAU node/network. This is because analysis is essentially a more complex process of being able to dissect and parse out the nuances and finer details of something. It is an act of delving more deeply within a topic or skill thereby helping one to be able to locate it more fully in its' larger context, perhaps even comparing and contrasting it with other topics or skills.

Evaluating, while similar to analyzing, has the added element of comparing a given topic for the purposes of making judgments. Such judgments might illuminate discrepancies, point to limitations, or highlight new directions that need to be taken. It is possible that all four basic types of CAU system change might occur as a result of this even more complex cognitive process. Finally, the ability to create represents what is considered in the Taxonomy to be the most complex set of cognitive processes. While it can and often does involve all of the other basic types of change, it is more fully concerned with the fourth kind of CAU transformation wherein something genuinely new is generated. It differs markedly from mere application because here the person must devise new knowledge, applications, et cetera in truly novel and creative ways.

As we can see, as each of these processes are increasingly complex when viewed through the CAPS model. In fact, search the Internet for images related to Bloom's Taxonomy and the majority of websites depict them in ascending order from remembering (being the more foundational and simplistic) to creating (being the pinnacle of one's ability to be able to process something cognitively) similar to what is shown in the figure below. In essence, such images capture the increasing complexity with which a person engages with a set of material. The underlying assertion here, then, is that these processes are directly linked to the increasing cognitive complexity noted by neo-Piagetians that we can have in relation to a specific area as discussed above. In other words, the more that we engage with material following the six processes outlined in the Taxonomy, the more complex, interrelated, and detailed our understanding of the material becomes. For educational purposes, the goal is to therefore help students to progress along these six processes so that their engagement with the material moves from more simple and superficial levels of learning to deeper engagement with it.

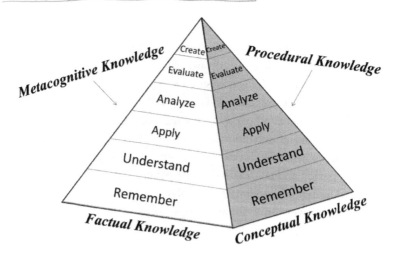

Figure 34. The Revised Bloom's Taxonomy.

For the workshop, then, these six processes can be very useful. We can use them to help us to identify some of the objectives that we have for participants, categorize activities that might foster one or more of these processes, and guide the kinds of assessments that we might develop. For instance, if we wanted students to engage with conflict mediation skills, we might choose activities that walk participants through each of the six Taxonomy processes. We might begin by introducing them to the stages of conflict mediation by lecturing on them, having them watch videos of role plays, et cetera. All of these may be designed to help them to re-member these stages. We might then break them up into small groups to discuss these mediation stages in relation to various conflict scenarios specifically having them to compare, contrast, make predictions, et cetera to ensure a deeper understanding of each of the mediation stages. Par-ticipants could also be asked to apply these stages to a specific conflict in their own lives. Based on this, they could then analyze and evaluate how the application went, compare it with some of the other mediations and role plays that they have seen in the workshop, and make suggestions for what they might do differently next time. Finally, participants could be asked to create their own version of these mediation stages, particularly ones that are more appropriate for their own local and cultural contexts.

Throughout such activities, participants can be led step-by-step to engage with the material in increasingly complex and interrelated ways. In the process, their CAU systems will be changing in significant and lasting ways that are increasingly interconnected and complex. As we can see, along with CAPS and neo-Piagetian developmental theories, this Taxonomy can therefore be a very powerful model for helping us to develop the other elements of the formation framework. As a result, this model is adopted as one of the primary models of reality for this strong model-based spirituality and peacebuilding workshop.

## Social Learning Theory Revisited

With these core models of cognitive change and development in place, we return briefly to Bandura's social learning theory discussed above. The central notion that was noted from this model was the idea of how people learn from one another. As it relates to these cognitive models, what is important to note is that each of the basic types of change, the increas-ingly complex cognition, and the Taxonomy's processes are all brought in relation to each other when people come together. In other words, as par-ticipants share their insights, reflect on their experiences, work together on projects, et cetera they will not only be modeling the Taxonomy's processes for one another, they will also be helping each other to foster the basic types of CAU system change in increasingly complex ways (ideally). Granted, while the workshop facilitator and fellow participants may not be the best mentors for one another in this, they will nevertheless provide many alternative ways of engaging, thinking about, applying, et cetera the workshop's material.

Since such interpersonal learning has been highlighted as being central for women's development, the minister will therefore need to intentionally design the program to foster the kinds of cognitive change discussed above primarily through social interactions among the group. What is important for this workshop, then, is to help participants to be exposed to one another's views, behaviors, et cetera in relation to the material. We can then help them to reflect on these different views and work towards refining and integrating them into their own lives. Some of this work, clearly, is the metacognitive knowledge covered in the Taxonomy. The majority of it, however, will be related to the other three domains of knowledge (factual, conceptual, and procedural). What is therefore helpful for us in preparation for this workshop is to be aware of the interpersonal CAUs that are shared amongst the participants and how they are integrating these into their own lives. Again, while not overly detailed, these additional insights will be helpful as we design this program.

## Theology

Our final underlying model of reality for the workshop is theology. Following the Trinitarian theology outlined in previous sections of this text, we can assert God to be present and active in these cognitive developmental processes and this workshop in incarnational, transcendent, and Deified ways. God may be conceived as the mysterious and utterly transcendent Ground that sustains and undergirds the workshop's existence and progression. Incarnationally, God may be understood to be non-dualistically present within and through the ever unfolding physiological-psychological processes, the social interactions and relationships among participants, the growth and development of the workshop's concepts, as well as the workshop as a whole. Finally, as Deity, it might be asserted that God continually provides the additional courage, motivation, healings, insights, et cetera that will be needed within and among the group's members and their respective communities in relation to the workshop's content and skills. Overall, then, we may theologically assert God's Life to be fully and continually active within, to, and beyond every part of the workshop.

While these kinds of general theological claims are helpful, we may go further in asserting where and how God might be at work in this program. We may assert that God seeks to manifest in the world in fully nonviolent ways. As a result, we can expect God to support the fundamental aims of this workshop. More specifically, the primary goal of this workshop may be conceived of as being to help its participants to come to partner ever more fully with God's nonviolent work in the world. In other words, the core spirituality and theology of the workshop is to help participants to be able to know how God is ever striving to work nonviolently in their own lives and communities so that they might become a more intimate and contributing part of this Divine work. Hence, by teaching participants nonviolent skills such as conflict mediation and restorative justice, for instance, we would be empowering them to work more harmoniously and intimately with God's nonviolent life in our world.

We may also conceive of God to be working to encourage the more holy and enduring CAU nodes and networks whilst also seeking to discourage and transform the more distorted ones. For instance, participants might initially believe in and support a revengeful "eye for an eye" approach to retributive justice. If it is accurate that God is fully nonviolent, then such beliefs and behaviors would be viewed as being distorted according to this theology. We would therefore expect God's Trinitarian Life to be working with these individual to change their views towards more of a forgiving, reconciling, and healing approach to restorative justice.

We might also expect the Spirit to be fully supportive, nurturing, and sustaining of the increasingly complex cognitive content and processes outlined above. We may conceive of God to be working to establish nodes, foster networks, and evolve meta-networks in the system. We might also assert that God is helping participants as they work to remember, understand, apply, analyze, evaluate, and create in relation to the peacebuilding material that they are engaging with.

In addition, the four basic types of CAU system change may be viewed as part of the primary ways by which God works within, to, and beyond a person's enduring inner life to nurture spiritualizing growth and development in these nonviolent topics and skills. In other words, it may be claimed, God will be working in Trinitarian ways to modify the existing knowledge and experiences that participants have, adding new ones as the workshop unfolds, combining concepts and creating connections between the material and the participant's own life, and nurturing genuine novelty and creativity as they strive to bring these nonviolent ways of life to their own lives as well as their communities.

Overall, then, it is the minister's role to continually reflect on and discern where and how the Spirit is working in the lives of the participants in relation to all of this. It is to look for the places where students are learning and growing in the material in increasingly complex ways. It is to discern the extent to which they are grasping, integrating, and applying the material to their own life and communities. However, it is to also look at those places where God's Life appears to be hindered or distorted. It is to look to those places where such development and progress is not happening smoothly and to those parts where participants do not seem to be absorbing or integrating the material into their life. These are the areas where the workshop may not be in harmony with God's movements as much as they could be.

Based on these spiritually discerning reflections, the minister must therefore decide where it is that God seems to be inviting the group to go next, which actions to take, what movements to discourage in the group, what to revamp or revisit, et cetera. The theology that undergirds this workshop is therefore a fundamental model that must shape not only the design of the workshop but also its continual unfolding. Furthermore, since we are exploring an example of a strong model-based approach to ministry in this part of the book, each of these models of reality will comprise the core foundation out of which each of the remaining parts of the formation framework will emerge as we shall now see.

## Goals & Objectives: Peacebuilding Empowerment

With these core models in place, we are now in a position to begin developing the rest of the framework's elements. When we think about the ideals that this workshop will work towards, there are really two levels of ideals to articulate: goals and objectives. In essence, the goals are the general horizons towards which we discern the workshop should head. Objectives, on the other hand, are the specific aims that we will work to achieve. These objectives are the ones that we will seek to concretely measure and evaluate the progress (or not) of the program and its activities. This is because we need to be able to assess in tangible ways where and how the workshop is unfolding. These objectives therefore have the purpose of setting the standards against which the assessments will be based on. Both of these levels of ideals are necessary to help guide the development of this program.

As we have developed the above models and explored the context for which this workshop is intended, some overarching goals have already been articulated. The overarching and most primary goal of this program is for this workshop *to help participants to learn about and participate more fully in God's nonviolent peacebuilding movements in their own life as well as in their communities.* As we just saw, a core theological assumption of this program is that God is seeking to act in the world in fully nonviolent ways. The education and the skills that this workshop will cover are therefore viewed as being a form of theological formation and empowerment. In other words, it is the core goal of this program to help participants to become an ever more fully part of these nonviolent movements of God.

As a result of this central goal, another one of the hopes is that the participants will grow in their ability to apply the nonviolent peacebuilding content & skills to their own lives. Additionally, there are also hopes that they will also become leaders in their community for this kind of peacebuilding work. As the models of reality show, there is also a need to address the development of each participant's increasing content and processing complexity. In other words, the workshop should help each person to develop in their understanding of the material at each of the levels being addressed (individual, relational, communal, and societal) in increasingly nuanced and interconnected ways. It should also help students to become more sophisticated in how they engage with and process this material following Bloom's model.

So, if we were to develop general goals for this workshop, they might begin to take shape as follows:

- Overall Goal/Ideal: Help participants to learn about and participate more fully in God's nonviolent peacebuilding movements in their own life as well as in their communities

- Goal #1: Knowledge of the Nonviolent Peacebuilding Content and Skills at Individual, Relational, Communal, and Societal Levels

- Goal #2: Processing of the Material with Increasing Complexity

- Goal #3: Personal and Leadership Development

While these goals are helpful horizons towards which to journey in this workshop, we will still need more concrete objectives in order to further define the specific milestones that the workshop will work to tangibly achieve. To help with the development of these, we turn to the models of reality for specific guidance and insight, something which is inherent for strong model-based methods of program development. In particular, the neo-Piagetian perspectives and Bloom's Taxonomy will be the central guiding models for the development of these objectives.

Beginning with the first goal, the hopes are that participants will be able to understand the material with increasing complexity and interconnectedness. As was discussed above, this would involve moving beyond simplistic definitions of violence, for instance, to seeing a typology of the various forms of violence that are prevalent in our world. Following Bloom's, there are four different forms of knowledge that such content-related complexity can develop along: factual, conceptual, procedural, and metacognitive. For the purposes of this workshop and the development of specific objectives in relation to this first goal, we will combine these into two general areas.

The first would be the specific peacebuilding content, which would be a combination of Bloom's factual and conceptual knowledge. Here, the workshop would work to develop each participant's knowledge of peacebuilding at each of the four levels. The second would be the associated peacebuilding skills, such as conflict mediation, restorative justice, et cetera. These would align most fully with Bloom's procedural knowledge. The metacognitive kinds of knowledge will be addressed in the third goal. What is important to note for this model-based case example is how each of the goals and objectives that are being developed are directly related back to models of reality.

Based upon this we are almost in a position to write an objective for the first goal. However, in order for it to be helpful it must be something that will be measurable or observable by the minister as discussed above. Educators recommend that such concrete objectives have at least three basic parts to them: a condition, a behavior, and a degree or criteria.[29] The condition is essentially the situation, teaching, et cetera that initiates the behavior that is to be observed. The degree or criteria is then the extent to

---

29. Holden, "A Guide to Developing Cognitive Learning Objectives"; Corporation, "Developing Clear Learning Outcomes and Objectives."

which the student is expected to perform; i.e., the criteria against which they will be compared. It is here that the list of verbs for Bloom's Taxonomy is helpful for it can provide us with concrete actions that may be observed and assessed. For this workshop, such a concrete objective might be written as: *After completing the learning module for each peacebuilding level, participants will be able to define the identified key terms and relate them to one another as covered in the module with 100 percent accuracy.* Here, the condition is completing the learning modules for each peacebuilding level. The behavior is their being able to define key terms and relate them to one another as covered in these modules. Finally, the degree or criteria is the 100 percent success rate in doing this. Since these learning modules will intentionally work to help participants to develop in their content complexity (i.e., in moving from simple concepts to more nuanced and interrelated ones), this objective therefore also addresses the neo-Piagetian part of the theories of change. In other words, this model of cognitive development directly shapes the objective for the first goal.

In regards to the second goal, we must develop a similarly concrete and measurable objective in relation to the cognitive processes of Bloom's Taxonomy. We are interested in how the participants engage with and use the peacebuilding material in terms of both the content and the skills for each of the peacebuilding levels. Recalling the verbs for the first two levels of the Taxonomy (i.e., remember and understand), we can see that the first objective covers these lower processing levels. As a result, this Goal #2 objective is more concerned with the remaining four (i.e., apply, analyze, evaluate, and create). Again, in order to help these objectives to be more concrete, they should specify the condition, behavior, and degree. For this goal, it may be helpful to separate these into four separate objectives that directly follow the Taxonomy:

- Applying Objective: *As a part of each peacebuilding learning module, participants will be able to explain how the specific peacebuilding content and skills may be applied to their own personal life and the communities of which they are a part. Participants will be able to demonstrate this by using one or more specific and detailed examples.*

- Analyzing Objective: *As a part of each peacebuilding learning module, participants will be able to compare and contrast specific peacebuilding content and skills with how conflicts are typically viewed and engaged in their own life and in their community. Participants will be able to explain this by using one or more specific and detailed case examples.*

- Evaluating Objective: *In light of what they are learning in each peacebuilding module, participants will be able to assess the effectiveness of how they and their communities currently engage with conflict. Participants will be able to explain this by using one or more specific and detailed case examples.*

- Creating Objective: *By the end of the workshop, participants will create a peacebuilding plan that may be implemented in their community to improve the effectiveness of nonviolent ways of engaging conflict at one or more of the peacebuilding levels.*

As we may see, each of these objectives specify the conditions under which the objective will be met, the behavior that is expected, and the degree to which each objective must be fulfilled. Following directly from Bloom's Taxonomy, each of these is intended to help the participants to engage with both the content and skills of the workshop with increasingly complex cognitive processes thereby fostering CAU system change. Again the underlying assumption here, according to our models of reality, is that by engaging in the Taxonomy's processes, they will grow in their understanding of the material in increasingly complex cognitive ways. In other words, these four objectives also help to support the objective for Goal #1.

Finally, turning to Goal #3, we find that the objectives just articulated fulfill this one as well. As it relates to nonviolent peacebuilding, this goal is primarily concerned with helping participants to reflect on and apply the content and skills of this workshop to their personal lives as well as to their communities. As we look back over each one of the objectives above, we can see that all but one has both of these elements to them. In other words, each learning module will intentionally incorporate these kinds of reflections and applications. For the creating objective, however, participants will only be asked to create a lesson plan for one of the peacebuilding skills that may be implemented in their community. This was chosen due to the time constraints of the workshop as well as of the participants, many of whom work at a full-time job. Developing peacebuilding lesson plans (as this section of the book demonstrates) can be very time consuming. As a result, participants will only be asked to create a single one. Since the mission of this nonprofit is focused on women's leadership development, participants will be asked to develop this plan for their community. Since these objectives cover the personal and leadership development ideals for this third goal, additional objectives are not needed. We might therefore combine these two goals into one: Increasing Cognitive Processing, Personal & Leadership Development.

Collectively, then, the goals and objectives for this workshop are compiled below. Emerging directly out of the models of reality, they provide a more tangible set of directives for the minister to pursue. These objectives will not only help her or him to develop assessments for each of them, they will also help to guide the kinds of activities that are chosen to help participants to move towards them. It is to the design of these activities that we next turn. But to recap, the following are the goals and objectives that have been derived following a strong model-based method:

- Overall Goal/Ideal: *To help participants to learn about and participate more fully in God's nonviolent peacebuilding movements in their own life as well as in their communities.*

- Goal #1: Knowledge of the Nonviolent Peacebuilding Content and Skills at Individual, Relational, Communal, and Societal Levels

    ◊ Content & Skills Objective: *After completing the learning module for each peacebuilding level, participants will be able to define the identified key terms and relate them to one another as covered in the module with 100 percent accuracy.*

- Goal #2: Increasing Cognitive Processing, Personal & Leadership Development

    ◊ Applying Objective: *As a part of each peacebuilding learning module, participants will be able to explain how the specific peacebuilding content and skills may be applied to their own personal life and the communities of which they are a part. Participants will be able to demonstrate this by using one or more specific and detailed examples.*

    ◊ Analyzing Objective: *As a part of each peacebuilding learning module, participants will be able to compare and contrast specific peacebuilding content and skills with how conflicts are typically viewed and engaged in their own life and in their community. Participants will be able to explain this by using one or more specific and detailed case examples.*

    ◊ Evaluating Objective: *In light of what they are learning in each peacebuilding module, participants will be able to assess the effectiveness of how they and their communities currently engage with conflict. Participants will be able to explain this by using one or more specific and detailed case examples.*

◊ Creating Objective: *By the end of the workshop, participants will create a peacebuilding plan that may be implemented in their community to improve the effectiveness of nonviolent ways of engaging conflict at one or more of the peacebuilding levels.*

## Approaches & Activities: Relationally & Critically Engaging

Following our systematic intentionality, where we seek to develop each new part of the framework in light of each of the other elements, we can begin to see what kinds of activities and approaches might be most appropriate for this specific program. Given the context of this being for women's leadership develop and the social-cultural learning theories, we already know that interpersonal activities must be a central set of approaches and pedagogies to draw from. This means that this program might include many small and large group discussions as well as collaborative activities. In addition, following the processes from Bloom's Taxonomy that will theoretically lead to the kinds of CAU network changes that we are working towards, we can have participants engage in activities as outlined by the Taxonomy. Indeed, and following systematic coherence, the objectives we just derived directly embody these processes from Bloom's. In fact, these objectives essentially outline the kinds of activities that we can have participants engage with. As a result, we are already well on our way to choosing these specific activities.

However, we can also look back to our deep learning and spiritual formation reflections in the previous part of this book. Here, we learned that such deep formation should: 1) foster significant change/learning of the concepts and/or skills, 2) be viewed from multiple perspectives and in multiple ways, 3) be adaptable to multiple contexts, 4) be directly relatable to the participant's own lives, and 5) be engaged repeatedly in spiral learning ways. While the objectives embody each of these characteristics, we want to be sure that we are not neglecting any of them. Overall, then, we are in a really good position to begin choosing the specific activities that will be used in this program.

As there are four levels of peacebuilding (individual, relational, communal, and societal) that this program will be walking with participants through, we will not design the entire course for each of these levels.

Instead, we will now consider only one of these levels (the relational level) to see how specific activities may be chosen following a strong model-based method in systematic ways. Overall, following spiral learning theory,[30] we would like for these four levels to build upon one another. One way of doing this is to begin with the individual level and move to the relational level, recognizing that a healthy inner life is emergently related to and foundational for healthy relationships. By doing this, we can therefore revisit and relate the learnings from the individual level to the relational one. Then, as the participants move on to the communal level, we can help them to see that healthy relationships and inner lives are foundational for healthy communities, all of which are subsequently foundational for healthy societies. In this way, we can revisit and deepen each of the previous level's core concepts and skills in each of the successive modules.

For the relational module, then, we will be building on the learnings from the individual level where participants will learn more about what a healthy inner life looks like and how to continually foster it in nonviolent ways. As we saw with the objectives, these are the essential concepts and skills that we will be working to nurture at each level of the program. For the relational level, then, this program will work towards these aims by building on what was learned at the individual level. From some of the literature on building healthy relationships,[31] there are at least three primary areas of content and skills that are important.

The first is exploring and knowing what healthy relationships look like and what some of the challenges and obstacles to these are. Participants need to learn, as stated above, that having healthy relationships is very much dependent on cultivating a healthy inner life. At a personal level, it is challenging for many to have the kinds of openness and vulnerability that are necessary for closer interpersonal relationships. The first part of this module can therefore focus on helping participants to better understand these concepts and how they relate to their own lives.

A second area of central importance noted in some literature on healthy relationships is the need for genuine communication. Here, participants need to learn the basics of the different kinds of communication that there are and what can obstruct or distort communication. They also need to learn some of the differences between just hearing someone else and deeply listening to and being present to one another. The ultimate

30. Ginsburg and Opper, *Piaget's Theory of Intellectual Development*, 232.

31. Barrick, *Sacred Psychology of Love*; Block, *Naked Intimacy*; Kraybill, *Peace Skills*.

goal of such deep presence is interpersonal attunement, or the feeling of truly being felt by another. Of course, such genuine communication can only occur when each person in the relationship opens themselves up internally to such attunement and connection, an openness that requires mature levels of vulnerability. As a part of this second area, then, is the engagement with active listening skills.

This deeper communication and attunement seems easier when things are going well with our relational partners, but what about when conflicts arise? A third central area of nonviolent peacebuilding at this level is therefore conflict mediation or transformation skills. Here, participants will learn the basic steps of mediation and how to apply these to different kinds of conflict. They will also come to see that the individual level (as well as the genuine communication skills they have already learned about) is essential for this area as well.

Overall, then, these are some of the foundational concepts and skills that participants will engage for this relational level of nonviolent peacebuilding. It should be noted that specific knowledge of this workshop's content was merged with the models of reality that are being considered herein. Following the deep learning and spiritual formation principles, we can also see that participants will be working to deepen their understanding and engagement of core peacebuilding concepts and skills as they move from the individual level to this relational one and then on to the other two modules (e.g., communal and societal levels).

We can also see that the overall development of this module so far requires that the practitioner already has a strong background in this area of learning or formation. Some educators assert that practitioners must have a strong background in the following four areas in order to develop educational programs: knowledge of the content area, pedagogical knowledge for the content area, general pedagogical knowledge, and a general knowledge of learning.[32] In this case, knowing the literature on relationship building helps one to know what core concepts/skills to focus on and how to sequence them in ways that build upon previous learning and engagement.

Hence, we have located this relational module within the larger landscape of this program's unfolding from individual to communal levels. We have also identified and sequenced the core concepts and skills that participants will engage as part of this particular module based upon relationship literature and some of our deep learning/formation principles.

---

32. Eggen and Kauchak, *Strategies and Models for Teachers*, 8.

What needs to happen next is the identification of the specific activities and pedagogies that participants will engage in for this module. As there are three core areas (i.e., knowing what healthy relationships looks like, et cetera), or sub-units, to this module we will only be taking one of these to better understand how a strong model-based method might be used to aid in the development of this program. For this, we will be looking at the first of these three sub-units, focusing on helping participants to better understand what healthy relationships look like and what some of the challenges and obstacles to these are.

In the previous module on peacebuilding at the individual level, participants will have learned about the necessity of being present to their inner life with greater awareness, sensitivity, and compassion. As we have heard, this relationship module will therefore seek to build upon these core peacebuilding concepts and skills as they apply them to their relationships. Returning to our models of reality, we are theoretically hoping to utilize these already existing CAU networks from the previous module to expand, reshape, combine, and add new ones to. For guidance in how to help foster these kinds of cognitive-affective changes, we look to Bloom's Taxonomy and the objectives that were directly derived therefrom.

In other words, we are looking for activities that will help participants to better understand, apply, analyze, and evaluate the concepts in this first sub-unit. In addition, following our social-cultural learning theories, these activities need to be interpersonally engaging. For this module, this is particularly important because having participants learn about relationships through relational engagement should work to further deepen their experiential understanding of this material. Finally, given the Trinitarian theology that is a part of this program's development and given that this program is focused on spirituality and peacebuilding, the activities chosen should have a more religious and theological tone to them than would be found in a secular version of it. Noting that participants are of different religious orientations, though, these resources and activities must allow for such diversity.

With these model-based foundations in place, the practitioner must now return to the literature and resources in this area to begin looking for activities that meet these criteria. At this point, program development now moves from being more of a theory-based science to more of an art form. This is because which specific activities to choose and how to precisely sequence them is dependent on a number of factors that are not exactly captured by these models of reality even though they are quite detailed. Such factors include each participant's specific background in relation to conflict and peacebuilding, unfolding contextual dynamics, how things have unfolded up until this point in the program, the resources available for the program, and many others. Experienced peacebuilding practitioners who have been teaching in this specific field for many years will have a better feel for which activities to choose and how to sequence them based on their extensive educational and experiential background. For novice practitioners, a greater reliance on resources, particularly those developed or offered by experienced practitioners, will be helpful.

For this first sub-unit, where participants will explore the nature of healthy relationships and some of the challenges to cultivating these, the minister chose the ensuing specific activities following the model-based guidelines above. Coming directly out of the individual module, participants will watch a Ted Talk by Brene Brown which discusses the importance of being vulnerable in one's life and relationships and what some of the consequences are of not doing so.[33] Following this, participants will discuss in dyads what they gained from this video clip and whether being vulnerable and open to others is difficult for them personally. After sharing some of these dyad reflections as a large group, participants will be given an "openness scale" test that was developed by clinical psychologist, Joel Block, who works on intimacy issues with couples.[34] Again returning to dyads to discuss their own results, participants will also talk about the "many faces of deception" that Block asserts that we sometimes use in our relationships and how these can negatively impact our lives.

As a large group, recognizing that "unhealthy" relationships are ones where there is little vulnerability and much deception, participants will begin brainstorming what more vibrant and intimate relationships look like. Here, a focus will be given to further clarifying what a more spiritual relationship is. Following these discussions, participants will return to their dyads where they will choose from a list of key ingredients that are needed to foster such healthy relationships that was developed by marriage and family therapist, Marlyn Barrick.[35] Being comprised of a list of fifteen such ingredients, participants will be asked to choose what they think are the top three and explain to their partners which three they chose and why they think that they are the most important ones for

33. Available at http://www.ted.com/talks/brene_brown_on_vulnerability; accessed 28 March 2014.

34. Block, *Naked Intimacy*, chap. 2.

35. Barrick, *Sacred Psychology of Love*, 208–11.

fostering healthy relationships. After these dyads have completed their explanations, the group will discuss these ingredients. One of the top ingredients on Barrick's list is communication and the minister will use this large group discussion to begin the transition into the second sub-unit on genuine communication. These discussions therefore complete this sub-unit as the group moves into the next one.

What is important to recognize here, more than the specific activities that were chosen or how they were sequenced, is how they begin to embody the models of reality and resulting objectives for this program. We can clearly see how each of the activities was directly related to each participant's personal life, something which is considered to be essential for deep learning and formation to occur. We can also see the centrality of social-cultural learning theories via the dyad and large group discussions. It is through these conversations that participants are modeling their understanding and deeper thinking in relation to the material being engaged. Following Bloom's Taxonomy, participants are also led from merely understanding the nature of healthy and more spiritual relationships via the video clips and readings towards applying, analyzing, and evaluating some of these concepts. The dyad and large group discussions are also designed to engage participants in these kinds of processes as they are asked to relate these concepts to their own life as well as to defend their choice of the top three ingredients that are needed to foster healthy relationships. Such critical and deeper engagement will then continue as the next two sub-units of this module unfold.

We can therefore see how these models of reality can be a very helpful aid to practitioners for knowing what kinds of approaches to choose. It is out of consideration of each of these models that specific activities may come to the surface from the content/skill specific resources. Once one has a set of such approaches to consider, they can then begin to engage in both systematic and intuitive reflections to help with choosing and sequencing the specific activities that they will use. This program is therefore one example of how strong model-based methods, based on the theological anthropologies that we synthesize, might be used to help further support our program development efforts.

## Monitoring & Assessment: Concept/Skill Tracking

As the title of this section suggests, there are two parts that we need to consider in the development of this program: the data that we will monitor and collect and the measures by which we will evaluate and assess this data. The models that we have outlined above should provide us with insights into the development of each of these. Overall, we are interested in tracking how the participant's understandings and applications of the core peacebuilding concepts and skills are progressing for them.

In terms of monitoring, the models can help us to realize that we are interested in how the peacebuilding concepts and skills for the participants are taking shape. These concepts and skills should therefore be expanded, reshaped, combined, increase in complexity, and even possibly result in the emergence of novel insights and creative applications. As a result, our monitoring system must track such developments. In addition, Bloom's Taxonomy encourages us to also monitor the processes by which participants are engaging with the material. Finally, our deep learning characteristics from the previous chapter help us to see the importance of making sure that participants are repeatedly engaging the material from multiple perspectives and contexts. This should be done in ways that relate to their own lives such that the details and nuances of the peacebuilding concepts and skills are being illuminated for them.

This might sound somewhat complex and abstract. However, we can look to our objectives for further guidance in these monitoring activities because these were developed based upon the models. Specifically, then, we are interested in monitoring and tracking how participants remember, understand, apply, analyze, evaluate, and ultimately create using the program's peacebuilding materials. Again, the underlying assumption is that these processes will foster the kinds of cognitive development detailed by the models of reality and deep learning characteristics. In addition, since these objectives describe the directions that the program should be headed towards, the data that is collected needs to provide the facilitator with insights into how participants are doing in relation to them so that the facilitator may modify the program as it unfolds. Hence, at a minimum, the data that is collected should be directly related to these objectives.

When it comes to collecting this data for monitoring and evaluation purposes, there are at least two avenues to use. The first is via the activities that we have participants engage in. For example, the small and large group discussions described in the previous section can provide the facilitator with valuable insights into how the participants are engaging with and making sense of the concepts and/or skills. A second source of such monitoring data are activities that are explicitly designed to collect specific kinds of data. An example of this would be exams, essay assignments, reflection questions, et cetera. These kinds of activities differ from the first kind because their primary intention is to gather specific kinds of focused data for the express purpose of assessing where students are in relation to the objectives. The first kind of activities, on the other hand, are primarily concerned with having the participants to engage with the material in ways that foster deeper formation but may also be used to gather data for assessment. As we can see, the data that needs to be gathered for a given program may be closely connected with the kinds of activities that one uses in the program. As a result, choosing the activities for each module should be done in close consideration of the kinds of data that need to be gathered. This is precisely why it is becoming increasingly accepted in the instructional design community to view program development work as a tightly integrated endeavor rather than as distinct phases (e.g., first choose the models, then set the objectives, next pick the activities, et cetera).[36]

So for this particular program, what kinds of data might need to be gathered? Turning once again to our objectives, we find that the following kinds of data need to be collected. For the content and skills objective, participants are expected to be able to describe key peacebuilding terms and to be able to relate them to one another. As a result, data gathering needs to include activities (of one or both kinds above) that provide the facilitator with insights into participant understandings of these key concepts and skills. Examples might include having students create concept maps, having them teach specific concepts and skills to one another, or have them take a quiz to check their understanding.

For the applying objective, participants should be able to show how the program's material may be applied to their lives and communities. Similarly, the analyzing objective requires that they also be able to compare and contrast specific concepts and skills in relation to their personal contexts. Finally, the evaluating objective states, "participants will be able to assess the effectiveness of how they and their communities currently engage with conflict." In addition, participants are expected to demonstrate each of these objectives by providing one or more specific examples. The data that is gathered must therefore provide the facilitator with a clear picture of the extent to which participants are able to do this.

36. Branch and Merrill, "Characteristics of Instructional Design Models," 8.

Examples might include having participants use conflict mediation or restorative justice skills in a specific relationship or having them interview members of their community and reflect on some of the common views of conflict and how it is dealt with. Again, the data that is gathered from such activities should help the facilitator to monitor how participants are doing in relation to the objectives as well as the cognitive, social, and deep learning dynamics that are described by the models of reality.

Once these channels of monitoring and data collection are decided upon, the next step is to decide how to evaluate and assess it. One of the primary purposes of assessments is to provide the facilitator with insights into how the participants are progressing (or not) specifically in relation to the objectives. There are a number of different kinds of assessments that can be developed and the reader is referred to these extensive resources for more detailed discussions of these. Here, only one example will be given in order to help demonstrate how one kind of assessment—known as "rubrics"—might be developed following strong model-based methods.

One way of using rubrics for this program is to develop a set of criteria for each of the program's objectives. Such rubrics could outline the developmental stages that participants are likely to progress through as they come to meet each objective in more substantial ways. For instance, consider an activity where the facilitator had the participants engage in analysis of how persons in their own families have typically handled interpersonal conflicts. This activity clearly aligns with the analysis objective and the data gathered from this critical reflection assignment can be used to assess how well the participants are doing in relation to this objective.

However, rubrics are not typically used as a "right or wrong" kind of assessment. Instead, rubrics can be used to evaluate the extent to which participants are showing competency in a given area. Consider the rubric shown in the table below.

| Area Assessed | Proficient | Proficient –Intermediate | Intermediate | Intermediate-Beginning | Beginning or Incomplete |
|---|---|---|---|---|---|
| *Critical Analysis:* Reflections critically analyze and are logical and complete. | a) Reflections critically analyze by comparing and contrasting course concepts and/or skills with other material, noting greater details and nuances, et cetera. b) Reflections are logical in that they are clearly connected to and supported by the references and discussions in the answer. c) Reflections are complete in that they follow through on questions, analyses, et cetera to their full and logical end. | a) Reflections critically analyze material. b) Reflections are logical. c) Reflections are complete but in less thorough ways than for the Proficient Level (i.e., critical analysis is begun and carried out to some extent, but not to its full development). | a) Reflections critically analyze, but in less thorough ways than at the Proficient Level. b) Reflections are logical, but in less thorough ways than at the Proficient Level. c) Reflections are complete but in less thorough ways than for the Proficient Level. | a) Reflections are only borderline critical, providing some analysis but in only very general ways. b) Reflections are far less logically supported and connected. c) Reflections are not complete or developed with much depth. | a) Reflections provide little to no critical analysis. b) Reflections lack a logical consistency. c) Reflections are not complete, but are stated very briefly. |

This rubric identifies the specific area that is being assessed, in this case critical analysis. In addition, however, it also defines what various levels of competency look like in relation to this specific area from beginning through intermediate to proficient. This development reflects the kinds of increasing cognitive complexity that we discussed in detail for the models of reality. We might therefore expect that certain concepts or skills participants will enter the program towards the beginning end of the scale. If this is the case and our program is effective in fostering the kinds of deep formation that we have designed it for, then we would expect that they would gradually move towards the proficient end of the rubric as the program unfolds. These are precisely the kinds of insights that our monitoring and assessing systems should provide us with. If it turns out that the majority of participants are not making progress, then the program needs to be modified accordingly in real-time. Overall, then, the models can provide us with useful insights and guidance in knowing what kinds of data to collect and how to construct assessments. As a result, we can again see how each element of the formation framework may be more systematically developed following a strong model-based method of program development.

## Discernment & Implementation: The Foundational Bedrock

When it comes to spiritual discernment, there are a number of resources that practitioners may draw from to help guide their prayerful reflections.[37] It is beyond the scope of this section to review these various processes. Instead, we will only be reflecting briefly on how one's own approaches to discernment might inform their program development efforts. We will also be considering how strong model-based methods might be implemented once a program is being implemented.

For initial program planning, one's own spiritual discernment processes may be engaged to help in the design and development of its various parts. As we heard at the beginning of this chapter, there are at least five different core program design methods that can be used to give shape to the specific programs that we are working to develop. As we have seen throughout this final section, these methods may be used to develop each part of the formation framework. However, this does not mean that we should use these design methods to the neglect of our own discernment

---

37. See footnote 21 on page 126 for a list of some of these kinds of resources.

processes. Rather, our ways of engaging in discernment and decision-making needs to form the very foundation of how we engage in program development using these core design methods.

Consider the section above where we reflected on how a strong model-based method might be used to help determine what kinds of activities to draw from and use for this specific program. While the models of reality helped to narrow down the range of activities that we might choose from, there were still a wide variety of interventions that we can choose from. This is where our own spiritual discernment processes should be helping to further inform and guide our decisions. For theists, the goal of all such processes is to help us to more clearly discern where it is God might be leading us towards, in this case which specific activities that God is seeking to work through in this program. Stepping back and looking more broadly, these discernment processes should also help to guide our choices of which core methods to use, what contextual factors to consider, et cetera. Through and through, from beginning to end, these processes should comprise the very foundational bedrock for how we engage in program development.[38] Indeed, spiritual discernment should form the very foundation for how we live and engage our lives on a daily basis in all that we are and do.

With this discerning foundation in place, we finally turn to implementation for strong model-based methods. Once a program is designed, developed, and launched, it is up to the practitioner to discerningly walk step-by-step with the program as it unfolds. Certainly, a part of this implementation entails an ongoing presence to and an awareness of the moment-by-moment dynamics of the program. However, each of the core methods might also be additionally seen as having their own specific implementation methods that are associated with them. Objective oriented programs are primarily concerned with progress towards the given standards and implementation should be focused on ensuring this. Pedagogy centered programs work to achieve a deep engagement with specific activities, processes, or skills and the practitioner needs to continually work to encourage such deep engagement. Data driven methods are more focused on following the dominant patterns, trends, and movements of the group and implementation needs to embody this adaptability. Authoritative sources are more concerned with adherence to the advice, insights, mandates, et cetera of the source(s) and the practitioner's

---

38. For more discussions on this, see Kyle, *Living Spiritual Praxis*, chap. 1.

role is to help the program to unfold following these lines. Of course, such implementation methods can and should also be blended to make for more holistic and robust program embodiment.

For model-based methods with programs such as this one, however, the practitioner's focus can turn to the models and seek to ensure that the program remains a strong model-based system if this continues to be appropriate and fruitful for the program's unfolding. This means that as the program progresses, the practitioner can continually modify and update the models of reality based on the in-vivo data that is being collected. As we have tried to show with this particular peacebuilding program, as these models are modified then so too might the other framework elements. Implementation for such strong model-based systems therefore becomes one in which we strive to maintain a close correlation between the insights that the models are providing us with about the participants and how the program is continually being carried out.

For example, if we were to add a model that addressed the affective dynamics of the group, then it would behoove us to revisit each of the framework elements and reflect on what some of the possible implications of such an addition might be for the program. Or, if it was discerned that one or more of our models was not accurately describing the dynamics of the program, then these models would need to be modified along with the program. Again, for a strong model-based systems, if the models change then so too might the other framework elements that were designed based on them. Such discerned data gathering, model validations, and program modifications form the basis for how strong model-based courses such as this one might be implemented.

## MODELS AND EDUCATION IN REVIEW

In this final chapter, we have attempted to demonstrate how the theological anthropologies that we have synthesized might be used to further inform our spiritual formation program development. The exploratory foundations of the first two parts of the book have provided us with general insights into and overviews of some of the major dynamics of human nature. However, as we saw in the beginning of this chapter, more guidance and details are needed in order to be able to develop a strong model-based program. Realizing this, we can and perhaps should be humbled by the immense complexity of human systems. While there are so many insights that our many historical western Christian and modern science models can and do provide us with, there is still so much that we do not fully understand in relation to human systems.

Yet, even in the midst of this, the little bit that we do currently know can provide us with enough insights to help us to construct better informed and, hopefully, more effective formation programs. Such model-based complexity can also help us to realize the need that there is for a solid historical and contemporary education in the areas that our own programs typically focus on. Practitioners working primarily with individuals should have strong foundations in neuroscience, psychology, et cetera. Those working with couples and team building should have knowledge of marriage and family therapy insights, sociological principles, et cetera. And so on.

However, even with such backgrounds, the synthesized theological anthropology, with as seemingly detailed as it was, could only provide us with a general landscape within which to locate the formative work of this particular program. We needed additional and more specific insights into the cognitive and social-cultural dynamics that this program was seeking to work with. As a result, spiritual formators need to be well aware of the kinds of programs that they prefer to develop and the anthro-cosmological areas that these typically address, be they at the individual, relational, communal, or other levels. Once identified, practitioners would do well to continually seek a stronger background in the study of these areas, particularly ensuring that such an education addresses each of the formation framework's elements. Doing so will not only equip the practitioner to develop strong model-based programs such as this one, but to also be able to utilize the other core program development methods when it is more appropriate and preferable to do so.

# Anthropological Afterthoughts

THIS BOOK HAS SOUGHT to walk practitioners and theorists through a process of exploring historical and contemporary theories of human nature in pursuit of insights into how these might then be used to support spiritual formation program development. Along the way, we have not only seen how we might begin to synthesize our own theological anthropologies in light of this background but we also developed a more generalized model for formation. Using these as the foundational landscape within which a strong model-based program was developed, it was clearly seen just how complex formation work with human systems is. If there is one major theme that has emerged from these writings, it is the realization of this complexity. We should therefore be quite humbled in light of this complexity and awed by the wonder of creation in general and for the human species in particular.

For formators seeking to conduct ministry at other levels (e.g., relational, communal, et cetera), similar research projects and model-based explorations are needed to support their work. This is of particular significance for those working in congregational ministry, where one regularly works at multiple levels. The background that is needed for such work is quite extensive. Unfortunately, the current state and trajectory of religion in the West has been one of decline thereby decreasing the educational and resource supports for ministers in these settings. The assertion that this book seems to support, however, is that in order to develop higher quality programs, a strong background in formation work is needed. As the supports continue to decline, though, and congregations and other under-resourced ministries continue to struggle to find adequately trained and equipped formators, we can expect the quality of their programs to likewise be in decline. It has become typical to end my books with a calling for our field of spiritual formation and for this particular work it is this: that our ministries need to continue to receive the adequate supports that they need to ensure more deeply transformative programs and spiritual formation systems. For as we have seen throughout this book, such supports are what is needed in order to help ensure ever deepening spiritual being and becoming.

# APPENDIX A

# Summary Table
# of Western Christian Views

| Source | Views of Human Nature | Views of the Divine in Relation to Humanity | Nature of Change For Humans, and God's Relationship to Such Transformation |
|---|---|---|---|
| Biblical (J. Green) | • Undivided Wholeness = "Soul" <br> • Embodied, Physicality <br> • Relational <br> ◊ God <br> ◊ Others <br> ◊ Creation <br> • Divine Image w/in <br> • Continual participation with sin | • Wisdom as a Pure Emanation <br> • Jesus as the Model and Transforming Foundation for humanity | • Change comes via the whole person <br> • A turning away from sin <br> • Change includes our relationships and communities <br> • It is a gradual, day-by-day, repatterning process of "thinking, feeling, believing, and behaving" <br> • Comes by means of Christ's and Divine Wisdom's transforming work in creation |

| Source | Views of Human Nature | Views of the Divine in Relation to Humanity | Nature of Change For Humans, and God's Relationship to Such Transformation |
|---|---|---|---|
| Augustine of Hippo (The Trinity) | • Elements<br>◊ Body<br>◊ Soul<br>◊ Rationality/Mind<br>◊ Will<br>◊ Inner person (understanding, reason, wisdom, wordless knowing), Outer person (sensation)<br>◊ When united with God: "three elements, God, soul, and flesh"<br>• Trinities<br>◊ Mind, Knowledge, Love<br>◊ Memory, Understanding, Will<br>• Sin<br>◊ Distortions from flesh<br>◊ Devil | • Christ<br>◊ Defeats Devil<br>◊ Pays our debt<br>◊ Model to our "outer man" and a<br>◊ Saving sacrament to our "inner man" "in order to refashion us to the image of God,"<br>◊ Standing as a mediator between us and God<br>• Trinity<br>◊ Eternal<br>◊ Omnipresent,<br>◊ Unchangeable,<br>◊ Uncreated "more excellent,"<br>◊ Invisible,<br>◊ Spiritual (meaning God "senses with mind not body")<br>◊ In control of all that transpires<br>◊ Relates to humans through wisdom, angels, Christ, other people | • Soul in need of redemption<br>◊ Weighed down by the "accumulated dirt of our sins"<br>• Liberation<br>◊ Via rational soul cleaves to God<br>◊ Aided by daily practicing the virtues and contemplation<br>◊ By the use of reason and self-knowing<br>• The Journey<br>◊ A gradual ascent from earth to heaven<br>◊ From the "outer man" to the inner one<br>◊ God as the source, sustainer, and culminator of this journey |

| Source | Views of Human Nature | Views of the Divine in Relation to Humanity | Nature of Change For Humans, and God's Relationship to Such Transformation |
|---|---|---|---|
| Maximus the Confessor (L. Thunberg) | • Emphasis<br>◊ Finding our end in God<br>◊ Wholeness, Mediation of various parts<br>◊ Humans as a middle position between matter and God<br>• Parts<br>◊ Mind - ("nous") as Unifying our various parts; "the primary instrument of [a person's] relationship to God"<br>◊ Soul – hypostatically/ inseparably united with body<br>  * Concupiscible Part = relationship to the "lower" world; responsible for the Fall of Humanity<br>  * Irascible Part – relationship to others<br>  * Rational Part – relationship to Intellect and Spirit; the Image of God in humans<br>◊ Body<br>◊ Passions – came in through the Fall of Humanity<br>◊ Will<br>• Sin<br>◊ From Human choices<br>◊ Devil's influences<br>◊ Caused by "ignorance, self-love, and tyranny"<br>◊ Essentially humanity choosing to find its pleasure in sources other than God | • Christological Focus<br>◊ Emphasis on Christ's Two Natures<br>◊ Model for Deification = Human and Divine Natures becoming One<br>◊ Christ as the Mediator, the Unifier of Creation<br>◊ Christ as the Model and Unifier of such Unity | • Deification Emphasis<br>◊ Humans as the Divine Likeness brought to bear in creation<br>◊ Central Role of Christ in the Journey<br>• Five Mediations, between:<br>◊ 1) Woman and man,<br>◊ 2) Paradise and the inhabited work,<br>◊ 3) Heaven and earth,<br>◊ 4) Intelligible and sensible things and<br>◊ 5) Finally between created and uncreated nature<br>◊ These mediations are needed because of the Fall, which caused separation and division<br>• Stages of the Spiritual Life:<br>◊ Vita practica = acquisition of the virtues<br>◊ Vita contemplative = pursuit of the true nature of things<br>◊ Vita mystica = "superknowledge," which is "a supreme ignorance through which God the Unknowable is made known" |

| Source | Views of Human Nature | Views of the Divine in Relation to Humanity | Nature of Change For Humans, and God's Relationship to Such Transformation |
|---|---|---|---|
| Thomas Aquinas (Summa, J.P. Torrell) | • Generally<br>◊ Inherently good, able to acquire perfect goodness<br>• Parts/Elements<br>◊ Body - form of the soul<br>◊ Soul:<br>  * Takes the form of the body;<br>  * Desires unity with the body, but can exist without the body<br>  * Has other ways of knowing beyond the senses<br>  * Incorporeal, incorruptible, and "the more noble part"<br>  * Created by God and makes the spiritual life possible<br>  * Gives life to the body<br>  * Powers:<br>• Vegetative<br>• Sensible<br>• Intellectual – memory, reason, understanding<br>◊ Free-Will – empowering, but limited<br>◊ Conscience = source of guidance<br>◊ Appetites:<br>  * Irascible<br>  * Concupiscible<br>◊ Community<br>• Sin<br>◊ The result of choosing counter to the God-given nature of things | • Relationship to creation<br>◊ There is a continuity between matter and Spirit<br>◊ "God's love makes being arise from nothingness – at every instant"<br>• God<br>◊ Utterly Transcendent and Unknowable<br>◊ Creator and Redeemer of Creation<br>• Christ<br>◊ The Model and the Mode for us achieving the Divine<br>◊ Friend to humanity<br>◊ The Visible manifestation of God<br>• Holy Spirit<br>◊ An aid and source of life and grace in creation | • Aims and nature of the Journey<br>◊ To return to God, from which we came<br>◊ The complete spiritualizing, harmonizing, and re-orienting of the whole of one's life towards the Divine<br>◊ Twofold movement:<br>  * Us becoming more like God<br>  * God coming to dwell more fully in us<br>• Stages:<br>◊ 1) A natural aptitude to know and love God<br>◊ 2) We know and love God actually and habitually<br>◊ 3) We know and love God actually and perfectly<br>• Needed for the Journey:<br>◊ Contemplation,<br>◊ Rationality,<br>◊ Following one's conscience, and<br>◊ Cultivating the virtues<br>◊ Supportive Community<br>• God and the Journey<br>◊ Holy Spirit led |

| Source | Views of Human Nature | Views of the Divine in Relation to Humanity | Nature of Change For Humans, and God's Relationship to Such Transformation |
|---|---|---|---|
| Martin Luther (Freedom, Mannermaa) | • Two-fold Nature:<br>◊ Bodily<br>　* Also known as the flesh, carnal, outer, and old person<br>　* Viewed as full of sin,<br>　* Pitted against the Spirit, and<br>　* In need of redemption<br>◊ Spiritual<br>　* Also known as the soul, inner, or new person<br>　* What it means to be a Christian,<br>　* Secure,<br>　* Subject to both none and all,<br>　* Created in the image of God,<br>　* Totally righteous, and<br>　* Ultimately replaces the old self or outer person<br>◊ Relationship between these:<br>　* On-going battle | • Christ is Central<br>◊ Viewed as bearing all our sins<br>◊ Wins the battle for the inner person<br>◊ Unites us and all of creation in substance with God<br>◊ Viewed as God's favor and God's gift<br>◊ Comes as God's Word<br>◊ He is grace itself<br>◊ The "greatest person" (maxima persona), in whom all human beings are really united<br>• Holy Spirit<br>◊ Viewed as the Spirit of Christ | • Aim, Nature of the Journey<br>◊ A battle between the inner and outer person<br>◊ To put off the old person and allow the new person to emerge<br>◊ Different for different persons<br>◊ Proceeds by faith in Christ alone<br>　* But works, or "means of grace," are still encouraged: Word, works, community<br>　* Emphasis on hearing the Word of God, particularly the Gospels<br>• Christ's Role<br>◊ Spirit of Christ fights for us against the flesh<br>◊ There is nothing a person can do of themselves to win the battle<br>◊ Christ becomes Present in one's faith, allowing Christ to win the battle for us<br>◊ Christ takes on our sins and transforms them for us |

| Source | Views of Human Nature | Views of the Divine in Relation to Humanity | Nature of Change For Humans, and God's Relationship to Such Transformation |
|---|---|---|---|
| *Immanuel Kant (Religion w/in Limits)* | • Generally<br>◊ Humans are inherently good, this is our original disposition<br>◊ Though we have fallen from an original "state of innocence"<br>• Parts, Elements<br>◊ Something in us that is able to individually access mystery<br>◊ Will – freedom to choose<br>◊ Dispositions – inclinations already present<br>• Nature of Sin<br>◊ The result of a combination of one's will and dispositions;<br>◊ Good or evil dispositions can be adopted or rejected by each individual | • Christology<br>◊ Jesus as a model; A<br>◊ An "archetype" to which we are expected to conform;<br>◊ The ultimate maxim that we are supposed to strive towards<br>• God<br>◊ As the omnipotent Creator of heaven and earth, i.e., morally as holy Legislator,<br>◊ As Preserver of the human race, its benevolent Ruler and moral Guardian, and<br>◊ As Administrator of His own holy laws, i.e., as righteous Judge | • Nature of the Journey<br>◊ Struggling against our fallness by the means of the goodness of God<br>◊ Rooted in rationality<br>◊ Oriented towards the moral good<br>◊ It is a long and gradual cultivation of virtuous living<br>• Needed for the Journey<br>◊ Knowledge of universal laws accessible to all via our rational faculties (he is arguing for a religion of pure reason)<br>◊ Virtuous communities and society<br>• God's Role<br>◊ Grace as giving that which nature cannot, providing comfort, freedom, and strength |

| Source | Views of Human Nature | Views of the Divine in Relation to Humanity | Nature of Change For Humans, and God's Relationship to Such Transformation |
|---|---|---|---|
| *Karl Barth (Dogmatics, Neder, Price)* | • Components<br>◊ Relationships<br>  * Others<br>  * God, Christ<br>◊ Consciousness, especially in response to grace<br>◊ Body<br>◊ Soul<br>  * "a rational and volitional structure for the animating force of the human body"<br>◊ Unity of Body and Soul = "an embodied soul and an ensouled body"<br>◊ "spirit" – of the person<br>  * This means that one is grounded by God<br>  * Both limits and unifies body and soul<br>◊ Spirit – of God<br>  * Sustains and orders the body and soul, as well as all of creation<br>• Sin<br>◊ A break in relationships<br>◊ A distortion and blinding of our abilities to see reality as it is | • Christ<br>◊ The restoring Image of God we are called to cleave to<br>◊ The core foundation for all of humanity in God; the very center of the divine-human relationship<br>◊ The Source and Origin of all things<br>◊ Divine Mediator who frees all by the Giving of Himself<br>◊ Participates in our suffering and fallen nature<br>• God<br>◊ Expresses Divinity in creation through Christ<br>◊ "is neither a part nor the whole of human nature. . ... But the whole which we are in this unity and order is not without God"<br>◊ Always revealed only under a veil of mystery | • Nature of the Journey<br>◊ A "mutual indwelling. . .the liberation of human action by God's sovereign grace"<br>◊ Imaged as a death to the "sinner" in us and the creation of a new person<br>◊ Such a death-to-life transition happens in God through Christ<br>◊ Relational unity in Christ is at the core of the Journey<br>◊ A path of growing in conformity to the Word of God<br>◊ Christ alone affects all that is necessary for our salvation and sanctification |

| Source | Views of Human Nature | Views of the Divine in Relation to Humanity | Nature of Change For Humans, and God's Relationship to Such Transformation |
|---|---|---|---|
| *Karl Rahner (Foundations)* | • Nature of Human Nature<br>◊ Bounded in history,<br>◊ Whole, neither re-ducible nor dividable<br>◊ "Transcendentality," ultimately unknow-able essence or "ground"<br>  * Through this we experience the "absolute closeness and immediacy" of God<br>◊ Free and responsible to choose,<br>◊ Dependent, and<br>◊ Oriented towards God<br>• Sin<br>◊ Can result from free-dom when under the influence of "original guilt" | • God's Nature<br>◊ Simultaneous transcendence and immanence of the Divine<br>◊ As transcendent, God is "the ontologically silent horizon of every intellec-tual and spiritual encounter"<br>◊ As immanent, God is "the ultimate and highest dynamism of this world and its history"<br>• God's Relationship to creation<br>◊ God's self-commu-nication happens most fully "in the fundamental unity of knowledge and love"<br>• Jesus<br>◊ Historically and biologically located<br>◊ Fully alive - a model and climax of human potenti-ality and hypostatic union with God's self-communication | • Nature of the Journey<br>◊ One towards both whole-ness and self-transcendence<br>◊ One of God permeating the entirety of one's being and history<br>◊ Includes self-awareness and self-actualization as well as a love which extends to one's neighbors<br>◊ It is one where we come to embrace our transcendentality<br>◊ Transformation never made in complete isolation, made in concert with the whole cosmos<br>• Needed for the Journey<br>◊ Must be open, oriented towards God<br>◊ Fully actualizing of our freedom and decision-making faculties<br>◊ Faith<br>  * Needed in order for God to enact God's salvific plans and in order for the individual to receive revelation<br>  * But it is a horizon to-wards which one travels<br>◊ Mediators of Grace<br>  * Community, guidance<br>  * Practices of the church<br>◊ Jesus = model and help, participation in His mystery |

| Source | Views of Human Nature | Views of the Divine in Relation to Humanity | Nature of Change For Humans, and God's Relationship to Such Transformation |
|---|---|---|---|
| Contemporary Theological Anthropologies | • Nature of human nature; Elements<br>◊ Multi-layered,<br>◊ Hierarchically and emergently arranged unity,<br>◊ May have an unknowable core<br>◊ Higher levels of integration possible<br>◊ Consciousness and personal subjectivity<br>◊ The importance of memories and schemas<br>◊ Emotions, feelings, and soul<br>◊ The formative role of relationships, environments – social & physical | • God's nature<br>◊ Non-physical entity<br>◊ All-knowing<br>◊ Everywhere present, fully active in history<br>　* Not contrary to laws of nature, works thru them<br>◊ Transcendent to creation<br>◊ Self-limiting<br>◊ Human-like qualities<br>　* Will<br>　* Memory | • Nature of the Journey; Elements<br>◊ Evolutionary<br>◊ Schema change and conditioning<br>◊ Environmental, social, and internal feedback loops<br>◊ Ultimately beyond our control |

| Source | Views of Human Nature | Views of the Divine in Relation to Humanity | Nature of Change For Humans, and God's Relationship to Such Transformation |
|---|---|---|---|
| Common Elements | • Physical - Body, sensations<br>• Affective - Passions, emotions<br>• Cognitive - Rationality, consciousness, will, memory, understanding, intellect<br>• Divine Connection - Made in the Image of God, Spirit within, Higher part, Inner/True Self, conscience (when guided by God), Mystery, "transcendentality," immanence<br>• Integration - Internally Interconnected, Wholeness, unified, ordered<br>• Relational - Communal, contextual: with others, environment, God<br>• Distortions - Presence of sin, disorder, competing pulls (e.g., matter vs. Spirit), lower parts, temptations<br>• Excluded:<br>◊ "Soul" - Different authors conceive of this in different ways that are captured or described by the other common elements above | • God:<br>◊ Transcendence - Invisible, eternal, unchangeable, utterly transcendent and unknowable, Mystery, Rahner's "the ontologically silent horizon," non-physical entity<br>◊ Immanence - Pure emanation, creation arises out of nothingness, source of life and grace, Omnipresence, all-knowing, works thru natural law<br>◊ Powerfulness – 1) All powerful – defeats Devil, wins our battles, Kant's holy Legislator; 2) Self-limiting<br>• Christ:<br>◊ Mediator – pays debt, bears sins, creates/restores intimate relationship to inner person, unites us with God<br>◊ Model - Visible manifestation of God, Model for us, Luther's "greatest person," Kant's ultimate maxim<br>◊ Human - Participates in suffering, historically and biologically located (some) | • Nature of Change:<br>◊ Divinely United - Becoming more Divine like, rejoined to God; A turning away from sin, weighed down by sin, battle with falleness; become more like God as God becomes in us; death to life transition, growth in conformity with Word of God, souls cleaving to God<br>◊ Gradual - day-by-day repatterning, Gradual ascent, allow new/inner person to emerge, schema conditioning<br>◊ Holistic – involves whole person, includes relationships and communities, Green's "thinking, feeling, believing, behaving," self-transcendence<br>• Necessary Supports Needed for Personal Transformation:<br>◊ Christ/God – source and sustainer, wins battles for us, provides strength, comfort, freedom, rooted in faith<br>◊ Virtues - Daily practice<br>◊ Contemplation<br>◊ Reason, rationality<br>◊ Self-knowing, following conscience, self-actualization<br>◊ Community - Virtuous and supportive<br>◊ Knowledge - of universal laws, Hearing Word of God, Jesus as Model<br>• Stages of the Journey:<br>◊ Augustine: From earth to heaven, from outer to inner person<br>◊ Maximus: Virtues practice, pursue true nature of things, Unknowable God<br>◊ Aquinas: desire to know and love God, do so habitually, do so perfectly |

# APPENDIX B

# Summary Table of Modern Science Views

| *View* | *Definitions, Characteristics, etc.* | *Nature of Change for this View* |
|---|---|---|
| *Trait-Disposition* | • Stable qualities of a person that are enduring across time and many situations<br>• But also flexible, malleable, and changing to some degree<br>• "Deeper psychological entities that can only be inferred from behavior and experience"<br>• Hierarchically ordered<br>• Evolutionary adaptations<br>• Examples: Neuroticism, Extraversion, Openness to Experience, Agreeableness, Conscientiousness | • Influenced by:<br>◊ Genetics<br>◊ Environment<br>◊ Social/cultural context<br>• Must work to repattern thoughts, feelings, and actions – Example: Allport's prejudice trait<br>• Questionable if some traits can be changed – else they are not, by definition, "traits" |

| View | Definitions, Characteristics, etc. | Nature of Change for this View |
|---|---|---|
| Biological | • Evolutionary<br>◊ "Focuses on the processes that have shaped the genes over the long course of the species' development"<br>◊ Human nature develops according to natural selection and evolutionary principles<br>◊ Core Q: How is this or that behavior related to the genes' efforts to both endure and spread?<br>• Genetic<br>◊ By-products of evolutionary history<br>◊ Nature and nurture play major roles<br>◊ Gene expression helps determine physiological development and functioning<br>◊ These give rise to adaptive behaviors, traits, etc<br>• Biological Brain (also see Neuroscience below)<br>◊ Partly a by-product of genetic expression; viewed by Wilson as a pre-programmed machine<br>◊ Correlations between neurophysiological functioning and behavior | • Human development is guided by nature and nurture<br>◊ Evolutionary history and gene pool surviving/thriving asserted to be part of what drives this<br>◊ Genetic expression influences physiological development and functioning (such as with the biological brain)<br>• Evolution can be altered by understanding its laws and principles |

| View | Definitions, Characteristics, etc. | Nature of Change for this View |
|---|---|---|
| *Neuroscientific* | • "Brain" – really distributed throughout the entire human body<br>• Building Blocks of the Brain: neurons, axons and dendrites, and glial cells<br>• Brain Meta-Regions:<br>◊ Brainstem and cerebellum - commonly associated with stimulus-response actions including "attitudes, emotional reactions, repeated actions, habits, conditioned behaviors, unconscious reflexes, and skills;" also drives for food, shelter, reproduction, and safety<br>◊ Limbic system - affective and emotional center of the brain; works to generate the emotions that we feel; "crucial of how we form relationships and become emotionally attached to one another."<br>◊ Cortex – our "thinking cap;" includes many of the cognitive functions that humans have such as developing ideas and concepts as well as the ability to consciously construct and process mental representations of such abstracts as time, self, and morality | • Brain develops in spurts, in a cyclical fashion, and across the lifespan<br>• Brain change follows the Hebbian Principle - "neurons that fire together, wire together"<br>• Other factors which contribute to brain change:<br>◊ Experiencing different external stimuli,<br>◊ Emotional arousal,<br>◊ Repetition of actions,<br>◊ Internal reflections and<br>◊ Mental rehearsals, and<br>◊ Focused attention |

| View | Definitions, Characteristics, etc. | Nature of Change for this View |
|---|---|---|
| *Psychodynamic-Motivational* | • Focused on unconscious drives, motivations, and goals (conscious and unconscious); two fundamental and interrelated drives that are "active in every particle of living substance": the death and life instincts; also the inferiority complex (Adler)<br>• Conflict driven - humans are fundamentally "torn by unconscious conflicts and wishes that pushes them in seemingly puzzling ways;" relationship conflicts are central (Horney)<br>• Three levels of consciousness - the conscious (what we have immediate access to), the preconscious, and the unconscious; pre- and unconscious levels are not readily "responsive to our deliberate efforts at recall"<br>• Psychic Structures:<br>◊ *Id* - an inherited, biological structure in the psyche that is the source of instincts, passions, and energy<br>◊ *Superego* - an "ego-ideal," a "conscience" or "morality judge," and it is the embodiment of all that a person "ought" and "ought not" to do<br>◊ *Ego* - that part of the our minds that exhibits conscious control on the psyche; seeks to bring Id into subjugation to itself in light of the superego | • Ego work to bring balance between Id and Superego<br>• We cannot ignore the unconscious, but must work with its motivations and drives<br>• Use of dream work and free association to access the unconscious<br>• We must seek to resolve conflicts by more directly addressing them |

| View | Definitions, Characteristics, etc. | Nature of Change for this View |
|---|---|---|
| Behavioral-Conditioning | • Focuses on exploring the relationship between an individual's behaviors and the conditions that give rise to them<br>• Behavior-response conditioning - using both positive and negative reinforcements in direct relation to specific behaviors to gradually condition people to behave in certain ways<br>• Conditioning applies to internal responses as well such as fears, drives, repressions, and even the use of reason<br>• Empirically focused experiments<br>• Four primary factors for learning:<br>  ◊ Drive – compel us to act<br>  ◊ Cue – initiate the drives<br>  ◊ Response – our resulting actions<br>  ◊ Reinforcement - ensures that a behavioral pattern either continues or is discouraged | • Behavior-response conditioning - using both positive and negative reinforcements in direct relation to specific behaviors to gradually condition people to behave in certain ways<br>• The road to recovery, and a fully healthy life, comes primarily through the use of discrimination, reasoning, and planned activity via gradual conditioning techniques<br>• Four factors of learning: drive, cue, response, reinforcement |
| Phenomenological-Humanistic | • Focus is to understand how people view and understand themselves and how they consciously and subjectively construe the world and their own personal experiences<br>• Active Co-Creators - each person is seen as a proactive participant and co-creator of their own experiences; human beings are autonomous and can do much to alter and direct the course of their own lives<br>• Human as whole and integrated organisms<br>• Self-created "Constructs" - intended to help us to make better sense of the world and to guide our future actions<br>  ◊ Self-constructs - the ones that people generate about themselves that they try to live in accordance with | • To uncover and modify self-constructs and the maladaptive effects these might be having on one's behaviors<br>• Therapy is focused on helping individuals to uncover and continually work with their self-concepts so that they are better able to live a more open and constructively adaptive life in relation to their environments<br>• Self-actualization as a core aim |

| View | Definitions, Characteristics, etc. | Nature of Change for this View |
|---|---|---|
| Social Cognitive | • Focused primarily on attempting to link external situations with "what goes on in the mind of the person – their thoughts or cognitions, emotions, goals, and motivations"<br>• Asserts that "the self is essentially social and interpersonal"<br>• Constructs or "schemas" and how they give shape to our perceptions and guide our lives, particularly in relation to our social world<br>◊ Situationally and culturally influenced - who we are and how we learn is heavily influenced by the particular situations, contexts, and cultures of which we are a part<br>◊ These not only influence such factors as one's self-esteem and how one relates to others, but they also have been shown to exhibit "a good deal of stability" | • Situationally and culturally influenced - who we are and how we learn is heavily influenced by the particular situations, contexts, and cultures of which we are a part<br>• "Learning phenomena resulting from direct experience occur on a vicarious basis by observing other people's behavior and its consequences for them" |
| Transpersonal-Parapsychological | • Focus is on unity with creation beyond one's self and/or experiences beyond the 5 physical senses<br>• Transpersonal experiences Include: mystical and unitive experiences, personal transformation, meditative awareness, experiences of wonder and ecstasy, and alternative and expansive states of consciousness<br>• Parapsychological experiences include: extrasensory perception (ESP) [telepathy, clairvoyance], psychokinesis (PK) [mind-matter interactions], and near-death (NDE) or out-of-body experiences (OBE)<br>• Assagioli's psychosynthesis approaches to unify one with their higher Self and foster super-conscious development as an example | • Use of imaginative and intuitive-based techniques to foster these abilities<br>• Assagioli's stages of development:<br>◊ Knowledge of one's personality<br>◊ Control of one's parts<br>◊ Emergence of truer Self<br>◊ Living life from this new Center |

| View | Definitions, Characteristics, etc. | Nature of Change for this View |
|------|-----------------------------------|-------------------------------|
| Essential Elements Across these Views | • Basic Characteristics of Human Nature:<br>◊ Enduring parts: traits, instincts, schemas, etc.<br>◊ Inner life/structures are hierarchically arranged; an ordered system: Traits-dispositions, Brain organization<br>◊ But also flexible, malleable, organismic<br>• Parts:<br>◊ Physiological: genes, brain, body, energies, etc<br>◊ Psychological: cognitive-affective, drives, motives, reasoning, memory, goals, conflicts, consciousness, "shoulds/oughts," fears, repressions, self-constructs, will/co-creators, etc<br>◊ Super-conscious: ESP, PK, OBEs, NDEs, etc<br>• Balance, harmony, integration sought: ego, humanistic, with higher Self<br>• Contextually responsive/influenced:<br>◊ Evolutionary adaptations<br>◊ Genetic Expression – in response to evolutionary history, context, and our responses to stimuli<br>◊ Stimulus-response patterns: behaviorism, instincts, positive/ negative reinforcement<br>◊ Socially and interpersonally located and influenced<br>◊ Transpersonal unity with creation<br>• Historically located: Survival of genes, inherited dispositions and propensities | • Aims: balance, integration, self-actualization, higher Self<br>• A general work of repatterning thoughts, feelings, actions, neuron connections, unconscious motives/ movements, conflicts, stimulus-responses, self-constructs, schemas<br>◊ Also foster change via understanding the laws/ principles that shape human development<br>• Influenced by: genetics, environment, social/cultural context and learning, nature and nurture, emotional arousal, repetition, cognitive focus and processing<br>• Some questions as to what can really be changed and to what extent; some development observed to occur in stages |

# Bibliography

Abe, Masao, and William R. LaFleur. *Zen and Western Thought.* Honolulu: University of Hawaii Press, 1985.

Ackerman, John. *Listening to God: Spiritual Formation in Congregations.* Bethesda, MD: Alban Institute, 2001.

Adler, A. *The Practice and Theory of Individual Psychology.* Translated by Paul Radin. New York: Harcourt, 1927.

Allport, G. W. *The Nature of Prejudice.* Cambridge, MA: Addison-Wesley, 1954.

———. *Personality: A Psychological Interpretation.* New York: Holt, 1937.

Anderson, Rosemarie. "Introduction." In *Transpersonal Research Methods for the Social Sciences: Honoring Human Experience,* edited by William Braud and Rosemarie Anderson, xix–xxxi. Thousand Oaks, CA: Sage, 1998.

———. "Intuitive Inquiry: A Transpersonal Approach." In *Transpersonal Research Methods for the Social Sciences: Honoring Human Experience,* edited by William Braud and Rosemarie Anderson, 69–94. Thousand Oaks, CA: Sage, 1998.

Aquinas, Thomas. *Summa Theologica.* Translated by Fathers of the English Dominicans Province. 1st complete American ed. 3 vols. New York: Benziger Bros., 1947.

Assagioli, Roberto. *Psychosynthesis: A Collection of Basic Writings.* Paperback ed. Middlesex, UK: Penguin, 1965.

Au, Wilkie, and Noreen Cannon Au. *The Discerning Heart: Exploring the Christian Path.* New York: Paulist, 2006.

Bandura, Albert. *Social Learning Theory.* Englewood, NJ: Prentice-Hall, 1977.

Barbour, Ian G. "Neuroscience, Artificial Intelligence, and Human Nature: Theological and Philosophical Reflections." *Zygon* 34, no. 3 (1999) 361–98.

Barrick, Marilyn C. *Sacred Psychology of Love: The Quest for Relationships That Unite Heart and Soul.* Corwin Springs, MT: Summit University Press, 1999.

Barth, Karl. *Church Dogmatics.* Vol. 3/2, *The Doctrine of Creation, Part Two.* Edited by Geoffrey W. Bromiley and Thomas F. Torrance. Translated by Harold Knight et al. Edinburgh: T. & T. Clark, 1960.

Bear, Mark F., Barry W. Connors, and Michael A. Paradiso. *Neuroscience: Exploring the Brain.* 3rd ed. Philadelphia, PA: Lippincott Williams & Wilkins, 2007.

Becker, Ernest. *The Denial of Death.* New York: Simon & Schuster, 1973.

Beitler, Michael A. *Strategic Organizational Change: A Practitioner's Guide for Managers and Consultants.* 3rd ed. Greensboro, NC: Practitioner, 2006.

Benet-Martinez, V., and Oishi, S. "Culture and Personality." In *Handbook of Personality: Theory and Research*, edited by O. P. John, R. W. Robins, and L. A. Pervin, 542–67. New York: Guilford, 2008.

Bilgrave, Dyer P., and Robert H. Deluty. "Stanislavski's Acting Method and Control Theory: Commonalities across Time, Place, and Field." *Social Behavior and Personality* 32, no. 4 (2004) 329–40.

Block, Joel D. *Naked Intimacy: How to Increase True Penness in Your Relationship*. Chicago: Contemporary, 2003.

"Bloom's Taxonomy Action Verbs." Office for Institutional Assessment, http://www.clemson.edu/assessment/assessmentpractices/referencematerials/documents/Blooms%20Taxonomy%20Action%20Verbs.pdf (accessed January 25, 2015).

Bourgeault, Cynthia. *The Wisdom Way of Knowing: Reclaiming an Ancient Tradition to Awaken the Heart*. San Francisco, CA: Jossey-Bass, 2003.

Bracken, Joseph A. *The Divine Matrix: Creativity as Link between East and West*. Faith Meets Faith. Maryknoll, NY: Orbis, 1995.

Branch, Robert M., and M. David Merrill. "Characteristics of Instructional Design Models." In *Trends and Issues in Instructional Design and Technology*, edited by Robert Reiser and John V. Dempsey, 8–16. Boston: Pearson Education, 2012.

Bransford, John D., et al. "Foundations and Opportunities for an Interdisciplinary Science of Learning." Chap. 2 in *The Cambridge Handbook of the Learning Sciences*, edited by R. Keith Sawyer, Kindle Locations 1159–966. Cambridge: Cambridge University Press, 2006.

Braud, William, and Rosemarie Anderson. "Conventional and Expanded Views of Research." In *Transpersonal Research Methods for the Social Sciences: Honoring Human Experience*, edited by William Braud and Rosemarie Anderson, 3–26. Thousand Oaks, CA: Sage, 1998.

Brice, John, and Celia Kourie. "Contemplation and Compassion: The Heart of a Fransciscan Spirituality of Clinical Pastoral Supervision." *The Journal of Pastoral Care and Counseling* 60, nos. 1–2 (2006) 109–16.

Britt, David W. *A Conceptual Introduction to Modeling: Qualitative and Quantitative Perspectives*. Mahwah, NJ: Erlbaum, 1997.

Canli, T. "Toward a "Molecular Psychology" of Personality." In *Handbook of Personality: Theory and Research*, edited by O. P. John, R. W. Robins, and L. A. Pervin 311–27. New York: Guilford, 2008.

Carter, Rita, and Christopher D. Frith. *Mapping the Mind*. Berkeley: University of California Press, 1998.

Carver, Charles S., and Michael Scheier. *On the Self-Regulation of Behavior*. Cambridge: Cambridge University Press, 1998.

Cassian, John. *John Cassian: The Conferences*. Translated by Boniface Ramsey. Ancient Christian Writers. Mahwah, NJ: Paulist, 1997.

Chudler, Eric H. "Brain Facts and Figures." http://faculty.washington.edu/chudler/facts.html (accessed January 25, 2015).

Churches, Andrew. "Bloom's Digital Taxonomy." Educational Origami, http://edorigami.wikispaces.com/Bloom%27s+Digital+Taxonomy (accessed January 25, 2015).

Clayton, Philip. *Adventures in the Spirit: God, World, Divine Action*. Minneapolis: Fortress, 2008.

———. *Mind & Emergence: From Quantum to Consciousness.* Oxford: Oxford University Press, 2004.

Clayton, Philip, and Arthur Peacocke, eds. *In Whom We Live and Move and Have Our Being: Panentheistic Reflections on God's Presence in a Scientific World.* Grand Rapids: Eerdmans, 2004.

Cobb, John B., Jr., and David Ray Griffin. *Process Theology: An Introductory Exposition.* Louisville: Westminster John Knox, 1976.

Collins, Allan. "Cognitive Apprenticeship." In *The Cambridge Handbook of the Learning Sciences,* edited by R. Keith Sawyer, Kindle Locations 2448–983. Cambridge: Cambridge University Press, 2006.

Conn, Joann Wolski. "Toward Spiritual Maturity." In *Exploring Christian Spirituality,* edited by Kenneth J. Collins, 355–78. Grand Rapids: Baker, 2000.

Corporation, Learning Management. "Developing Clear Learning Outcomes and Objectives." http://www.thelearningmanager.com/pubdownloads/developing_clear_learning_outcomes_and_objectives.pdf (accessed January 25, 2015).

Damasio, Antonio R. *The Feeling of What Happens: Body and Emotion in the Making of Consciousness.* 1st ed. New York: Harcourt Brace, 1999.

Dawkins, Richard. *The Selfish Gene.* 30th anniversary ed. Oxford: Oxford University Press, 2006.

Descartes, Rene. "Discourse on Method." In *The Study of Human Nature,* edited by Leslie Stevenson, 84–89. Oxford: Oxford University Press, 2000.

Dietrich, Dietmar, et al., eds. *Simulating the Mind: A Technical Neuropsychoanalytical Approach.* Morlenbach, Germany: SpringerWienNewYork, 2009.

Dispenza, Joe. *Evolve Your Brain: The Science of Changing Your Mind.* Dearfield, FL: Health Communications, 2007.

Dollard, J., and N. E. Miller. *Personality and Psychotherapy: An Analysis in Terms of Learning, Thinking, and Culture.* New York: McGraw-Hill, 1950.

Dougherty, Rose Mary. *Group Spiritual Direction: Community for Discernment.* New York: Paulist, 1995.

Downs, Perry G. *Teaching for Spiritual Growth.* Grand Rapids: Zondervan, 1994.

Eggen, Paul D., and Donald P. Kauchak. *Strategies and Models for Teachers: Teaching Content and Thinking Skills.* 5th ed. Boston: Pearson/Allyn and Bacon, 2006.

Eysenck, H. J. "Genetic and Environmental Contributions to Individual Differences: The Three Major Dimensions of Personality." *Journal of Personality* 58, no. 1 (1990) 245–61.

Faber, Roland. "De-Ontologizing God: Levinas, Deleuze, and Whitehead." In *Process and Difference: Between Cosmological and Poststructuralist Postmodernisms,* edited by Catherine Keller and Anne Daniel, 209–34. Albany: State University of New York, 2002.

Franklin, Gene F., J. David Powell, and Abbas Emami-Naeini. *Feedback Control of Dynamic Systems.* Addison-Wesley Series in Electrical and Computer Engineering: Control Engineering. 3rd ed. Reading, Mass.: Addison-Wesley, 1994.

Freud, Sigmund. *The Ego and the Id.* London: Hogarth, 1927.

Gilligan, Carol, Nona Lyons, and Trudy J. Hanmer, eds. *Making Connections: The Relational Worlds of Adolescent Girls at Emma Willard School.* Cambridge, MA: Harvard University Press, 1990.

Ginsburg, Herbert P., and Sylvia Opper. *Piaget's Theory of Intellectual Development.* Upper Saddle River, NJ: Pearson, 1987.

Gould, Stephen Jay. "Challenges to Neo-Darwinism and Their Meaning for a Revised View of Human Consciousness." In *The Richness of Life: The Essential Stephen Jay Gould*, edited by Paul McGarr and Steven Rose, 222–37. New York: Norton & , 2007.

Green, Joel B. *Body, Soul, and Human Life: The Nature of Humanity in the Bible*. Studies in Theological Interpretation. Grand Rapids: Baker Academic, 2008.

Griffin, David Ray. *Parapsychology, Philosophy, and Spirituality: A Postmodern Exploration*. Suny Series in Constructive Postmodern Thought. Albany: State University of New York Press, 1997.

———. *Reenchantment without Supernaturalism: A Process Philosophy of Religion*. Ithaca, NY: Cornell University Press, 2001.

Hart, Tobin. "Opening the Contemplative Mind in the Classroom." *Journal of Transformative Education* 1 (2003) 1–19.

Hauser, Richard J. *Moving in the Spirit: Becoming a Contemplative in Action*. New York: Paulist, 1986.

Heer, Rex. "A Model of Learning Objectives–Based on a Taxonomy for Learning, Teaching, and Assessing: A Revision of Bloom's Taxonomy of Educational Objectives." Center for Excellence in Learning and Teaching, http://www.celt. iastate.edu/teaching/RevisedBlooms1.html.

Hippo, Augustine of. *The Trinity*. Translated by Edmund Hill. Brooklyn: New City, 1991.

Holden, Jolly T. "A Guide to Developing Cognitive Learning Objectives." The Government Alliance for Training and Education by Satellite, http://gates.govdl. org/docs/A%20Guide%20to%20Developing%20Cogntive%20Learning%20 Objectives.pdf (accessed January 15, 2015).

Huebner, Dwayne E. "Spirituality and Knowing." In *Learning and Teaching the Ways of Knowing: Eighty-Fourth Yearbook of the National Society for the Study of Education*, edited by Elliot Eisner, 159–73. Chicago: National Society for the Study of Education, 1985.

Hull, Bill. *The Complete Book of Discipleship: On Being and Making Followers of Christ*. Colorado Springs: NavPress, 2006.

Hunter, Charles, and Frances Gardner Hunter. *How to Heal the Sick*. New Kensington, PA: Whitaker House, 1981.

"Introduction to Quantum Mechanics." http://en.wikipedia.org/wiki/Introduction_to_ quantum_mechanics (accessed January 25, 2015).

Irwin, Harvey J., and Caroline A. Watt. *An Introduction to Parapsychology*. Jefferson, NC: McFarland, 2007.

Isenhower, Valerie K., and Judith A. Todd. *Living into the Answers: A Workbook for Personal Spiritual Discernment*. Nashville: Upper Room, 2008.

Kant, Immanuel. *Religion within the Limits of Reason Alone*. Translated by Theodor M. Greene and Hoyt H. Hudson. 1793. Chicago: Open Court, 1934.

Kegan, Robert. "What "Form" Transforms? A Constructive-Developmental Approach to Transformative Learning." Chap. 2 In *Learning as Transformation: Critical Perspectives on a Theory in Progress*, edited by Jack Mezirow, 35–69. San Francisco: Jossey-Bass, 2000.

Krathwohl, David R. "A Revision of Bloom's Taxonomy: An Overview." *Theory Into Practice* 41, no. 4 (2002) 212–18.

Kraybill, Ronald S. *Peace Skills: Manual for Community Mediators*. San Francisco: Jossey-Bass, 2001.

Kretzmann, John P., and John L. McKnight. *Building Communities from the Inside Out: A Path toward Finding and Mobilizing a Community's Assets*. Evanston, IL: Institute for Policy Research, Northwestern University, 1993.

Krueger, R. F., and W. Johnson. "Behavioral Genetics and Personality: A New Look at the Integration of Nature and Nurture." In *Handbook of Personality: Theory and Research*, edited by O. P. John, R. W. Robins, and L. A. Pervin. 287–310. New York: Guilford, 2008.

Kyle, Eric. *Living Spiritual Praxis: Foundations for Spiritual Formation Program Development*. Eugene, OR: Pickwick, 2013.

———. "The 'Paradoxical-Transcendent' Mind: Is a Cognitive-Neuroscientific Understandingof Mystical Thought Possible?." AAR/WR Annual Meeting 2011, Whittier College, Whittier, California, 2011.

———. *Sacred Systems: Exploring Personal Transformation in the Western Christian Tradition*. Eugene, OR: Pickwick, 2013.

Langer, Ellen J. *The Power of Mindful Learning*. Reading, MA: Addison-Wesley, 1997.

Lawrenz, Mel. *The Dynamics of Spiritual Formation*. Ministry Dynamics for a New Century Series. Grand Rapids: Baker, 2000.

Lichtmann, Maria R. *The Teacher's Way: Teaching and the Contemplative Life*. New York: Paulist, 2005.

Linn, Marcia C. "The Knowledge Integration Perspective on Learning and Instruction." In *The Cambridge Handbook of the Learning Sciences*, edited by R. Keith Sawyer, Kindle Locations 9236–998. Cambridge: Cambridge University Press, 2006.

Luther, Martin. "The Freedom of a Christian." Translated by W. A. Lambert. In *Three Treatises*, 261–316. Philadelphia: Fortress, 1970.

Mannermaa, Tuomo. *Christ Present in Faith: Luther's View of Justification*. Minneapolis: Fortress, 2005.

Maslow, A. *Motivation and Personality*. 2nd ed. New York: Harper & Row, 1970.

Matlin, Margaret W. *Cognition*. 6th ed. New York: Wiley & Sons, 2005.

May, Gerald. *Will & Spirit: A Contemplative Psychology*. San Francisco: Harper & Row, 1982.

McCrae, R. R., and P. T. Costa Jr. "The Five-Factor Theory of Personality." In *Handbook of Personality: Theory and Research*, edited by O. P. John, R. W. Robins, and L. A. Pervin, 159–81. New York: Guilford, 2008.

McGrath, Alister E. *A Fine-Tuned Universe: The Quest for God in Science and Theology: The 2009 Gifford Lectures*. 1st ed. Louisville: Westminster John Knox, 2009.

Metcalf, J., and W. Mischel. "A Hot/Cool System Analysis of Delay Gratification: Dynamics of Will Power." *Psychological Review* 106, no. 1 (1999) 3–19.

Mischel, W. "Personality Coherence and Dispositions in a Cognitive-Affective Processing System (Caps) Approach." In *The Coherence of Personality: Social-Cognitive Basis of Consistency, Variability, and Organization*, edited by D. Cervone and Y. Shoda, 37–60. New York: Guilford, 1999.

Mischel, W., and Y. Shoda. "Toward a Unified Theory of Personality: Integrating Disposition and Processing Dynamics within the Cognitive-Affective Processing System." In *Handbook of Personality: Theory and Research*, edited by O. P. John, R. W. Robins, and L. A. Pervin, 208–41. New York: Guilford, 2008.

Mischel, Walter, Yuichi Shoda, and Ozlem Ayduk. *Introduction to Personality: Toward an Integrative Science of the Person.* 8th ed. Hoboken, NJ: Wiley & Sons, 2008.

Morinis, E. Alan. *Everyday Holiness: The Jewish Spiritual Path of Mussar.* 1st ed. Boston: Trumpeter, 2007.

Morra, Sergio, et al. *Cognitive Development: Neo-Piagetian Perspectives.* New York: Erlbaum, 2008.

Mursell, Gordon. *The Story of Christian Spirituality: Two Thousand Years, from East to West.* 1st Fortress Press ed. Minneapolis: Fortress, 2001.

Neder, Adam. *Participation in Christ: An Entry into Karl Barth's Church Dogmatics.* Louisville: Westminster John Knox, 2009.

Nelson, Charles A., Michelle De Haan, and Kathleen M. Thomas. *Neuroscience of Cognitive Development: The Role of Experience and the Developing Brain.* Hoboken, NJ: Wiley, 2006.

Odin, Steve. *Process Metaphysics and Hua-Yen Buddhism: A Critical Study of Cumulative Penetration vs. Interpenetration.* Suny Series in Systematic Philosophy. Albany: State University of New York Press, 1982.

Osborn, T. L. *Healing the Sick: A Living Classic.* Tulsa: Harrison House, 1986.

Ostow, Mortimer. *Spirit, Mind, & Brain: A Psychoanalytic Examination of Spirituality and Religion.* Columbia Series in Science and Religion. New York: Columbia University Press, 2007.

Palmer, Phoebe. *The Way of Holiness, with Notes by the Way; Being a Narrative of Religious Experience Resulting from a Determination to Be a Bible Christian.* Michigan Historical Reprint. New York: Lane & Tippett, 1854.

Parker, Stephen E. *Led by the Spirit: Toward a Practical Theology of Pentecostal Discernment and Decision Making.* Journal of Pentecostal Theology Supplement. Sheffield, UK: Sheffield Academic, 1996.

Peacocke, Arthur. *Paths from Science towards God: The End of All Our Exploring.* Oxford: Oneworld, 2001.

Pickover, Clifford A. *The Physics Book: From the Big Bang to Quantum Resurrection, 250 Milestones in the History of Physics.* New York: Sterling, 2011.

Price, Daniel J. *Karl Barth's Anthropology in Light of Modern Thought.* Grand Rapids: Eerdmans, 2002.

Radin, Dean I. *The Conscious Universe: The Scientific Truth of Psychic Phenomena.* 1st. ed. New York: HarperEdge, 1997.

Rahner, Karl. *Foundations of Christian Faith: An Introduction to the Idea of Christianity.* Translated by William V. Dych. New York: Crossroad, 1982.

Rasmussen, Ane Marie Bak. *Modern African Spirituality: The Independent Holy Spirit Churches in East Africa, 1902–1976.* London: British Academic, 1996.

Reid, Daniel P. *A Complete Guide to Chi-Gung: Harnessing the Power of the Universe* Boston: Shambhala, 1998.

Richey, Rita C., James D. Klein, and Monica W. Tracey. *The Instructional Design Knowledge Base: Theory, Research, and Practice.* Kindle ed. New York: Taylor and Francis, 2011.

Rogers, C. *Client-Centered Therapy, Its Current Practice, Implications, and Theory.* Boston: Houghton-Mifflin, 1951.

Rosenzweig, Steven, et al. "Mindfulness-Based Stress Reduction Lowers Psychological Distress in Medical Students." *Teaching and Learning in Medicine* 15, no. 2 (2003) 88–92.

Roughgarden, Joan. *Evolution's Rainbow: Diversity, Gender, and Sexuality in Nature and People*. Berkeley: University of California Press, 2004.

Russell, Robert John, et al., eds. *Neuroscience and the Person: Scientific Perspective on Divine Action*. Vatican City: Vatican Observatory, 1999.

Ryan, R. M., and E. L. Deci. "Self-Determination Theory and the Role of Basic Psychological Needs in Personality and the Organization of Behavior." In *Handbook of Personality: Theory and Research*, edited by O. P. John, R. W. Robins, and L. A. Pervin. 654–78. New York: Guilford, 2008.

Sagan, Carl. "Can We Know the Universe?: Reflections on a Grain of Salt." In *Science and Its Ways of Knowing*, edited by John Hatton and Paul B. Plouffe, 3–7. Upper Saddle River, NJ: Prentice-Hall, 1997.

Sawyer, R. Keith. "Introduction: The New Science of Learning." In *The Cambridge Handbook of the Learning Sciences*, edited by R. Keith Sawyer, Kindle Locations 484–1154. Cambridge: Cambridge University Press, 2006.

Schneiders, Sandra M. "Theology and Spirituality: Strangers, Rivals, or Partners?" *Horizons* 13, no. 2 (1986) 253–74.

Schultheiss, O. C. "Implicit Motives." In *Handbook of Personality: Theory and Research*, edited by O. P. John, R. W. Robins, and L. A. Pervin 603–33. New York: Guilford, 2008.

Siegel, Daniel J. *The Mindful Brain: Reflection and Attunement in the Cultivation of Well-Being*. 1st ed. New York: Norton, 2007.

———. *Mindsight: The New Science of Personal Transformation*. 1st ed. New York: Bantam, 2010.

Slavin, Robert E. *Educational Psychology: Theory and Practice*. 9th ed. Boston: Pearson, 2009.

Smith, Adrian B. *God, Energy and the Field*. Ropely, Hants, UK: Hunt, 2008.

Suchocki, Marjorie Hewitt. *God, Christ, Church: A Practical Guide to Process Theology*. Eugene, OR: Wipf and Stock, 1989.

Thompson, Bard. *Liturgies of the Western Church*. 1st Fortress Press ed. Philadelphia: Fortress, 1980.

Thunberg, Lars. *Microcosm and Mediator: The Theological Anthropology of Maximus the Confessor*. Chicago: Open Court, 1995.

Torrell, Jean-Pierre. *Saint Thomas Aquinas*. Vol. 2, *Spiritual Master*. Translated by Robert Royal. Washington, DC: Catholic University of America Press, 1996.

Torrey, R. A. *The Power of Prayer and the Prayer of Power*. Grand Rapids: Zondervan, 1971.

Van Kaam, Adrian L. *Fundamental Formation*. Formative Spirituality. Pittsburgh: Epiphany Association, 2002.

Westen, D., G. O. Gabbard, and K. M. Ortigo. "Psychoanalytic Approaches to Personality." In *Handbook of Personality: Theory and Research*, edited by O. P. John, R. W. Robins, and L. A. Pervin. 61–113. New York: Guilford, 2008.

Whitehead, Alfred North. *Adventures of Ideas*. 1933. Reprint, New York: Free, 1961.

Wilber, Ken. *Integral Spirituality: A Startling New Role for Religion in the Modern and Postmodern World*. Boston: Integral, 2006.

Willard, Dallas. *Renovation of the Heart: Putting on the Character of Christ*. Colorado Springs: Nav, 2002.

Wilson, E. O. *On Human Nature*. New York: Bantam, 1978.

Wink, Walter. *Engaging the Powers: Discernment and Resistance in a World of Domination*. Minneapolis: Augsburg Fortress, 1992.

Wolpert, Daniel. *Leading a Life with God: The Practice of Spiritual Leadership*. Nashville: Upper Room, 2006.

Wong, Eva. *Taoism: An Essential Guide*. Boston: Shambhala, 2011.

Wynn, Charles M. "Does Theory Ever Become Fact?" In *Learning and Teaching the Ways of Knowing: Eighty-Fourth Yearbook of the National Society for the Study of Education*, edited by Elliot Eisner, 60–63. Chicago: National Society for the Study of Education, 1985.

# Index

Made in the USA
Middletown, DE
18 August 2020

15571927R00176